An Approach to Building

FINESCALE TRACK

in 4mm

by IAIN RICE

WILD SWAN PUBLICATIONS LTD.

DEDICATION

To Ken Northwood, gentleman, craftsman, and creator of the 'North Devonshire' – inspiration to at least three generations of railway modellers.

ISBN 1 874103 00 3

Designed by Paul Karau
Printed by Amadeus Press, Huddersfield

Published by
WILD SWAN PUBLICATIONS LIMITED
1–3 Hagbourne Road, Didcot, Oxon OX11 8DP

INTRODUCTION

If there's one thing that serves to delineate the gulf that still exists between 'mainstream' and 'finescale' railway modelling, it's the very different approach to trackwork. Not only does the finescale devotee wear the hair shirt of authenticity in PW matters, he's also expected to build the dratted stuff – a prospect daunting enough, it would seem, to deter many a ripe convert. For the building of track – proper, finescale track, with chairs and easements and scale ballast, writhing itself into fearsome complexities of slips and overlapped turnouts – has been ever wrapped about with a sort of mystic aura; the suggestion is that entry to the select order will involve years of dedicated study, the mastering of fearsome techniques and possibly the acquisition of a few of the Black Arts.

It was always like that. Certainly, back in the days when Beatties were the Southgate Hobbyshop, with an E93A Ford sidevalve van and a gaggle of seedy suburban lock-ups, the gulf between my grey Rovex sectional track and what was then described as 'scale' track was wide indeed; 'Wrenn Universal' was about all that the likes of Rice could aspire to – and I won't have to remind older readers just how horrible *that* was! One was dimly conscious, in the mists of the far, 'scale' shore, of wondrous, fabulous things: EM gauge, whatever *that* was, track with 'scale' rail, individual sleepers, proper ballast, and, talked of with bated breath by aspirant acolytes, the wonders of ABC 'Chairway'. Real chairs, points that looked like points, with proper fabricated 'frogs', code 95 rail – and 8s 6d per yard! Heavens, that was twice the price of Welkut, and we thought that pretty exotic!

Such expenditure was quite beyond the sparse Rice coffers, which were lucky to top the heady heights of five bob. Even Wrenn, at 3/11d a yard, strained the exchequer, added to which the fibre sleepering warped before your eyes and the rails rusted as soon as you'd cleaned them a time or two. Then, one winter Saturday, about the year 1959, there came my way a very second-hand copy of *A Study of the Model Railway – Facts and Features of OO Model Railway Construction,* by E. Rankine Grey (2nd edition, 1951). This was a description of Grey's big exhibition model railway at Bournemouth, which gave a detailed account of the ERG track system. Whether it was Grey's airy prose and general self-assurance, or my natural optimism, I can't remember. But the contents of the coffers, hitting a post-birthday high that must have included at least one ten-bob note, were converted into postal orders, and an order dispatched to Bournemouth.

While waiting for the GPO to do its stuff, I collected about me those tools I thought appropriate to the job: a battle-scarred pair of pliers, father's old RAF-surplus 65W Solon soldering iron, a file or two, Bakers fluid, solder and a massive 18oz claw hammer. The ERG track parts, when they arrived, consisted of fibre sleepers in an odd red-brown hue, punched to take tinned boot-brads, and designed to be mounted on pre-cut wooden track bases about ¼in thick. And, to top it all – scale rail! Code 95 nickel-silver bullhead in a long wax-paper package with the red ERG label around its midriff, like the seal on an expensive cigar.

After a few false starts, I got on quite well with these components. Nailing the sleepers to the wooden track-base with the boot-brads was no problem, not with my monster hammer! Soldering on the rail was a bit trickier, trying to hold it all in place with one old Hamblings track gauge while sploshing Bakers Fluid on the fibre sleepers (which made them swell up obscenely) and spraying drops of molten solder off the wobbling, drooping bit of the Solon. But somehow I got it done, all ballasted with fish glue and mawseed. I thought it looked wonderful – at least, I did until the Bakers Fluid, attacking the steel brads, molehilled a blob of rust around every solder joint. Notwithstanding this small drawback, the ERG track ran my trains far better than the mix of Wrenn and Rovex that preceded it. I eventually aspired to a few turnouts that seemed no more inclined to derail things than did the Wrenn equivalents.

This ERG system was the ancestor of Joe Brook-Smith's boot-brad-and-ply-sleeper EM track, which was further refined by the P4 pioneers of the Model Railway Study Group, who substituted a hollow copper rivet for the boot-brad, and code 75 rail for the old code 95 – a scale rail that *was* scale, at last! This ply and rivet track has served well in the intervening 21 years, gaining such refinements as cosmetic chairs on the way. I've used the ply system pretty much the whole of that time, after a brief dalliance with printed circuit board in the early 1970s, and though I've recently tried the all-plastic track developed by C & L's Len Newman, I found that I got on best with a combination of the two systems, using the plastic chairs solvent-welded to the ply sleepers, with a riveted sleeper every now and then for strength.

Things have progressed a long way from Rankine Grey's boot-brads, and it is now simpler and cheaper to build a track that is as near as dammit dead to scale than it ever was to work with the cruder approximations of thirty years since.

There's still a lot of scope for improvement, mind. Maybe not in the track as such, but I've long felt that the way in which we use these wonderful components doesn't get the best out of them in practical terms. I've spent a lot of time – and built quite a few layouts – exploring different approaches to track construction and tracklaying, resilient underlays, trackbed systems, and the baseboards that lie beneath it all. What I present here are some conclusions from my enquiries and experiments, intended as a practical guide to the construction of 4mm finescale track, mostly of the traditional bullhead variety. In the course of my usual ramblings, I touch on many matters, of both theory

and prototype fact. Of necessity, I have been somewhat superficial in my treatment of some of these topics; strictly speaking, you don't *need* to know a lot of the 'why', but I find it helps to qualify the 'wherefore'. So – apologies to the experts I shall doubtless offend as I ride, roughshod, o'er their hallowed turf in my prosaic and pragmatic quest for perfect permanent way.

I don't suppose that the particular combination of techniques and design solutions that I've evolved will suit everybody. The nub of the whole business – the actual construction of the track – has a pretty wide relevance, and is anyway the result of broad consensus among a good many 4mm finescale modellers. The close replication of prototype appearance is, obviously, a main plank of the finescale philosophy, and to date the approach described seems among the most successful. It is in endeavouring to more closely replicate the way in which real track behaves under a train that I appear to differ from many of my colleagues. Likewise, my obsession with the search for quiet track – which any modeller brought up on foam-bedded Peco Streamline will expect as a right – distances me somewhat from pundits of the conventional wisdom that calls for a great solidity in the underpinnings.

As usual, I shall disclaim any universal wisdom. If this book helps the odd toe-dipping Peco convert to a successful entry to the finescale fold, I'll be well pleased. And if my half-baked arguments stir some better-equipped researcher into the formulation of a really effective underlay and ballasting system, I'll be delighted.

Thanks are due to sundry friends for help and elucidation in PW matters, both real and miniature, especially to Bernard Weller and Ray Hammond, who know a thing or two between them. I'm also indebted to the Swindon and Cricklade and South Devon Railways, who have furthered my quest for prototype information. Lastly, I must acknowledge the contribution of my old friend Mike Sharman, if for no other reason than that he has successfully broken more of the rules of PW design and construction than most of us have ever heard of, which must go to prove that trackwork is essentially a practical subject, whatever the theorists might have to say!

Iain Rice
Chagford, Devon

CHAPTER ONE

TRACK FACTS AND FINESCALE FICTIONS

Never has a word been so abused over the years as that well-worn, over-worked adjective, 'scale' – at least, in so far as it has been applied to model railways. A scale, according to my 1934 (rev. 1950) edition of the 'Concise Oxford', is defined as: 'Relative dimensions, ratio of enlargement and reduction . . .' So, presumably, 'scale' track must be held to bear a direct, numerically linear, relationship to the real thing. Certainly, a lot of the trackwork sold as 'scale' over the past thirty years bore scant relationship, numerical or otherwise, to anything existing in the practice of the full-sized railway.

So, in the context of model railways, the description 'scale model' has become ambivalent indeed. While a 'scale model' boat might be expected to be accurate in dimension and proportion, according to the ratio of reduction quoted, a model locomotive could be accepted as 'scale' even if it incorporated such trifling errors as a 13% deficiency in the gauge to which it was built, coupled with a like discrepancy in wheel size and 22% excess in tread width. And what of 'scale' track? In all probability, the sleeper size and spacing bore no relationship to the prototype, while the rail size employed and the method of fastening were both dimensionally gross and at best only approximate in form and proportion. For many years, then, the term 'scale track' has been applied to track whose only virtue was that it was slightly less obscenely innacurate than that purveyed by the makers of toy trains.

And then, to add to this literary abuse and etymological excess, we manufacture this wonderful adjective 'finescale'. If a scale is a ratio or proportion, then just what in the dickens is 'finescale?' The word is a nonsense! Well, the whole business is a nonsense, of course; it is the long-standing abuse of the reasonably concise description 'scale model' that has led to the need for a term to differentiate 'scale' models that actually are to scale from those that aren't. But even now, in strict terms, we continue to misuse these descriptions, for we will bless with the distinction of 'finescale', models which still incorporate errors of dimension or proportion. Which has led a few meticulous souls to coin an even more absurd term, in 'exact scale'. As a scale is, in itself, a totally exact thing, you can't really have an inexact scale, can you? An inexact *application* of a scale, certainly; this is the root of all the bother; but to be didactic (which some of these gentlemen most certainly are), we can't qualify the word 'scale' used as an adjective.

Having enjoyed myself with all this argument, I'm going to add to the general confusion by keeping the terms, but adding my own definitions to them. This I do on the basis that use modifies meaning, and I think that certain things are now understood by the various 'scale' descriptions. So, if we accept a 'scale' model as one that resembled a prototype without incorporating gross distortions, while not necessarily being particularly accurate in dimension – as in the average modern R-T-R model – then we can argue that a 'finescale' model is something 'one up' on that.

WHAT IS FINESCALE?

Actually, rather than trying to define the quality and accuracy of a model by reference to its scale and the conformity thereto, I'd like to consider it as a measure of the success with which it represents its prototype. Perhaps this might be best served by reviving another description much bandied about in years gone by. 'Authentic Scale Model', a claim emblazoned on the box-lid of many a model or kit, seems to me to sum up those attributes that we look for in a successful miniature. The concept of authenticitiy, of truth to an original or source, seems to me the principle which lies behind the railway modelling concept of 'finescale'.

So, in my definition, a 'finescale' model is one that successfully portrays its subject, on as many levels as possible. It is as much about an approach, an attitude of mind, a way of proceeding from direct and detailed observation of the prototype through linear scaling and interpretation to a skilled and convincing rendition in miniature. And, as can readily be observed at any model railway exhibition, the mere adherence to numerical accuracy in scaling down reality is no guarantee of realism in the final result. I can cite any number of layouts that succeed against substantial numeric errors, and a possibly greater number that fail with great precision! There's a lot more to building my type of 'finescale' model than merely being a whizz with a micrometer.

Applying this rationale to the particular case of track, I would cite authenticity of appearance and a commensurate quality of running as the criteria by which I would judge 'finescale' track. This does not preclude that well-worn chestnut, 'finescale' OO track, which on the face of it might appear as anachronistic as atonal music or illiterate literature. 'OO' track is 13% under gauge, so therefore it can't possibly be finescale, can it? Well, say I, if it looks convincing and is viewed from such an angle that the deficiency in the gauge is not apparent, then I'm happy to award it the dubious accolade of 'finescale track', assuming, of course, that those deficiencies in the wheel-to-track relationship, which usually mitigate against OO track providing the quality of running that I would also be looking for, have been likewise attended to.

This is an interesting point, for the success of a model as a realistic portrayal of its subject has a lot to do with the manner in which it is viewed. Traditionally, we have looked down on model railways from a great height, a viewpoint that equates to the experience of a balloonist or steeplejack in the real world. From such a viewpoint, the deficiencies of 'dublo' are all too apparent. I have long argued that this is the wrong way to look at a model railway, and that something more closely approaching a natural eye level viewpoint will both enhance the authenticity of the model and diminish the impact of many of the compromises we have to make. Layouts like Dave Elbourn's excellent 'Scotland Street' do not lose greatly in authenticity because they are under-gauge, although this is not to say that there would be no benefit in applying more accurate wheel and track standards. There would, but the difference would be subtle rather than stunning. Why? Because, in most respects other than gauge, the track is already authentic. The twin blights of over-hefty rail and ill-proportioned sleepers have already been banished. With a viewing height that lets you look *across* the track, not down at it, the lack of inches between the railheads is less apparent than the size and proportions of the track components.

So, here is a definition of 'finescale' track that might serve, as describing track constructed from components that are in themselves accurate in their scale dimensions. A rail of correct size and form, carried on sleepers of appropriate length and width (although not necessarily correct as to depth, visually unapparent except on unballasted track), and incorporating representations of rail fixings, fishplates, ballasting and other PW features, should produce track of authentic appearance. Note that I have called for sleepers of *appropriate* dimensions – for placing rails at 16.5mm centres on sleepers dimensioned for track to 18.2 or 18.83mm gauge will only serve to point up the error in the gauge. The appropriate dimension in this case seems to me to call for the maintaining of the rail-to-sleeper-end distance at a correctly-scaled value, while slicing an appropriate allowance out of the portion between the rails.

If this suggests that building 'finescale' OO track is less than straightforward, then I must reinforce this impression. The whole business of 'finescale' OO is set about with difficulties arising from the fact that there is no established standard to which to work. The old BRMSB OO standard has largely fallen by the wayside, and was anyway pretty flawed, as it failed to address certain dimensions and relationships that are quite critical to the proper functioning of trackwork. But, while EM has (eventually) benefited from the setting out of a fully-defined set of standards, and while P4 started out as just such a standard, OO has been left in the cold – a situation that I have attempted to remedy in my 'standards' appendix. The criteria governing standards, and their derivation from first principles, receive a line or two in the next chapter.

CHOICE OF STANDARDS

I suspect that a goodly proportion of the luckless souls ploughing through all this verbiage will be modellers who, having reached the end of the Peco-tracked road of 'mainstream modelling', seek some enlightenment as to where they might go next. This being so, many will be uncommitted as to the gauge and standards they wish to embrace; there may even be some confusion as to what, exactly, is on offer. There will also, like as not, be some apprehension as to the practical difficulties to be overcome in actually doing the embracing, and in the manner in which these difficulties might be supposed to escalate in the progression from Peco to P4.

So far as standards go, I suppose that I had better come clean, and 'declare an interest', as they say at the Parish Council meeting when councillor Bloggs' application to demolish his listed cottage and replace it with a burger bar comes up for discussion. Well, I've no intention of attempting to demolish 'EM' or even 'finescale OO', but having adhered to the P4 standard since 1969, and finding myself currently serving on the committee of the society foundedto promote it, I can't claim impartiality! However, I'll try, and I feel perhaps the best precept upon which to invite practical and aesthetic comparisons of the 4mm scale modelling standards is to set out their history, derivation and characteristics, albeit briefly.

A BRIEF HISTORY OF 4mm FINESCALE

The British 4mm scale, which has spawned the most sophisticated modelling standards and arguably established the world-wide 'state of the art' for small-scale work, is a pure historical accident. As is probably well-known, 4mm scale evolved from HO, that widespread miniature standard derived simply by halving the old 'O' gauge dimensions. HO developed originally on the Continent, most particularly in Germany, from whence came the first mechanisms and components suitable for miniature use. Unfortunately, they weren't all *that* miniature, and mechanisms that could be accommodated in the generous proportions of a big-boilered loco built to the continental 'high, wide and handsome' loading gauge tended to burst out of the far smaller British engines in a most unseemly manner.

It is Henry Greenly who is widely attributed with having the notion of increasing the scale – to make the bulk of the models greater – while retaining the HO gauge and standards. The result, as we all know to our cost, was that unhappy misfit, 'OO' – a grossly inaccurate scale/gauge ratio with which British modellers have had to come to terms for the last half century. 'OO' hadn't been long established when the Second World War more or less put a stop to modelling activity – but it was long enough for Meccano Ltd to launch the OO Hornby Dublo system. And when the war was over, and there were no more HO 'mechs' to be had, bar a trickle from the USA, it was the Dublo range that formed the lynchpin or popular railway modelling in this country.

While World War 2 may have put a stop to most practical railway modelling, it also gave birth to the small-scale hobby's first 'think tank', the Model Railway Standards Bureau, which set out to devise some standards for the emergent 4mm scale. This official-sounding body started its deliberations somewhere around late 1940 or early 1941, but made slow progress. However, somewhere between 1941 and February 1945, 'EM' was born, for on page 27 of the *Model Railway Constructor* for that month, we find the late Mike Longridge describing the first in a series of 'BRMSB True Scale 4mm GWR Models' – to 18mm gauge. (This model, by the by, built of ply and 'whitewood' on a brass chassis, was a GWR 14-ton 'Toad A', and is quite exquisite, fully comparable with the best of today's work.)

The BRMSB Standards created quite a stir when they were published – in dribs and drabs, so far as I can make out – in 1945–6. At all events, the January 1947 *Constructor* had an interesting 'leader' on the 'BRMS Bureau Dimensions', which, among much interesting comment, noted that the bureau had been criticized for basing its track dimensions on a gauge equivalent to 4′ 6″ instead of 4′ 8½″; there were evidently P4 aspirants in 1946! The BRMSB standards were pragmatic, and were based upon the interesting notion of scale/gauge ratio. Thus, the prototype, with a scale of 12in–1ft on a gauge of 4′ 8½″ had a ratio of 56½″/12″ = 1:4.71. This was held to be a workable relationship from ¼in/ft scale up, but for miniature scales the ratio was compromised at 1:4.5, giving a track gauge of 4.5ft or 18mm at 4mm scale. This compromise was established by experiment (in 7mm, scale, as it happens), and was intended to give adequate clearances and allow for manufacturing tolerances without unduly compromising the model.

The BRMSB Standards

The grandly-named bureau set about the business of providing standards for all the modelling scales then in use. Consisting of the experts of the then current model railway magazines (Maskelyne of the *News*, chairman; R.J. Raymond and F.W. Chubb, editor and proprietor of the *Constructor*, and G.H. Lake, editor of *Railways*), the Bureau embraced the aim of 'drawing up dimensions that will provide trouble-free operation, and to labour for correct appearance'. However, in practice, this got a bit watered down, as for both 7 and 4mm scales, dual standards were produced, described as 'Standard' and 'Scale'. Thus, for 4mm, we have 'Standard OO', which perpetuated Greenly's horrible hybrid, as well as the 'Scale OO', yet to acquire the distinguishing title of 'EM'. There was also a 'Scale HO' standard, and, for interest, I reproduce these standards as set out in the Rev. E. Beal's 1947 *New Developments in Railway Modelling*.

So, in the mid-1940s, the BRMSB was recommending a pragmatic but eminently workable EM standard which, it was hoped, would form the basis of post-war development in 4mm modelling. But, alas, it was not so, for the model trade ignored the wise counsels of the senior members of the hobby, and opted for Greenly's bastard, probably in false hopes of export sales to the rest of the (HO) world. In which case, one might ask, why didn't they adopt HO outright, given that good-quality miniature motors were, by then, available? Could it be that Binns Road had a hand in the matter? Whatever the cause, the effect was the growth of that strange phenomenon that I have already touched upon, 'scale' OO that certainly wasn't 'Scale OO' as the BRMSB had set it out! Very confusing!

The Growth of EM Gauge

This confused state of affairs distressed many leading modellers, particularly those working to the 18mm gauge 'Scale OO' standard. So, in 1955, a number of interested parties, including such figures as Joe Brook-Smith of plywood sleeper fame, met in a North London pub, and formed a society for those working to the BRMSB's 'scale' 4mm standard. To avoid further confusion, they adopted the term of 'EM' (for 'Eighteen Millimetre') to describe the gauge, which

BRMSB Standards for 3.5 and 4mm scales.

	Scale "HO"	Scale "OO"	Standard "OO"
Scale	3.5 mm.	4.0 mm.	4.0 mm.
Gauge (Straight)	16.5 mm.	18.0 mm.	16.5 mm.
Rail height	2.0 mm.	2.0 mm.	2.5 mm.
Rail width	.75 mm.	.75 mm.	1.0 mm.
Distance between running and check rails	1.5 mm.‡	1.5 mm.‡	—
	1.25 mm.*	1.25 mm.*	—
Flange thickness	.5 mm.*	.5 mm.*	.5 mm.*
Flange depth	.75 mm.*	.75 mm.*	.75 mm.*
Overall wheel thickness	2.0 mm.	2.0 mm.	2.5 mm.
Wheel back to back	15.0 mm.	16.5 mm.	14.5 mm.
Sleeper sizes	32 × 3.5 mm.	36 × 4 mm.	32 × 3.5 mm.
Sleepers on main lines	9.0 mm.§	10.0 mm.§	—
Sleepers on sidings	10-12 mm.§	12-14 mm.§	—
Sleeper Thickness :—			
Non-ballasted track	.76 mm.	.76 mm.	.76 mm.
Ballasted track	2.0 mm.	2.0 mm.	2.0 mm.
Standard 6-ft. way :—			
Main line	40.0 mm.§	45.0 mm.§	50.0 mm.§
Sidings	50.0 mm.§	50.0 mm.§	50.0 mm.§
Height of conductor rail above running rail	2.5 mm.	2.5 mm.	2.5 mm

The radius of curves is measured from the inside edge of the outer rail.

The distance of the conductor rail from the running rail (centre to centre) is 4.0 mm. in each case.

* Max. † Straight. ‡ Curves. § Centre to centre

logical move both clarified the situation, and also created the 'mystique' which surrounded finescale modelling in the balmy days of my youth.

So, while EM was alive and well and thriving in the Euston Road, things went from bad to worse in 'OO'. One of the flaws of the BRMSB standards was that, while they gave a fairly full set of dimensions, they didn't specify any tolerances. This was a wondrous loophole for the trade, which could then claim that any old thing that bore a remote approximation to the BRMSB dimension was 'scale'. This is always a problem with standards that aren't fully defined, and it led to a situation where all sorts of bits and pieces were being bandied about under the BRMSB banner which in no way conformed to the standard. As the EM modeller was largely dependent on the mass-OO market for his components, he too was saddled with a lot of very dubious equipment.

Up in Manchester, they didn't think a lot of this. The Manchester Model Railway Society has always counted a good number of talented engineers among its members (and still does), and a group within the MMRS that had adopted the 'EM' standard set about the business of refining the BRMSB dimensions, and producing components to much more closely-defined tolerances. With men like Alex Jackson, Sid Stubbs and John Langan, all highly skilled practical modellers, the 'Manchester' standard soon emerged as something quite above the general run of things elsewhere in 4mm scale, and I well remember being utterly stunned by both the appearance and the remarkable running achieved on John Langan's 'Presson' layout. This standard, officially christened 'EMF', employed a far more prototypical wheel profile, and for the first time properly addressed the vital wheel/track relationship of the check gauge, on which the BRMSB had only really done half a job.

'EMF' was adopted by the emergent Pendon Museum when that magnificent model railway started out on its present ambitious projects, but, due to the scope of the work, they felt it necessary to get wheels and other components manufactured commercially to the new standards. This led, eventually, to Brian Rogers' 'Ultrascale' wheel, with Mike Sharman adopting the same profile when he started wheel manufacture in 1978. A decade earlier, another key development by a commercial firm had produced the other component essential for the growth of EM and the Birth of P4. This was the introduction of code 75 BH rail, originally in the context of the 'Kingsway' system of finescale 4mm track. Previous to the introduction of this rail, the standard had been the old Code 95 BH, far too heavy. EM modellers were split between those who stuck with an overscale rail of correct section, and those who adopted the Peco FB3X 'conductor rail' (equivalent to their current Code 60 FB), accepting the wrong section for a scale rail height.

All these developments were watched over by the elder statesmen of the EM Gauge Society, who were also keenly aware of the emergent Protofour standard, of which more in a page or so. The early 1970s was a period of confusion, with three '18mm' standards in use – BRMSB, the 'Pendon' EM, and the new P4. In 1977, the EMGS altered its rules, with 'Object 1' being 'To popularise the use of track gauges between 18mm and 18.83mm for 4mm railway models ... to encourage more accurate modelling'. A new EM wheel profile, based on the 'Pendon' development, was drawn in 1976, with a much better (and fully defined) flange profile and a wheel width of 90-thou (down from the 100-thou of the old BRMSB 'Standard OO' wheel which had been forced on EM by the manufacturers, notably Romford; no-one would make the 'scale' BRMSB wheel width of 2mm, the dimension subsequently adopted for P4). Read in conjunction with EM Manual Sheet 1.1.0 'Standards, Trackwork', there was at last a fully-defined, fully-dimensioned EM standard. There are still no tolerances quoted, but the improvements in manufacturing standards since the 1950s (and, with the advent of legislation, a stricter ethic with regard to the description of manufactured goods) mean that the tolerances offered by the trade are more than adequate for practical purposes.

So, the EM waters are perhaps a tad muddy. The old BRMSB standard, corrupted by the use of the 'Standard OO' wheel, is still around, living alongside the newer, and much better, 'modern EM' standard, which I would commend to all aspirant EM modellers. It works well, and looks good from most points of view. There are a full range of track gauges to support it, and a wide range of wheels and other components available from the trade. Thus, more than thirty years after it was first mooted, the sort of 'Scale OO' that the BRMSB pioneers had in mind has taken root and gained a wider acceptance than, one suspects, they would ever have dreamed possible.

The Model Railway Study Group and P4

By the early 1960s, the poor old BRMSB was in poor shape. In spite of their best efforts, 4mm modelling was anything but standardized, and their work had been corrupted almost beyond recognition by certain sectors of the trade. A fresh impetus in the development of scale railway modelling was needed, and that impetus came from the Model Railway Study Group. This was a much less official body than the old Bureau, composed of practical modellers rather than journalists, and with a much more defined aim: the investigation and evolution of an 'ultimate' 4mm scale modelling standard, and the promulgation of, and production of components for, that standard.

That they succeeded beyond all doubt is now a matter of record. News of the new standard first 'broke' in the pages of the *Model Railway News*, in August 1966, followed by a lengthy series of articles in the multi-coloured pages of the *Constructor*. The MRSG had done a thorough job, and, under the 'Protofour' banner, a society and a manufacturing organization were set up. I'm not going to go into the politics and personalities of those pioneering days, which were perhaps a touch on the bumpy side; the upshot was that, late in 1975, the Scalefour Society was formed by a group of disaffected P4 modellers, while others were finding refuge under the EMGS umbrella. More recently, the original Protofour Society has merged with the Scalefour Society, so the bandwagon rolls on! But through all these upheavals, the P4 standard remained constant, and gradually gained adherents and wider trade support.

The Protofour standard was not only fully defined, including a set of tolerances for each of the critical dimensions, but was accompanied by both a detailed theoretic exposition, and by a manual of techniques by which the theory could be put into practice. The work of the MRSG was nothing if not thorough, and those of us who took the plunge in the early days found that, as with cooking, if you followed the recipe and observed the stipulations, the end result was a model railway that not only looked better, but ran better too. It wasn't perfect, of course – cosmetic chairs were still in the future, let alone flexible track and all the modern goodies. But the basis of it – Joe Brook-Smiths' ply-sleepered track (yes, Joe was a member of the MRSG too!) was familiar territory, refined by the adoption of rivets in place of rail nails.

The track gauge, 18.83mm, is an exact scale reduction of the nominal 4ft 8½in prototype mean (it varies at full size, as we shall see). Following on from the EMF boys, it incorporated gauge-widening for curves, also provided in the 1976 EM standard. The crossing flangeway gaps and running clearances, while not exactly to scale, were very close; the difference is not readily detectable with the unaided eye. P4 is, to all intents and purposes, an accurate scale rendition of prototype practice. It was based on prototype theory, adapted as necessary, but addressing fully all those critical relationships upon which the functioning of real railways depend.

Hand in hand with the new standard came a new attitude to modelling in general and track in particular. After all, if you were going to the trouble of using scale wheel profiles and a track gauge expressed to two decimal places of a millimetre, then it rather behoved one to ensure that what you were modelling was likewise as accurate as possible. Gone forever were the old *laissez-faire* days of 'near enough is good enough'; we became aware of the need to adopt a far more uncompromising attitude to such things as PW design and layout, the correctness of details such as wagon running gear and locomotive wheels with the right number of spokes and crank throw.

The result has been that quantum leap in modelling standards which I believe, places the British finescale model in its full flowering at the pinnacle of achievement in small-scale (sub 'O') modelling anywhere in the world. The 'knock on' effect all this has had extends these days right through the hobby; the R-T-R model of today would eclipse all but the very cream of the 'scale' crop of not so many years since.

Even P4, with its minimal departure from strict scale practice, has failed to satisfy one or two exacting spirits, notably Ray Hammond and Bill Richmond. Ray produced his own 4mm standard, which he christened 'Scale Four' – abbreviated to S4 – which took out the P4 compromises and tightened up the tolerances still further to become, to all intents and purposes, an exact reduction of the prototype dimensions. Ray has made gauges available for this 'ultimate' standard, but it has not gained a wide following, mainly, I suspect, because it differs so marginally from established P4. However, there has, inevitably, arisen some confusion between the nature of the S4 standard and the Scalefour Society, with an unfortunate coincidence of names to help the muddle along. Just to set the record straight, the Scalefour Society recommends the P4 standard as set out by the MRSG, and it is for this standard that the Scalefour Stores supplies gauges and components.

PRACTICAL DIFFERENCES BETWEEN STANDARDS

So far as the construction of trackwork goes, there are essentially *no* differences between 'finescale OO', EM, and P4, in that the materials and techniques used will be the same irrespective of standard. However, it is a fact that the hardest row to hoe here is that of 'Finescale OO', for, as I've already pointed out, these days nobody promulgates any proper standards for this scale/gauge combination. It would seem to me to be not without the brief of the Scalefour Society (which welcomes *all* scale modellers working in 4mm scale, irrespective of gauge) to do so, and I hope that perhaps by the time that this book appears, such a course may have been adopted by the Society. In the interim, I have set out the 'fine OO' standard that I evolved for my 'Bringewood' project, undertaken in 1984 for the old *Model Railways* magazine.

The snag is, of course, that there are no gauges to go with this set of dimensions, while the OO wheelsets on the market conform to no one standard, some adhering to the old BRMSB profile, others to the current EM outline, and many others resembling no known wheel, actual or model! However, by going back to first principles, it is possible to achieve a workable result in the face of these difficulties, and I explain this process in my next chapter.

Otherwise, the differences in difficulty, or in the work involved, between the various standards do not lie in the area of track, but rather in the construction of locomotives and stock, particularly in the need for suspension systems in the finer standards. I cannot start to discuss the ramifications of suspension here, other than to observe that having all of the wheels firmly in contact with both of the rails all of the time has got to be a huge advantage, irrespective of scale or gauge. You can 'get away' with rigid locos and stock in EM; to try and do so in P4 is pointless, as it will so compromise the whole delicate business of trackholding as to render the adoption of the finer standard fruitless. EM is also a little more tolerant of such conditions as slightly misaligned rail-ends, out-of-kilter crossing noses and imperfectly 'housed' point blades than is P4. But for any of these standards to attain their full potential, careful work is needed in both track and stock.

The choice of 4mm modelling standards is, obviously, a personal one, influenced by many factors. There is a great deal of difference in the situations of the uncommitted modeller with maybe a couple of locos and the odd item of stock to convert, and that of a man with twenty years mainstream OO behind him and a stud of fifty locos.

In the latter case, the arguments for staying with OO and concentrating on improved track and some minor adjustment to the rolling stock will be unanswerable. But, if you aren't that committed, the course of action I would advise might suggest that a start be made with some modest project in Finescale OO, taking the opportunity to improve standards and acquire techniques without a wholesale change that will outdate all the locos and stock overnight. For, don't forget, 'Finescale' according to Rice applies equally to all aspects of the layout. Better structures, accurate signalling, improved scenics and a higher standard of detailing on the stock are just as relevant as a more accurate track gauge.

Then, perhaps, with experience and confidence gained and techniques acquired, a loco or two and a bit of stock might be converted, and either a new layout commenced or, more pragmatically, the fine OO track lifted and replaced by EM or P4. Use of separate track sub-bases as advocated in this book, and a little skilful salvage, will render much of the PW material reclaimable for re-use at the finer standard, now that we all use the same components. A progression of this nature is, I think, far more likely to produce a satisfying and workable layout than a wholesale plunge into the unknown! But while I'm quite happy to acknowledge the role and validity of 'Finescale OO', this doesn't mean that I don't find it wanting. I would always advocate a move to EM or P4 if at all possible – the rewards are greater than a few odd millimetric fractions might suggest.

CHAPTER TWO
TRACKWORK BASICS

The design of permanent way is a complex and subtle business, much hedged about with formulae and equations and mathematical tables of fearsome complexity. I'm not going to try and blind you with science and muddle you with maths in some esoteric exploration of the convoluted ins-and-outs of prototype PW design practice – for a start, once I get past the fundamentals, I haven't got a clue what it's all about; and anyway, most of it isn't relevant to the building of scale model railway track. There are already plenty of detailed – if somewhat dry – texts on these topics, so I shall stick with what I know – the basics.

Unlike the authors of the learned treatises aforementioned, I am quite unqualified in prototype PW matters. All that I know I have culled from books, mainly from the excellent *Modern British Permanent Way,* penned by the estimable C. J. Allen, and published by the Boswell Printing and Publishing Co (proprietors of the magazine *Railway News*) in 1915. This is a comprehensive but blessedly comprehensible survey of PW design and manufacture at that period – the very zenith of steam-era practice. As C. J. A. was a professional PW man turned journalist, I'm happy to regard his book as the 'horse's mouth' on PW matters. Were one of those publishers specializing in facsimile editions to reproduce this volume, he'd be doing all railway modellers a great service.

THE THEORY OF TRACKHOLDING

'No feory wivvout facts', as my old physics master used to quip as he unleashed potted Einstein on us. So it is with trackwork. On the face of it, a flanged wheel riding on an upright rail is a simple enough proposition, but things are a good deal more subtle than that. For a start, that wheel is not just flanged, it's coned. The tread is inclined from the horizontal at 1 in 20 (or 1 in 22 on the Midland, apparently; awkward lot!). It is this coning which serves to 'guide' the wheels on the rails – any departure from the centred position involves 'climbing' the coning of the wheel, which gravity resists; so the wheel tends to sit centrally on the rail. (This is a gross oversimplification of what is actually a very complex interaction, but it'll do for our purposes.)

But what of the flanges in all this? Are they not the means of guidance? Well, most of the time – no, they're not. They are a sort of *in extremis* insurance policy when it comes to staying on plain track. Their real significance comes, as we shall see, in the safe negotiation of crossings in pointwork. On any plain track short of a grindingly sharp

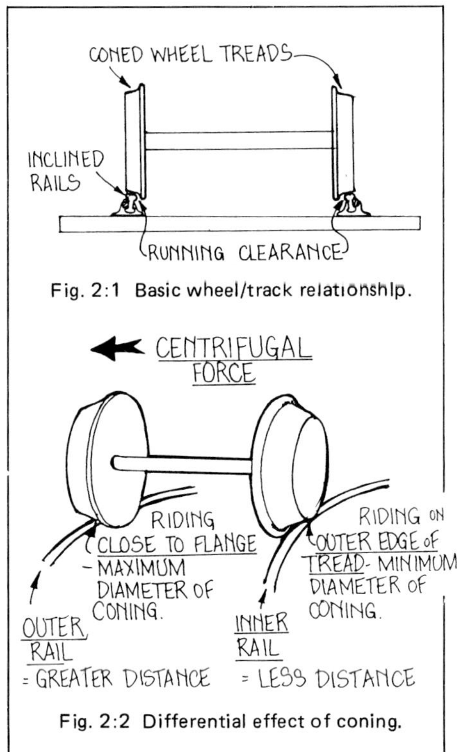

Fig. 2:1 Basic wheel/track relationship.

Fig. 2:2 Differential effect of coning.

curve, the flanges *should* not come into contact with the rail-head at all, the coning being arranged to prevent this. Additionally, on real track, the rails are inclined in at an angle to match the coning, so that the wheel tread and rail-head are in contact over as wide an area as possible, to reduce the loading – and hence wear – of the contact patch.

Even without rail inclination, largely ignored in 4mm scale, it is the coning of the wheels that provides the guidance, which is one reason why tiny P4 flanges aren't as ineffective as most people are apt to assume them to be. The reason for the use of a coned tread for guidance can be summed up in one word: friction. The legendary low rolling resistance of the 'iron road' would be negated at once if the flanges were in constant contact with the railheads, especially when centrifugal force added its tuppenceworth on curved track.

This was the only fundamental bloomer that Meccano Ltd dropped when designing Hornby-Dublo trains. The result, as any Dublo buff can testify, is that a train which cheerfully rockets down straight track at marginally less than the speed of sound then has a job to drag itself round the ensuing curve at anything much better than strolling speed for a lame tortoise. The friction generated when all those flanges bear against the inside of the outer curved rail, coupled with the skidding load caused by lack of differential effect (of which more in a moment) is often enough to stall the train completely, the legendary 'grunt' of Dublo locos notwithstanding. All for want of a bit of coning, Dublo wheels being unrelentingly flat-treaded to the last. These days, I'm glad to say, almost all R-T-R stock has coned wheels, so like problems should not arise.

THE ESSENTIAL DIFFERENTIAL

Lack of coning introduces other undesirable behaviour. The wheels of a railway 'wheelset' (pair of wheels on an axle) are firmly shrunk in place; they are not free to move on the axle in any way. Fine on straight track, where both wheels need to travel the same distance and hence revolve at the same speed; not so clever on curves, where the wheel on the outer rail has a greater distance to travel than the inner wheel fixed to the same axle. Flat tread wheels in this situation 'skid' on one side or the other, setting up more friction.

Coned wheels, on the other hand, tend, under the action of centrifugal force, to move towards the outside of the curve, where the outer wheel, riding on that part of the coning close to the flange (and hence of maximum effective diameter) will need to revolve fewer times to cover the increased distance. The inner wheel, conversely, will be riding on the outer part of the coning (where the effective diameter is less), and thus needs to revolve more quickly to cover its shorter distance. These two effects cancel each other out. The wheelset automatically takes up a position on the track such that the effective diameters of both wheels call for the same speed of rotation to cover the different length of path both must traverse. This, in turn, limits the extent to which the wheelset will move to the outside of the curve, thus continuing the guidance role by ensuring that only under extreme situations (very tight curves) will the flange contact the railhead. I said it was subtle!

RUNNING CLEARANCE

There is, of course, one further consideration to be recognized in the search for the Elysian 'friction free' running of our stock, and that is the matter of 'running clearance', or 'flange clearance'. Reference back to good old *Fig. 1* will show that the outer faces of the flanges of our wheelset do not touch the inside faces of the running rails, by an amount (surprisingly small in full-size practice; I was amazed how many PW dimensions are quoted to $\frac{1}{32}$in) that is sufficient to ensure that, under normal conditions, the action of the coning already described can keep the flange face clear of the rail.

This is a simple enough consideration on straight track but, as usual, as soon as you get to a curve, problems arise. Consider *Fig. 3* for a moment, which should show how the fixed wheelbase of a railway vehicle (and even a bogie has a fixed wheelbase of quite significant length in this context) can all too easily take up the running clearance when a curve is encountered. I've noted that this clearance is quite small, to prevent vehicles 'hunting' on straight track under some conditions, so it doesn't take much of an 'angle of attack' between the wheel flange and the rail to use it up – when instant friction will result. As the wheels cannot move on their axle to maintain the necessary clearance, this is achieved by easing the track gauge, by an amount dependent upon the severity of the curve.

The finer modelling standards, where the 'running clearance' is similarly set to fine limits (one of the major differences from the coarse 'OO' standard, which allows a lot of 'slop' in this dimension), require provision to be made to introduce gauge widening on curved track, one of the factors taken care of in the proper design of track gauges. It is this use of a fine running clearance that endows stock built to finescale standards with a superior running quality, free from the 'shimmy' that often characterizes coarse-standard OO stock; conversely, it is the large running clearance that helps get OO stock around far-tighter-than-scale curves without impossible levels of friction. However, there is absolutely no reason at all, where 'fine-scale' OO track is being built, why the same criteria that, applied to EM or P4 standards, result in smooth running, cannot be incorporated into 16.5mm gauge track, and the stock simply modified to suit by adjusting the 'wheel check gauge' to a suitable value. More on that in a page or two; it is first necessary to destroy a 'false idol' peculiar to railway modellers – the worship of that deceitful deity 'back-to-back'.

THE GREAT BACK-TO-BACK MYTH EXPOSED!

It is quoted, it is measured, it is checked, it is bandied about on all sides – and it's about as meaningful as a politician's election promise. Generations have assumed that, provided this 'magic number' is OK, then they have taken care of all those vital relationships between wheelsets and track – never mind the bumping and boring, the straight-line shuffle and the lurching through curves and over pointwork. The back-to-back measurement is only *part* of the equation – for really good running all the wheelsets in use should confirm to the same standard and have profiles with an *identical* flange thickness. I have already cited the

Fig. 2:3 Flange binding on curves.

LOSS of RUNNING CLEARANCE

N

N= NOMINAL TRACK GAUGE

importance of the distance over the faces of the flanges, and their relationship to the running clearance. It is the dimension, measured from the rear of one flange to the face of the opposing flange, and known as the 'wheel check gauge', that is the vital constant in assuring the correct relationship of wheels to track (*Fig. 4*).

This is where the 'fully defined' standards, the current EM and the P4 systems, have a huge advantage over largely unregulated OO. With only one 'approved' wheel profile in use, then the back-to-back dimension can be usefully used to check and set the critical check gauge. But where wheels of differing profiles or flange thicknesses are in use, then the back-to-back must *vary* if the wheel check gauge is to be *constant*. In this context, a 'front-to-front' gauge would be of more use, but even this does not answer the complete case, as the situation through crossing work, where the wheel has to be 'checked' by 'check rails', has not been addressed. And this is the most critical situation in this whole trackholding business, which can only be properly resolved by getting that 'vital constant', the wheel check gauge, right.

THE IMPORTANCE OF CHECK GAUGE

This business of check gauge and wheel guidance through crossing work is at the very nub of reliable trackholding, and is the one relationship which, once mastered, will not only enable you to build track that functions well, but will enable you to work out the why and wherefore when things go wrong! I don't know what percentage of derailments on model railways occur when negotiating a 'common' or 'acute' crossing in pointwork (that unit known to generations of modellers as a 'frog', which term PW engineers delude themselves refers to a small, slimy amphibian) in a facing direction, but I'd bet it must be on the high side of 75%. These derailments, usually due to the flange of one wheelset striking or riding over the 'nose' of the crossing, are caused by an inaccurate

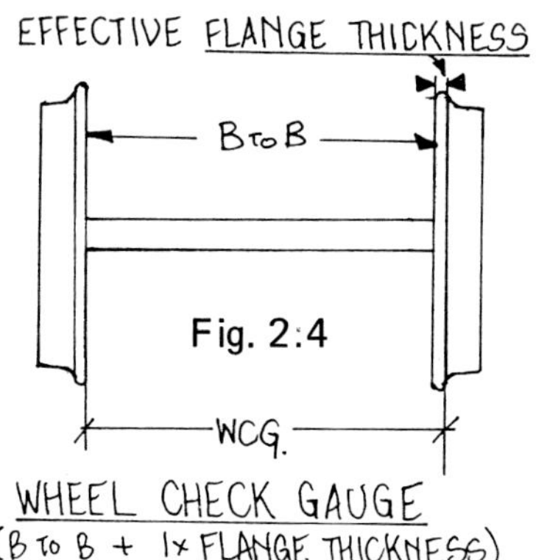

Fig. 2:4

setting of the check gauge – a breakdown of the fundamental relationship between wheels and track.

As I've already claimed, the negotiation of a common crossing in the facing direction is the most critical situation in the relationship between train and track. It is the occasion upon which all the complexities and subtleties of permanent way and wheel design come together to ensure that the wheel goes accurately and smoothly through the formation. Rather than being a single happening, the negotiation of a crossing is a sequence of events, which must complement each other if all is to go well.

Diagram 5 is the key to all this. Here, we have a wheelset about to pass through the crossing, and it is possible to visualize the sequence quite simply. The actual crossing point of the rails, where the knuckles flare out to embrace the finely-tapered 'V' nose of the crossing, is cited as the weakest and most vulnerable location in any PW formation; in the prototype, there are massive special chairs, cast gauging blocks and heavy cross-bolting here, all designed to reinforce this vulnerable gap in the rails' continuity. The ultimate disaster is for a wheel-flange to strike the crossing-nose directly – with the massive inertia of a train behind it, such an occurrence would smash the crossing and result in a mighty accident. Even at 4mm

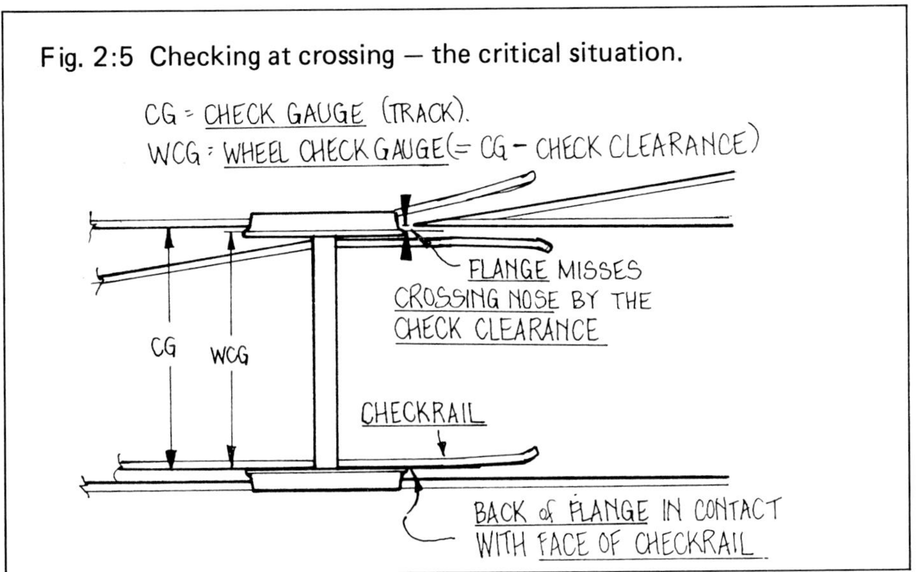

Fig. 2:5 Checking at crossing — the critical situation.

scale, it makes a derailment almost inevitable.

To ensure that this cannot happen, the wheelset is 'checked' and guided so that, even under extreme conditions, with the wheel as far over to the 'crossing' side as the coning and flanges will permit, there will still be the necessary clearance between the face of the flange and the crossing nose. This is accomplished by the 'check rail', which must be accurately set to accomplish this task. The 'flare' at the end of the check rail gradually closes toward the stock rail, guiding the wheelset across to align the flange for its passage through the crossing nose. This lateral movement is limited by the action of the crossing knuckle, where the transition from running rail to crossing wing rail takes place. This transition acts in a similar way to the flare on the end of the check rail, and stabilizes the wheelset in a 'centralized' position on the track. This position is optimized so that the face of the flange encountering the crossing nose will miss it by the desired amount, known as the 'check clearance'. At the actual point where the wheel is passing from the knuckle onto the crossing nose, it is thus located very precisely; once the critical moment is passed, the wing rail, then the check rail, are 'flared away' from the crossing nose and stock rail respectively, releasing the wheelset to establish its own alignment with the rails.

In the reverse direction, the alignment needed to pass the wheel smoothly from crossing nose to knuckle rail is established by the flares on the check and wing rails acting to 'centre' the wheelset, although with only the obtuse angle of the knuckle to clobber, rather than the acute angle of the crossing nose, matters are less critical in this direction. The check clearance still needs to be maintained as far as possible, however, or a very high rate of wear of the knuckle rails would be experienced, not to mention a pretty horrendous lurch and a percussive shock that would do little to inspire confidence in the fare-paying passengers!

A moment's reflection on the process just described will show the importance of the interaction of the check rails with the 'check gauge' of the wheelset. It is this measurement – the *back* of one flange to the *face* of the opposing flange, that *must* be a constant, (or at least vary only by a tiny tolerance – a matter of 'thou' at 4mm scale, even in EM) or the check rails will not be able to guarantee the maintenance of the vital check clearance at the crossing nose. And loss of that clearance is the road to disaster.

It is the very tight control of these factors – wheel check gauge, check-rail setting, check clearance – that lies at the heart of high-quality running on a model railway. This is precisely what the P4 system achieves to very fine limits; with the narrow flanges of the P4 wheel, allowing small flangeway gaps (more on those in a moment), plus a small but consistent check clearance, it is possible to obtain completely smooth running through crossings. The more you relax these dimensions and tolerances, the bumpier and less certain becomes the running.

'UNIVERSAL' TRACK

Another hoary old chestnut that I feel is long overdue for towing out to sea and sinking with a well-placed salvo! As far as I'm concerned, the whole concept of 'universal' track is an utter nonsense, as I hope the above analysis of the goings-on at a crossing will serve to demonstrate. 'Universal' track, we are led to believe, will accept a variety of wheelsets, differing in many characteristics, but especially in their check gauge, and guide them accurately and smoothly through the complex process just described. I suggest that 'universal' track abrogates the vast majority of the functions of real track, and allows the flanges alone – with luck – to keep it all on the planet. That the result is characterized by a bouncing, lurching ineptitude and a predilection for 'inexplicable' derailments should come as no surprise! The only inexplicable thing about 'universal' track in my book is that the guardians of the Trades Descriptions Act have not moved against the perpetrators of such nonsense!

No, in the context of our 'finescale' approach, we can only accept a single, consistent check-gauge dimension, to which the track is properly matched. It is not possible to consider either trackwork or wheel standards in isolation, something the modelling world has long been guilty of. If the pioneers of P4 had done nothing beyond making the railway modelling world aware of these 'facts of life', they would still have made possible a far better standard of running and trackholding, for it is not difficult to apply these criteria from 'first principles'; indeed, this is what I have long advocated for OO, the standard most in need of some proper regulation.

SETTING UP TRACK AND STOCK FROM FIRST PRINCIPLES

Sounds daunting, but it isn't. You can start at either end of the equation, either by setting a track standard, and matching the wheels to it, or by selecting one wheel type as your 'standard', and using that to determine the track settings. I originally described this process, as applied to OO R-T-R stock, back in the early 1980s, in a series of articles in *Model Railways* magazine under the collective title of 'The Bringewood Tales'. What I was aiming to do there was to maximize the potential of the 'new wave' of R-T-R stock, by taking much of the 'slop' (excessive running clearance, already noted) out of off-the-shelf OO, running it on trackwork specified to suit. With the quoted BRMSB 'back-to-back' figure of 14.5mm, most OO wheels, I found, measured between 15 and 15.5mm check gauge, from 15.5–16.0mm over the face of the flanges. R-T-R stock, I found, generally had a check gauge of some 14.5–15mm, about 15–15.5mm over flange faces, ie, a 'running clearance' of up to 1.5mm on the 16.5mm gauge. That's $4\frac{1}{2}$ inches at full size! All this slop was clearly unnecessary, so I decided on a running clearance no greater than $\frac{1}{2}$mm. With an average flange thickness of $\frac{1}{2}$mm, this gave a wheel check gauge of 15.5mm (and a back-to-back measurement ranging from 14.5–15mm), which I settled on as standard.

To set my various wheelsets to this common check gauge, I made up a simple Plastikard gauge as in *Fig. 6*, and used this to match the wheelsets. Non-adjustable wheelsets, of the 'two wheels moulded on an axle' variety, were junked, and replaced by either Romford or Maygib wheels, also adjusted to conform. Loco wheels were likewise eased outwards to the desired setting – it was usually quite simple to get the requisite ½mm or so a side without disturbing the wheel setting or quartering. Locos treated included an Airfix 4F, a Hornby 'Jinty', and a Mainline 2251. Obviously, if you're prepared to re-wheel or re-chassis locos and change stock wheels to a common type, then all this is made much easier, and it may be possible to produce a back-to-back gauge suited to your check gauge setting, thus arriving at the situation pertaining to the defined finescale standards.

It then becomes simply a matter of setting up your pointwork to match your now 'regulated' wheelsets, with their common check gauge. Put bluntly, all that you really need to ensure is that you set the check rails so that, with the wheelset pushed hard over in the 'crossing nose' direction, the face of the flange just misses the crossing nose. I decided on 10-thou clearance, about ¼mm, easy to set with a feeler gauge. This takes care of the basic and critical situation, but there are a few other factors to consider.

A further desideratum of finescale pointwork is the minimizing of flangeway gaps, both for reasons of appearance (prototype wing rail-to-crossing nose gap: 1¾in, barely more than ½mm at 4mm scale), and because smaller flangeways give a shorter break in the support and electrical continuity given to a wheel as it passes from the knuckle to the crossing nose (see *Diagram 7*). This gap can become a major problem in wide-radius points built to coarse-scale standards, as they lengthen in proportion to the narrowing of the angle of the crossing 'V'. I have seen OO points with a knuckle-nose gap of more than an inch! You could lose a whole loco down a hole like that, more than likely! To give you an indication, this gap is about 14in on a prototype 1 in 8 crossing, although the wheel will be supported over part of its width for most of this distance as the wing rail turns away.

I got my flangeway gaps down to 0.75mm on the 'Bringewood' OO track, about half the normal dimension for OO; this alone gave a huge improvement in the quality of running through the (PCB-based) pointwork; coupled with the accurate wheel/checkrail relationship, I arrived at OO track that gave a running quality approaching that which I had come to expect on my P4 layout, with commensurately improved appearance. I have set out these 'Bringewood' standards for OO gauge in the 'standards' appendix. They may not be the ultimate, but they are workable and proven, and as no-one else seems to have a set of finescale standards for OO, I offer them for what they're worth. Used with Maygib or Gibson wheels on that 15.5mm check gauge, I think they would answer very well for the bloke who wants to stay with 16.5mm gauge, but would like the appearance and running qualities associated with EM and P4. However, I would point out that there will be just as much work involved building OO track to this standard as for the more accurate gauges, and that due attention will need to be given to considerations such as gauge widening on curves. And, as yet, you can't buy gauges, templates and so on for this standard.

Fig. 2:6 The effect of flangeways on wheel support at crossings.

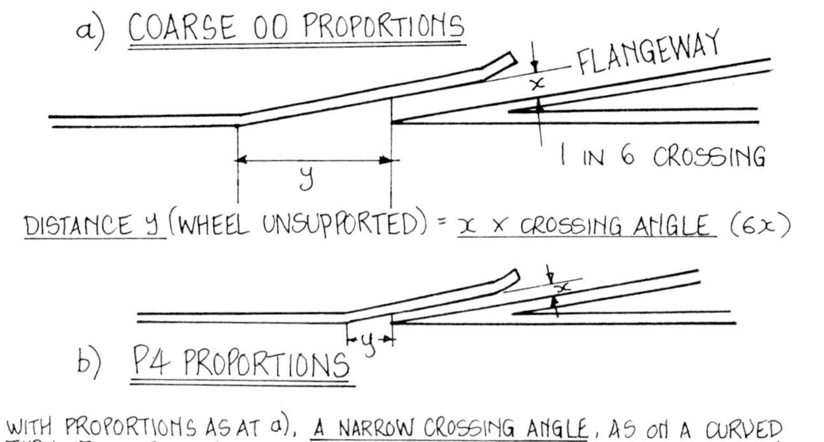

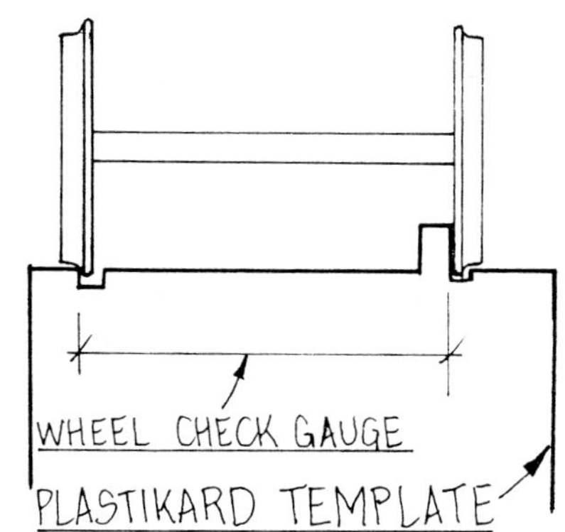

Fig. 2:7 Check gauge template.

SUMMARY OF BASICS

I have gone into these rather theoretical considerations at some length, as I firmly believe that it's a lot easier to build good track if you know *why* you're doing what you're doing. I also hope that I have shown that track cannot be considered in isolation, but rather forms part of a complex and subtle mechanical system. Most of what I have set out here is *fact* – it is the railway engineer's recognition of the laws of physics, and his solution to the problems posed by intractables such as mass, inertia, gravity, centrifugal force, and Murphy's Law.

So, what we have, in essence, is a coned, flanged wheel riding on a rail (which should be inclined to match the coning, to spread the wheel load and reduce wear, but which we can safely make vertical as our loads are tiny and you can't see the inclination at 4mm scale). The coning provides the primary guidance system, and also gives the necessary differential effect on curves. The flanges provide additional 'on the limit' guidance and also come into play in aligning the wheelset to pass it through the crossings of pointwork or diamond formations. There is an exact and critical relationship between wheel profile, rails, check gauge, track gauge, flangeway width, check rails and crossing knuckles which ensures at all times that proper clearances are maintained between flanges and railheads.

That's not all, of course. The prototype PW engineer has a lot of other factors to consider, such as drainage and resilience, maintenance, a smooth ride for the passengers and profit for the shareholders, resistance to wear and corrosion, and consistent performance under wide temperature variations. He has to worry about rail creep and hammer blow and fatigue fractures, about woodworm in his sleepers and rust in his fishplate bolt-holes. Some of these factors, such as the desirability of resilience and consistent performance at temperature extremes, concern us too, while we have concerns, mainly electrical, that need not trouble our full-size counterpart.

Full-size or model, there's a lot more to track than meets the eye. However, while we need to apply some of the theory, what we're basically setting out to do in building finescale model track is to replicate the appearance of real track as well as its performance. Some study of the physical nature of prototype track seems to be a logical 'next step'.

CHAPTER THREE
A PEEP AT THE PROTOTYPE

Having bored you with a load of regrettably essential technical mumbo-jumbo on the *workings* of track, I can now relax a bit and ramble on about what the real stuff *looks* like, which, in the context of our finescale model railway, is just as important as the mechanical functioning of the system. In this respect, track is just like any other aspect of our subject; we examine the prototype, and try to replicate it as convincingly as possible in model form. So, as well as the individual components that go to make up the trackwork, we're also going to be interested in the way it relates to the rest of the landscape, the peripheral systems (point rodding, drainage cesses, crossing infills, bridges and other structures) associated with it, and, importantly, its colouring and weathering.

It's not much use producing beautiful finescale track in the context of a historical model railway if we end up with the wrong type of permanent way for the trains being modelled, so perhaps I'd better start out by sketching the evolution of track. After all, getting such a fundamental aspect of the railway as 'right' as possible is an established cornerstone of the finescale 'credo' – all within limits, of course. I am talking here of the overall 'type' and appearance of the track, rather than minutiae such as chair-bolt-head radii or precise spike-head shape.

A POTTED HISTORY OF PERMANENT WAY

The iron edge railway dates from 1789, when Jessop produced his first cast-iron T-section rails at the Butterley Ironworks. T-section rails, usually of wrought iron and often of the 'fishbelly' pattern, were the earliest 'standard', usually secured to stone block sleepers, a hangover from plateway practice. Indeed, on parts of the Liverpool & Manchester, the 'T' rails, set in cast-iron chairs, were fixed directly to the living rock! The fishbelly rails were difficult to manufacture, and were soon replaced with the ancestor of the familiar 'bullhead' rail, the 'double headed' rail. The idea behind this was simple; with a symmetrical section, once the running surface of one head was worn, the rail could simply be inverted for further service using the other 'head'. Fine in theory, but in practice, the unyielding nature of early stone-sleepered track produced a wonderful hammer-action in the chairs that all but castellated the surface of the lower head!

It was fairly soon realized that the track needed to be a good deal more resilient than was possible with an all-stone substructure, and timber cross-sleepers soon became the standard, except on the GWR (and I'm not going to be diverted into dissertations on the 'baulk road', interesting though this topic is). I think that it is not generally realized by modellers that the *track*, rather than the suspension system on the locomotives and stock, was the principal springing medium on the steam-age railway. A moment's thought will suggest that a coupled steam locomotive cannot have much in the way of suspension travel, as vertical displacement of the wheels effectively alters the axle centres, which are then at odds with the coupling rod centres. More on all this in the section on underlays and track bases in Chapter 5.

So, by about 1850, most railways were running on timber-cross-sleepered road with wrought-iron double-headed rails of about 45lb/yd keyed into iron chairs with iron or wooden keys. The rails were in quite short lengths, typically about 24ft, with the joints arranged in 'joint chairs', rather than being fishplated. Sleeper-spacings varied widely from company to company, being as wide as 5ft centres on some lines; and as for turnout design, the variety was endless! There were stub points, single bladed points, unequal points (one blade longer than the other), cast crossings, fabricated crossings, crossings without wing rails, crossings with internal and external check rails (check rails outside and above the level of the running rails), and crossings with no check rails at all! Some of these early P & C formations are drawn in Alan Prior's excellent book: *19th Century Railway Drawings in 4mm Scale.*

Mind you, if you're modelling early PW, a lot of the details are of only academic interest, as the usual practice was to ballast right up to the rail-heads, thus obscuring the sleepering and rail-fastenings! I have modelled this sort of track with Peco Code 60 'Z' rail (to give a nice fine head, suggesting a light section) soldered to PCB sleepers, infilled with card, and given a top dressing of suitable ballast. Simple – and cheap.

THE BIRTH OF BULLHEAD

Gradually, the 'double headed' section gave way to the common 'bullhead', which put more metal where it was needed – in the wearing part of the railhead – and reduced the foot to a proportion suited to the lesser loads in that area of the rail. It became principally a locating device. Steel bullhead rails were first rolled in 1857, giving greater strength for the same section. Nevertheless, the rapidly increasing speed and weight of trains in the period from about 1865 until the First War led to a steady increase in the section of bullhead rails. The Settle and Carlisle, laid in 1875, used 24ft rails weighing 83lb/yard. By 1893, the Midland was using 85lb/yard rail in 30ft lengths; by 1896, the rail was up to 100lb/yd rail in 36ft, then 45ft lengths. By the time Allen's book was published in 1915, most of the principal companies were using bullhead rail of 90–95lb/yd, in 45ft lengths, with only the LNWR and NER on 60ft.

In 1904, an event of significance took place, when the British Engineering Standards Committee met, and formulated the 'Standard Section Railway Rail', the familiar 95lb/yd bullhead which remained the norm right up until the introduction of heavy section FB rails. There were other BS rails, of 85lb and 100lb/yd sections, but these varied only in height (and that by fractions of an inch), so in 4mm scale, our standard code 75 (75 thou high) rail serves to represent them all. The length of rails in the pre-grouping period rarely exceeded 45ft, with many lines retaining 30ft, 32ft (Caledonian), 36ft, 40ft, and 48ft (Caley again). 'Short' lengths, for use on the inside of curves, were sometimes supplied; otherwise, rails were cropped *in situ*.

SLEEPERS

Sleepering, too, gradually became more standardized. Timber was the usual material, with many types being tried, hard and soft wood, untreated, dipped and pressure-impregnated with creosote. In the pre-grouping period, the length became standardized – more or less – at nine feet, and the section at 10in wide by 5in thick for plain track. On pointwork, where there was need to secure chairs 'on the skew' rather than in line with the long axis of the sleeper, the width was increased to 12in and the thickness to 6in. Some railways – most of the Scottish companies and the GER notable among them – did not employ special sleepers for point and crossing work, preferring to 'interlace' standard sleepers, thus keeping all the chairs 'square'.

As well as the common timber sleeper, experiments were undertaken with 'rot-proof' sleepers in pressed steel (LNWR), cast iron and ferro-concrete. All these, for one reason or another, were found wanting, and the timber sleeper has remained in widespread use up until recently. The successful production of concrete sleepers did not really get away until the 1950s, though some of the mainline companies – notably the GWR – were working on them before the war. After the grouping, the length of the timber sleeper was reduced from 9ft to 8ft 6in; this may seem a rather petty reduction, until you consider the number of

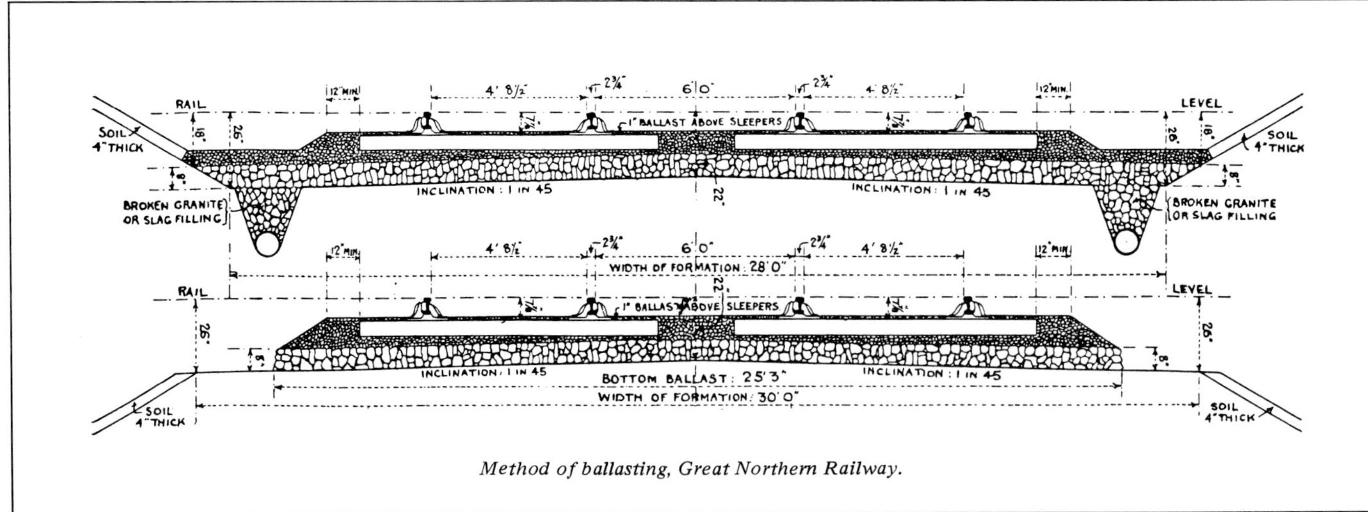

Method of ballasting, Great Northern Railway.

sleepers in use and required annually for replacement, when it becomes apparent that 6in a sleeper represents a pretty substantial saving in timber costs. However, sleepers, particularly pressure-impregnated ones, have a pretty long life, and it's quite appropriate to use 9ft pre-group sleepers on post-grouping layouts, particularly in sidings.

BALLASTING

The practice of ballasting 'all over' was called into question during the latter years of the 19th century. It was not, anyway, a universal practice; the LNWR's much-trumpeted 'dustless' PW was rarely ballasted above the sleeper-tops. Much seems to have depended upon the material used for ballast. The wealthy LNW, with its crushed and washed stone, could afford a quality of road that was beyond the means of impecunious companies like the GER or the notorious South-Eastern. The mighty Midland, too, with ample supplies of clean-draining crushed limestone available, laid a low-ballasted road. The NER used ash and clinker, ballasted level with the sleeper tops, as did the GCR. The GNR used broken slag, crushed, and ballasted 1in above the sleepers. The Brighton used beach shingle, as did the Cambrian amongst others. In this transitional period – 1885–1914 – it is best to consult photographs to establish the ballasting practice of your chosen prototype at a given date; the subject is far too complex to dissect in detail here.

By the grouping in 1923, the functioning of ballast was much better understood, and the use of crushed stone, usually granite or other hard igneous rock, became standard for running lines, though ash, slag and gravel continued in use on sidings. This type of ballasting continues to the present, though modern heavyweight high-speed PW with continuous welded rail calls for much heavier ballasting, with as much as a yard (depth) of stone being employed. Modern track is far more rigid than traditional steam-era bullhead, as the modern practice is for a solid track with soft, long-travel suspension with hydraulic shock-absorbers on the stock – no problem on an all-diesel or electric fleet. This fundamental change in PW practice is a major factor in the demise of the traditional British short-wheelbase 4-wheel wagon, which needed a resilient road to ensure trackholding; they can (and did!) bounce themselves clean off of rigid track. It also accounts for the restrictions on the routeing and speed of preserved steam locos, likewise unsuited to so inflexible a road.

DEVELOPMENT OF POINTWORK

These days, we modellers are all wordly-wise in the matter of what PW engineers refer to as 'P & C' work (point and crossing). We talk glibly of B7L and C12Rs as though 'twas ever thus, and assume that it's all taped in a nice matter of standardization, probably found on a stone tablet unearthed during the excavation of Tring Cutting.

Well, this is far from the truth. The more-or-less standard P & C work that characterizes most post-grouping track only evolved after the actual grouping took place. Prior to that date, the various companies all had their own practices, and there was very considerable variety in P & C design. Obviously, the fundamental rules that I discussed in the last chapter still pertained, but as with any rules, there are many ways of interpreting them. So, while the essentials remained the same, the details varied a lot. I've already mentioned the interlaced sleepering favoured by some companies, and the arrangement of point timbering is one aspect of P & C design that was far from standard. Allen devotes much space in his book to the differing practices of the main companies, without ever mentioning a 'B' switch (or any other such standard component). The number and type of slide chair, length of switch blade, throw of blades, use of 'joggled' or 'rebated' stockrails, type of knuckle chair and crossing chair, length and positioning of wing rails and check rails, length and angle of checkrail flares – all were a matter of company practice and individual design.

The further you go back, the more variety there is. I've already mentioned some of the primary turnout designs used in the early days of the railways, but some of the complex formations that were laid out in the 1860s and 1870s have to be seen to be believed. Many of them would just not be possible with the standardized components familiar to modellers. Much of this trackwork breaks what are now considered to be basic rules – curved crossings, check and guard rails willy-nilly or not at all, horrific curvature, point blades stacked one upon another, crossing angles all over the place, fouling clearances between tracks – you name it, they did it. Such carefree trackwork is rarely modelled by today's serious-minded finescale modeller, only by the utterly frivolous Mike Sharman, but if you're building an 1870s-period layout (in fact, any pre-group layout up to about 1914), then the sort of ultra-standardized trackwork which so many modellers tend to produce is as inappropriate as a Morris Oxford at the level crossing gates.

So, our standardized PW formations really only apply to the period 1925–1960, or thereabouts. Subsequent to that date, the gradual changeover to heavyweight FB track has brought about substantial design changes in P & C work. At first, the FB pointwork was very similar to the bullhead it superseded, although tending to be rather clumsier. By its very nature, FB rail is less suited to intricate P & C work, where the bulk of the wide, flat foot gets in the way somewhat. It's also much more of a job to replace individual components in FB pointwork, so recent years have seen a change to one-piece cast crossings in ultra-hard-wearing manganese steel, a solution only adopted at locations of exceptional wear in the bullhead era. Contemporary P & C work is also characterized by its sparsity, reflecting the greatly reduced scope and intricacy of the traffic patterns. A further modern development is the high speed turnout, characterized by some very long leads (see 'anatomy' section), up to as much as a $\frac{1}{4}$ mile. Just think, a 4mm turnout measuring 17ft from tiebar to crossing nose!

THE 'BIG FOUR' AND THE EARLY BR PERIOD

This is the most popular period with modellers, covering the years 1920–1965. There was little major change in the basic form of PW prevalent in Britain over this period, and it is track of this era which is most readily catered for by the modern finescale flexible track, principally from C & L, and by the various component systems. The templates widely supplied by the specialist societies are likewise appropriate to P & C work for this period, when only minor differences existed between the practices of the different groups – or, indeed, 'regions' of BR. I have called this track 'standard bullhead', though I stress that this is my own term for it, not some official description. It is with the modelling of 'standard bullhead' that the bulk of this book is concerned, though I dabble a bit with concrete sleepers and a spot of flat-bottom here and there.

As with any other aspect of the prototype, it pays to take a long, hard close look at just what it is you're trying to model. In the context of 4mm scale, there is a fairly general cut-off point beyond which further refinement and superfine detailing is lost on the viewer. But some 'minor' differences are all too apparent, even at normal viewing distance. The extra bulk and foursquare baseplate of a GWR modern 2-bolt chair contrasts strongly with the more compact, round-based 3-bolt chair, and that's the sort of detail worth getting right if you can. Likewise, the differing shapes of checkrail flares or wing rails are readily apparent, and again repay trouble. But, by and large, provided you get the basics right, your track should satisfy the eye.

ANATOMY OF 'STANDARD BULLHEAD' – PLAIN TRACK

This is really pretty straightforward. For most of the period under review, new track used BS 95lb/yd bullhead rail in 60ft lengths, with suspended fishplated joints incorporating an expansion allowance (quoted as 9/32in at 60°F for a 60ft rail), carried in keyed cast-iron chairs on timber or, latterly, reinforced concrete sleepers. The design of the chairs was one aspect that did differ from company to company and subsequently within BR. The tendency was to increase the area of the baseplate, to spread the load on the sleeper, while the introduction of fang-bolts in place of screw-spikes and trenails led to the widespread adoption of 'two-bolt' wide-base chairs, pioneered by the GWR. To be pedantic, we're usually incorrect in talking about three or four-*bolt* chairs; almost certainly, these multiple fixings would have consisted of a pair of screw-spikes, to locate the chair laterally, and one or two oak 'trenails' to hold it down to the sleeper.

All these chairs will, as the accompanying illustrations show, have provided for the 1 in 20 inward inclination of the rails; they will also have raised the foot of the rail clear of the sleeper by between $1\frac{1}{2}$ and 2in, a small gap that nevertheless is visually very significant, even in 4mm scale. This is one of the drawbacks of PCB (printed-circuit board) based track, where the rail is soldered direct to the surface of a copper-clad paxolin sleeper, thus eliminating this gap. In the ply & rivet system, the thickness of the rivet-

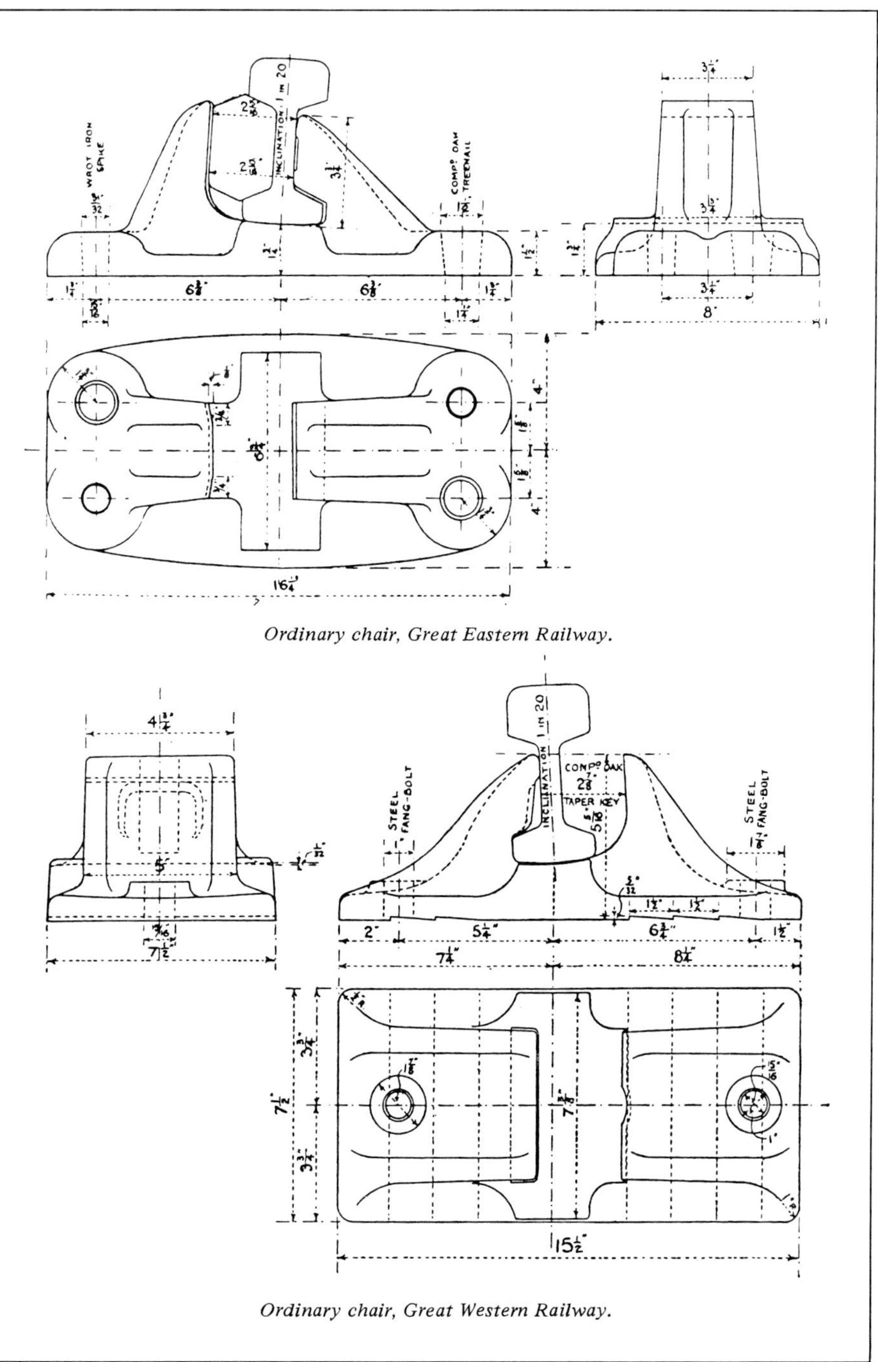

Ordinary chair, Great Eastern Railway.

Ordinary chair, Great Western Railway.

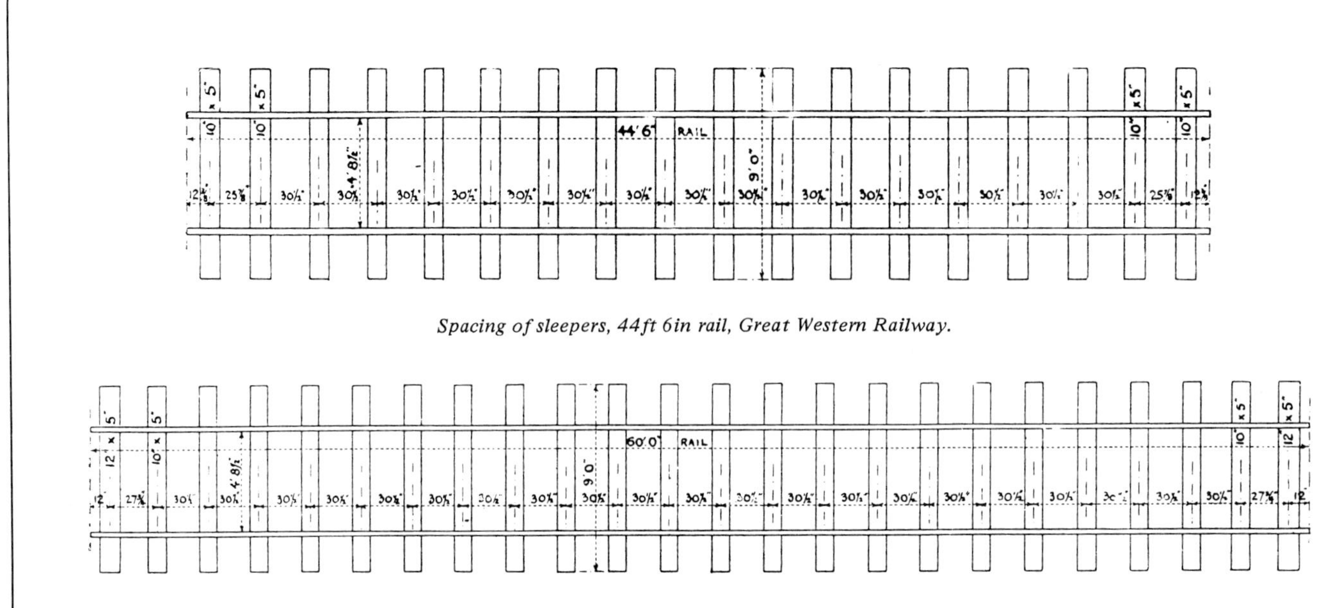

Spacing of sleepers, 44ft 6in rail, Great Western Railway.

Spacing of sleepers, 60ft rail, London and North Western Railway.

head above the ply sleeper provides the necessary clearance, while it is, of course, built-in to the C & L chairs – as is the 1 in 20 cant, a nice touch.

The rails are held into the chairs by tapered or sprung 'keys'. For most of the 'standard bullhead' period, these were of wood, usually oak or teak, and were quite subtle in shape. The C & L chairs incorporate excellent representations of these keys, and come in two 'hands'; key inserted from the left, or key from the right. The reason for this 'handing' is the propensity of rail, particularly bullhead rail, to 'creep'. That is, it tends to move in the chairs, gradually advancing in the direction of the traffic over the line. The effect is not spectacular – we're only talking inches of movement here, not the whole West of England main line making a beeline for the bufferstops at Penzance! But it was significant, as it tended to close up all the expansion joints in the track, which could lead to trouble. Hence, the practice was to drive all the keys into the chairs in the direction from which the traffic came, so that as the rail tried to 'creep', it had the effect of *tightening* the keys in the chairs, rather than easing them out. On single tracks or bi-directional running lines, keys were sometimes driven left and right on alternate chairs along the length or on opposite hands on adjoining lengths. Correct key orientation is quite apparent from a normal viewing distance, so is worth getting right.

The later sprung-steel type of key is much shorter than its wooden counterpart, and was designed to be driven right into the chair, flush with the edges of the chair-jaw. Unlike the wooden key, it is not tapered, relying on its spring action to provide firm rail location. The C & L and Ratio plastic

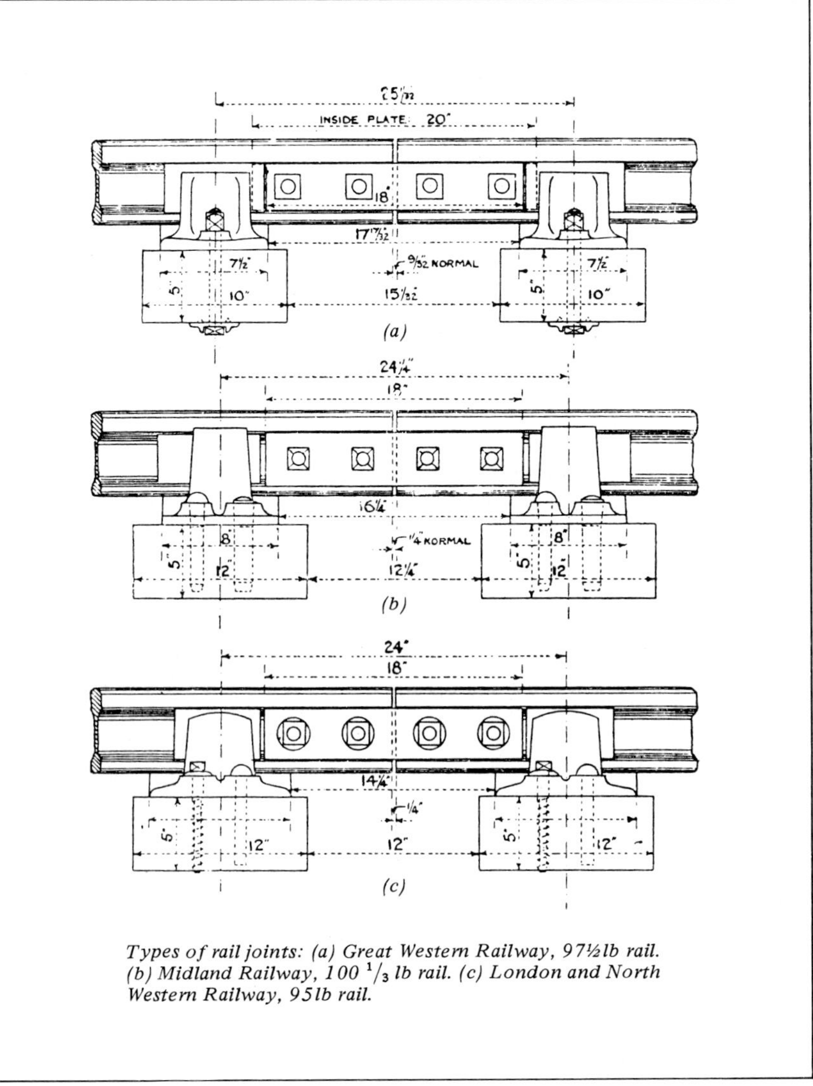

Types of rail joints: (a) Great Western Railway, 97½lb rail. (b) Midland Railway, 100 ⅓ lb rail. (c) London and North Western Railway, 95lb rail.

chair/sleeper strip, and flexible track made from it, has keys flush with the chair-jaws, for mould-release reasons, and so strictly speaking is more representative of track laid with metal keys, more common in the post-war period.

The 60ft lengths of track, known as 'panels', were joined by fishplates, of the 4-bolt BS pattern on all running lines (2-bolt fishplates could be found in sidings). These fishplated joints were of the 'suspended' pattern; that is, they were located between two adjacent sleepers and their accompanying chairs, rather than being situated *over* a sleeper in a special 'joint chair', as had earlier been common practice. These suspended joints were obviously a 'weak point' in the track, and the adjacent sleepers were usually closed up in spacing to afford more support to the joint. These 'joint spacings' are given on many of the plain track templates provided for track construction, and in the context of finescale track, are a 'must'. Incidentally, contrary to common modelling belief, fishplates do not 'grip' the rail in any way, and the bolts holding them are deliberately kept slack rather than being tightened. This is to ensure that the rail can move longitudinally – the holes in the rail-web are oval or oversize to allow the bolts to accommodate this. The function of the fishplates is to maintain the alignment between railheads and to add further support at this weak point in the track, not to join rail-lengths rigidly one to another.

Sleeper-spacing is another general feature separating finescale from 'toy train' track. The practice in the 'standard bullhead' period varied slightly from company to company, or with local conditions. Soft ground, for instance, might call for a closer sleeper spacing to improve support for the rails, and to spread the 'pumping' load over a greater area of sub-base. Generally speaking, with 95lb/yd bullhead, sleepers were on no more than a 2ft 6in centre-to-centre spacing, with, as noted, a closer centre distance adjacent to joints. The easiest way to get this right is, as already mentioned, to make use of track construction templates. Sources for these are listed in one of the appendices at the end of the book.

Whilst the 60ft track panel was the norm for renewals or new construction throughout the 'standard bullhead' period, branch lines often used older PW material downgraded on relaying, so the use of 45ft or even 30ft rails in these situations is not inappropriate. Sidings, yards, light railways, mineral and industrial lines all made use of 'pensioned-off' mainline material, and short rail lengths with pre-grouping chairs and sleepers lasted in such locations until quite recently. I remember finding several 30ft panels of ex-MR *inside-keyed* 75lb/yd bullhead at Kilmersdon Colliery in Somerset in 1975, which must have dated from the mid-1860s or thereabouts!

As described in the 'potted history', by the time 'standard bullhead' had appeared on the scene, ballast was generally of hard crushed stone with a riddle size of about 2½in (would pass through a 2½in ring on the smallest diameter). The broken edges of this ballast 'keyed together' well, while the many gaps between the stones ensured it was free-draining. The colour, though, varied considerably, depending upon the source, from hard grey granite through golden-brown to almost white. Getting the ballast colour correct is one of those small touches that can make a big difference to the final appearance of model trackwork, and can help 'fix' the geographical location of the model with ne'er a train in sight. Sidings, loops and such lesser trackage used less substantial ballasting; old, dirty mainline ballast, ash, cinders, slag and quarry waste could all be found, while in many instances the 'ballast' was soil and a due complement of grass and weeds.

Failure to differentiate between running lines and sidings is one of the most common failings on model railways, and the back coal siding that looks like a 'prize length' on the East Coast Main Line is a classic modelling chestnut. Apart from anything else, it adds a spot of variety to the often repetitive work of trackbuilding if you can ring the changes with some short track panels, pre-group 9ft sleepers, 2-bolt fishplates, ash ballast and some ground-foam weeds. Even in the 'standard bullhead' era, track still exhibited considerable variety of appearance, something that can be effectively exploited in model form.

One or two ancillary track items that are rearly modelled put in an appearance either before, or during, the 'standard bullhead' era. Train detector or point-locking bars, catch points (foot of falling gradients on uni-directional lines), detonator placers and AWS ramps can all be found in conjunction with standard bullhead track. Again, worth exploiting to add interest to finescale track.

STANDARD POINTWORK

I'm going to describe this in some detail, as it forms the basis for most of the ensuing 'nitty gritty' constructional sections of this book. The terminology of the various components is something it pays well to get right, as P & C work is a precise business rich in technical jargon. Obviously, much of what I'm on about here is not specific to bullhead track, as the principles are common to *all* P & C work. The main feature that sets bullhead P & C work apart is the use of numerous special chairs, each designed to fulfil a specific function in building up the formation. As many as 13 different chairs may be involved in the construction of one simple turnout; when you get onto complex formations including obtuse crossings, slip roads and tandem switches, the fun gets fast and furious! Thank goodness that most of the differences between these different 'special' chairs are subtle, and mostly unapparent at 4mm scale.

However, back to basics. Consider for a moment a plain turnout, as in the diagram. This can be negotiated in either direction – 'trailing', when the vehicle encounters the crossing before the switch, or 'facing', when the switch comes first. The two ends of the turnout are referred to as the toe end – where the blades start – and the heel end, where the two roads diverge beyond the crossing. A single line of rails is always known as *a* 'road'; if a PW engineer refers to '*the* road',

Typical 'standard bullhead' PW, here with wide base 2-bolt chairs and traditional hardwood keys. Note closer spacing of sleepers at joint in left foreground, and alternate direction of keys. Ash and cinder ballast suggest a secondary location.

he means the whole track, ballast, sub-base and all, in a very general sense, in other words, what should be described as the 'permanent way' (to distinguish it, during railway construction, from 'temporary way', track laid down to facilitate the works and later removed).

A turnout such as the one illustrated – a 'plain turnout' – has two roads, a 'straight' road, and a 'diverging road'. It consists of four basic units: the two 'stock rails', straight and curved respectively; a pair of 'switches', or point blades; a 'common' or 'acute' crossing, complete with 'check' or 'guard' rails; and the 'closures', those sections of rail serving to connect the heel end of the switches with the nose end of the crossing. All *pointwork,* however complex, is constructed from these four basic units, used in combination.

CURVES IN POINTWORK

There are a number of factors determining the severity of the curve by which the diverging road leaves the straight road. We have become used, in the general model railway sense, to the concept of defining pointwork by quoting a radius for this curve – a '3ft radius right-hand' or whatever. The radius of this curve is of obvious significance when it comes to running trains over the pointwork, but things are not quite as simple as merely following part of a circle. For a start, prototype track does not, by and large, use fixed-radius curves. It is normally laid out on transitions – curves that start on a very wide radius and gradually get tighter. So, normally, only the 'mean', or theoretical average, of the curve can be quoted as an 'off-the-cuff' indication of the degree of curvature. The limitation on trains, though, is the 'tightest' point on the curve. As with any other factor restricting the operation of trains (gradients, clearances, etc.), the tightest curve in a formation – or on an entire route – is known as the 'ruling radius'. If a loco can get round the 'ruling radius', it can negotiate the whole formation.

While PW engineers are, obviously, concerned with the radius of curvature included in pointwork, this is not the only factor by which a turnout is defined. Three other criteria are always specified: the switch length, the crossing angle, and the 'lead' of the turnout. This, of course, is related to fundamental considerations as to the nature of the turnout. Plain turnouts, with one straight and one curved road, must be differentiated from curved turnouts, where both roads are curved on the same hand, and 'Y' turnouts, where the roads are curved on opposite hands.

TURNOUT DESCRIPTIONS

Taking these various criteria separately, it is possible both to determine the effect each has on the turnout, and to use them to describe it accurately. The length of the

Fig. 3:1 Anatomy of a turnout.

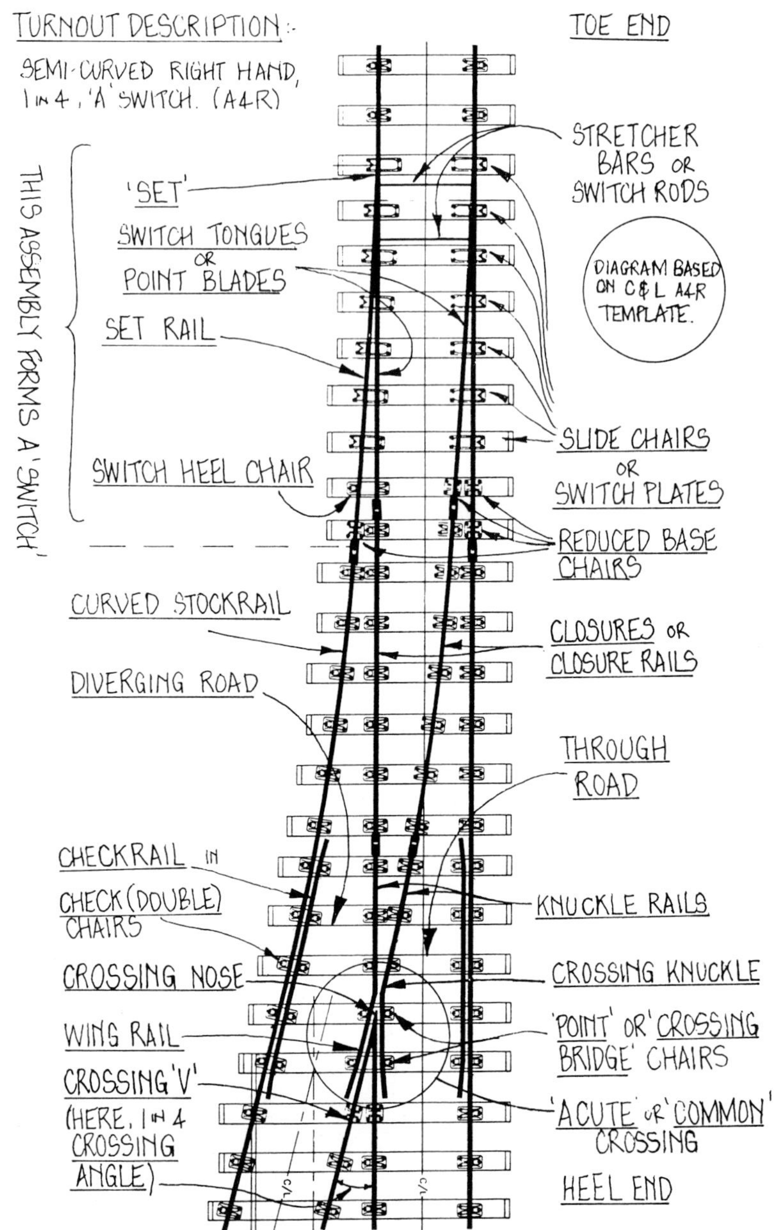

switches, for instance, will determine the rate at which the train is diverted from its mean path. Short switches give a rapid initial change of direction, and are those only suited to situations where speeds are low and wheelbases modest. Longer switches give correspondingly gentler guidance, but are inherently weaker. For very long switches, it is necessary to provide additional support with special chairs, and often to use a heavier section of rail. Switches in 'standard bullhead' are classified by a letter, with the shortest switches being 'A', and so on down the alphabet. I'm not quite sure what the longest are – I've come across reference to 'K' switches, which sound pretty lengthy!

The crossing angle is the other fundamental, and is quoted as a 'gradient', as in the diagram. Hence, a crossing in which the *diverging* road takes eight feet to reach a distance of one foot from the straight road is quoted as a '1 in 8'. The crossing itself is normally straight, from the toe end of the knuckle rails to the heel of the 'V' – so there's no question of measuring distances along a curve to arrive at the crossing angle. A point incorporating such a crossing would be described by the numer 8, as in B8L. This is describing a plain left-hand turnout using 'B' switches and a 1 in 8 crossing. But it's not the whole story, as it doesn't give you the 'lead' of the point. Now, to a large extent, the sharpness or otherwise of the crossing angle determines the 'lead' – the distance between the tip of the switch blades and the nose of the crossing. The 'lead' and the nominal radius of the turnout are directly related, and under 'standard practice', a B8 turnout will be quoted as being of a certain 'lead' or 'nominal radius', which is taken from a standard set of tables. These are the dimensions used to prepare turnout templates.

But there are circumstances, such as where the position of the switches and crossing are fixed due to their inclusion as part of a complex formation, when the lead has to be varied. Thus, it is possible to encounter a 'long lead' turnout, where the lead has been extended above the standard value; while curved turnouts will often end up with a shorter lead than standard – more on this on the section on using and adapting templates in Chapter 5. In terms of the materials and components used, there is no difference between a plain and a curved turnout, and the classification under the system just described will remain as 'B8R' or whatever. But it is useful to amplify this bald description by quoting either the respective radii of the two roads, or the outer radius and the 'lead'. By quoting these qualifiers, the nature of the turnout can be described exactly.

Fig. 3:2 Measuring crossing angles.

5 UNITS
DIVERGING ROAD
1 UNIT
1-IN-5
STRAIGHT ROAD

Fig. 3:3 Special P & C chairs.

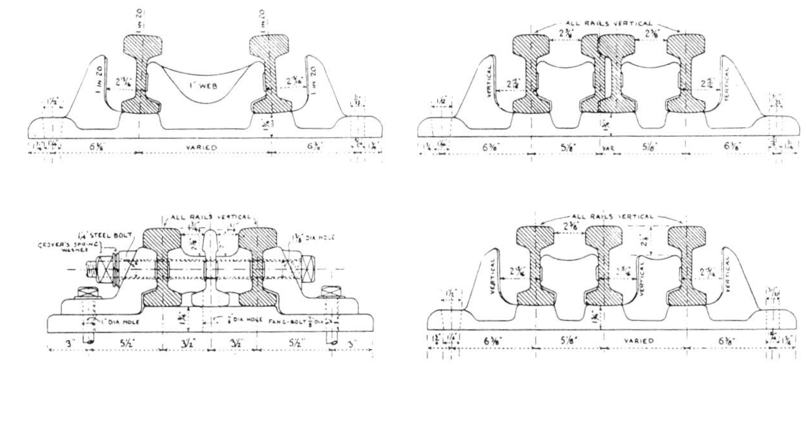

SPECIAL CHAIRS

As I've already mentioned, bullhead P & C work involves the use of numerous special chairs. The most obvious of these are the 'slide chairs' or 'slide plates', on which the point blades move when the switch is thrown; the 'crossing set', consisting of special chairs and cast-iron spacer blocks used to support and align the knuckle rails and crossing 'V'; and the 'checkrail chairs', a double-chair to take two rails and the associated keys. In addition to these, there are some less apparent 'specials'. The chairs supporting the 'point' and 'splice' rails that go to make up the crossing 'V', and the chairs of the knuckle rails beyond the actual knuckle are situated where the diverging rails are still too close together for the bases of standard chairs to be accommodated on the timbers, and so have specially shaped bases. The nature and number of these 'specials' will vary with the crossing angle of the turnout – the more acute the crossing angle, the more 'specials'. Fortunately, it is possible to replicate most of them quite adequately in 4mm scale by taking a scalpel to the standard C & L chair mouldings.

TIEBARS AND POINT LOCKS

These are two further items of prototype hardware of concern to the modeller of finescale track. While the 'mainstream' modeller may be happy to accept extra moving sleepers and other such anachronisms, it is obviously not appropriate in the finescale context

A common crossing in 'standard bullhead', showing the massive crossing nose chair and the cross-bolting of the crossing assembly. The crossing nose itself has a 'blunt' profile, while the point timbering is at a close centring on this short-lead 1 in 4 turnout.

to deviate so radically from prototype practice. Real BH turnouts have a number of 'stretcher bars' linking the two switch blades, so that they move as a unit. The tiebar is the stretcher nearest the tip of the blades, and receives the drive from the point actuating mechanism. As these bars are quite small, not being heavily loaded components, their 4mm scale equivalents would not be sufficiently robust to perform these tasks reliably – the more so as two-rail electrification rules out a continuous metal bar. The normal convention with finescale 4mm pointwork is to employ a robust hidden tiebar assembly beneath the trackbed, representing the prototype bars only cosmetically.

The other piece of equipment found in the tiebar area of prototype turnouts is a facing point lock. These were made mandatory for facing points in running lines under the Regulation of Railways Act and subsequent legislation. They are of two basic types – interlocked, and self-locking. The interlocked variety, more common in the 'standard bullhead' period, is, as its name suggests, controlled from a signal box, where its action is included in the locking frame. Matters are so arranged that only under the correct combination of signal indications and point settings may the point be unlocked and 'reversed'. It is thus interlocked with the rest of the signalling and PW installation, providing a double safeguard, in that a turnout so locked cannot be thrown except as part of a predetermined 'safe sequence', while the point lock also performs the primary function of ensuring that the point blades cannot move while a train is passing over them. The self-acting lock performs only this last function, and is activated by a 'lock-bar', a long treadle situated just inside the running rail on the approach to the turnout, where it is depressed by the flanges of the approaching train, engaging the point lock.

Fig. 3:4 'K' or obtuse crossing.

There are very many variations on the basic design of these point locks, but fortunately for us they are invariably concealed under stout timber covers, designed to protect them from anything dragging beneath a train, such as a disconnected brake rod. So, any facing point on a running line, which is any point on a single track or other bi-directional road, will need its lock, or at least some representation of the protective cover. By running line, I mean any track on which through traffic passes; sidings and shunting yards, mineral-only branches and other lesser lines do without.

DIAMOND CROSSINGS

The other 'plain' formation encountered is the diamond crossing, where two roads cross at an angle. This angle is measured exactly as for the common crossing of a turnout, as a diamond uses a pair of similar crossings. The other unit, or track sub-assembly, used in a diamond is the 'obtuse crossing', often known as a 'K-crossing' due to its resemblance to that letter. This is illustrated in *Fig.*3:4, and its relationship to the common crossings is shown in the sketch of the com-

Switches of a standard turnout – an A5 as it happens. Note how short these are – just five slide chairs and a single double 'heel' chair. Two flat-section stretcher bars are fitted. This is a hand-thrown turnout. The heel of the switch-rails are fishplated to the closure rails.

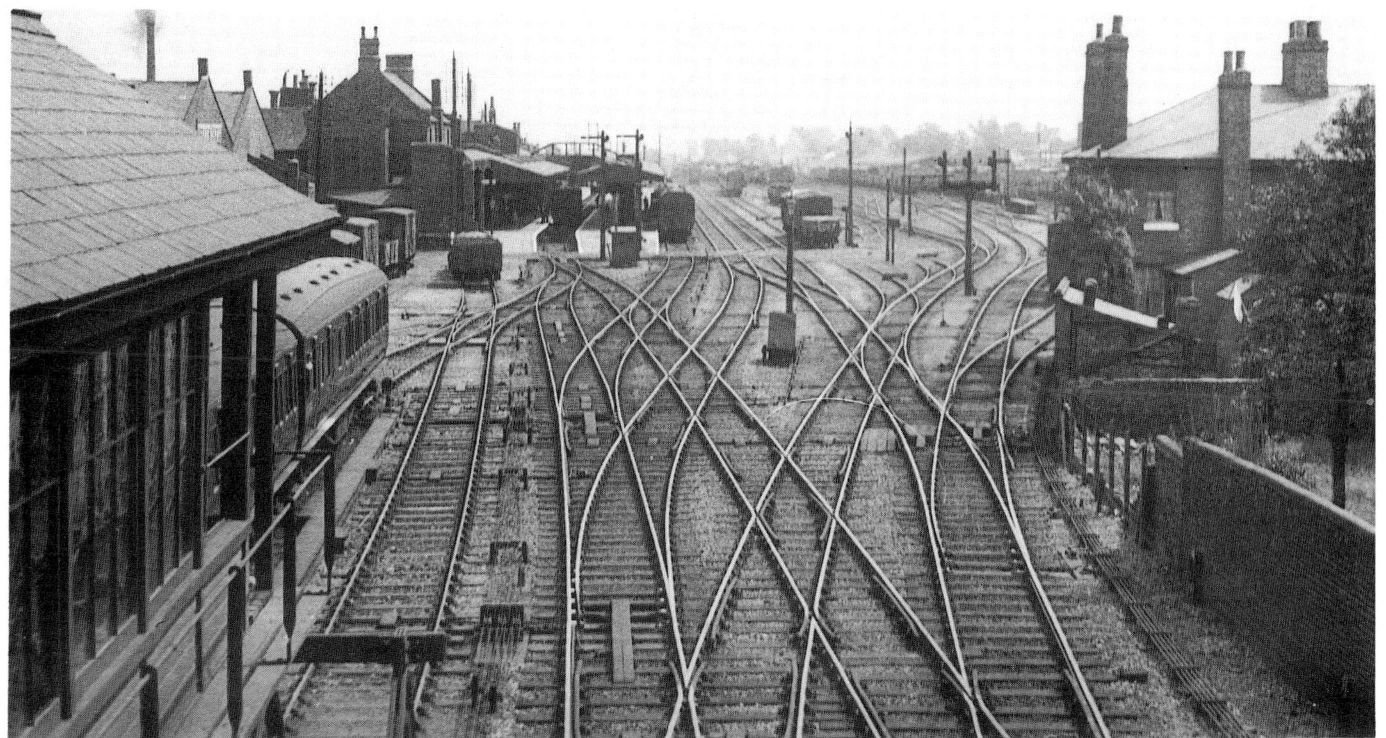

A delightful complex of standard bullhead at Peterborough East, ex-GER, photographed in June 1931. Note the wide provision of point locks on the facing road at left, and the trap points inserted in the siding exit turnout on the right. This was the west end of the GER's considerable complex at Peterborough, and reflects that company's liberal use of slip diamonds and comprehensive connections between all running lines.
L & GRP, CTY. DAVID & CHARLES

A GWR-pattern facing point lock with cover removed, showing the locking bolt passing through the drive and locking stretchers. Note also the ultra-close spacing of crossing timbers, and the tiebar fitted to maintain the gauge against spreading. This point lock is worked from the lever frame and forms part of the interlocking.
AUTHOR

plete crossing. It is rare, though not impossible, for either road through a diamond to be curved. Such a situation will almost certainly require the fabrication of special 'odd number' crossings, and may call for special chairs. Often, where curved diamond crossings are called for, the location may also be one of very heavy traffic wear, and specially-cast one-piece manganese steel crossings, both common and obtuse, may be provided. Two famous examples of such special crossing work may be quoted – at the East end of Newcastle Central, involving no less than 17 diamonds, two of which have further roads crossing in a superimposed 'double diamond'; and at Borough Market Junction, where the Cannon Street and Charing Cross lines diverge beyond London Bridge.

Study of the diagram of the 'K-crossing' may suggest that, if the angle between two roads becomes too acute, a problem can arise where the wheels, instead of passing from the knuckle of the crossing to the nose, will follow the knuckle around, 'swapping roads'. This does indeed happen from time to time, and, to avoid this possibility, plain diamonds are not used at crossing angles more acute than 1 in 8. Below this, the 'K crossing' is replaced with a 'switch crossing', with movable switches to 'close the gap'.

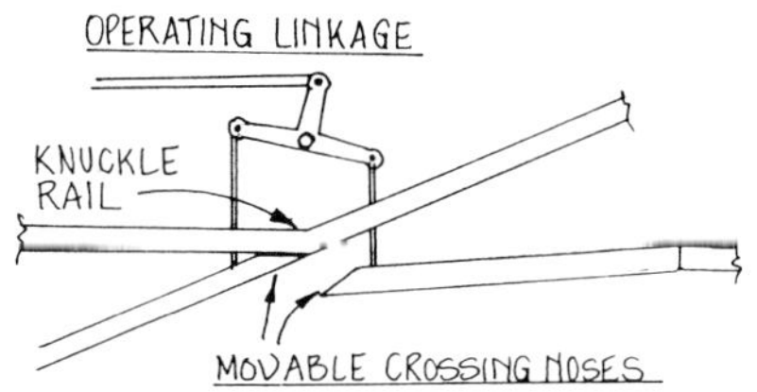

Fig. 3:5 Moving obtuse crossing for switched diamond.

This arrangement may also be used on crossings above 1 in 8 where speeds are high. It is rare to see a 'switch diamond' (as such a formation is termed) in model practice, which I find puzzling.

COMPLEX FORMATIONS

These come into two categories: 'standard formations', and 'specials'. Standard complex formations include the various varieties of 'three way' or 'interlaced' turnouts, sometimes referred to as 'compounds'; single and double slip points, properly referred to as 'slip diamonds'; and combination formations such as scissors crossings and double junctions. There are also such other delights as 'opposed interlaced' and 'superimposed' turnouts, which can be built up from standard switch and crossing components. I've sketched a selection of typical standard complex formations in *Fig.* 3.6.

Some situations, however, cannot be met by 'mixing and matching' standard com-

Facing page: *Special situations galore! This wonderful photo illustrates the sort of PW complexity found at some locations. Even describing some of this takes a bit of headscratching – as well as normal compound and slip turnouts, we have a 'tandem half scissors', or is it a 'double compound full scissors'? Note the complexity of the timbering, especially in the scissors formation, where there is some interlacing as well as through-timbering. The loco spur has trap points, and there is extensive checkrailing. All this and outside third rail! London Bridge, west side, in SR days, I believe.*
This page: *A curved scissors, which formed part of the infamous 'Crewe curve' at Shrewsbury, carrying a 10 mph speed restriction. This view, dating more or less from the grouping, shows a fine example of traditional BH practice. Note the huge difference in 'lead' between the curved and semi-curved turnouts in the scissors, which have the same crossing angle.* AUTHOR'S COLLECTION and NATIONAL RAILWAY MUSEUM

Switched diamond crossings at Old Oak Common (GWR). Notice that these, too, have locking mechanisms to ensure that they cannot move under traffic. Their use here has more to do with speed and smooth riding than the acuteness of the crossing angle. NATIONAL RAILWAY MUSEUM ponents, and here the PW engineer has no option but to design and 'customs build' P & C work to suit. The two junctions cited a paragraph or two back are classic cases, and there are, obviously, many more. But such a solution is costly, and would only be undertaken where there was no alternative, and the traffic justified the expense. Certainly, given the sort of subject most modellers are able to tackle, then the most complex formation that is likely to raise its ugly head is an interlaced turnout or double-slip diamond, neither of which is particularly difficult to build.

SPECIAL TRACKWORK

This is the last general aspect that need concern the modeller – but it is an area where we often fall down. While the 'standard bullhead' PW I have been describing forms the vast majority of the trackwork that would be encountered on the classic steam-era railway, there are certain situations where a different form of PW would be provided. Chief amongst these locations are bridges, where the conventional cross-sleepered road was very often replaced by a longitudinally-timbered 'bridge road', similar in many respects to Brunel's famous broad-gauge track. Special chairs with a narrow base to suit the width of the bridge longitudinals, or 'rail bearers', were used, and check (inside) and guard (outside) rails pro-

The goods yard exit at Brimscombe (GWR) is by means of this semi-outside single slip, a very characteristic piece of GW P & C work. It is my favourite formation, and I built one for my Cornish GWR essay, 'Trerice', described in Chapter 8. There was another fine example at Chipping Norton, beautifully modelled by Keith Armes on his 2mm finescale version of that station. L. E. COPELAND

Fig. 3:6 Complex formations.

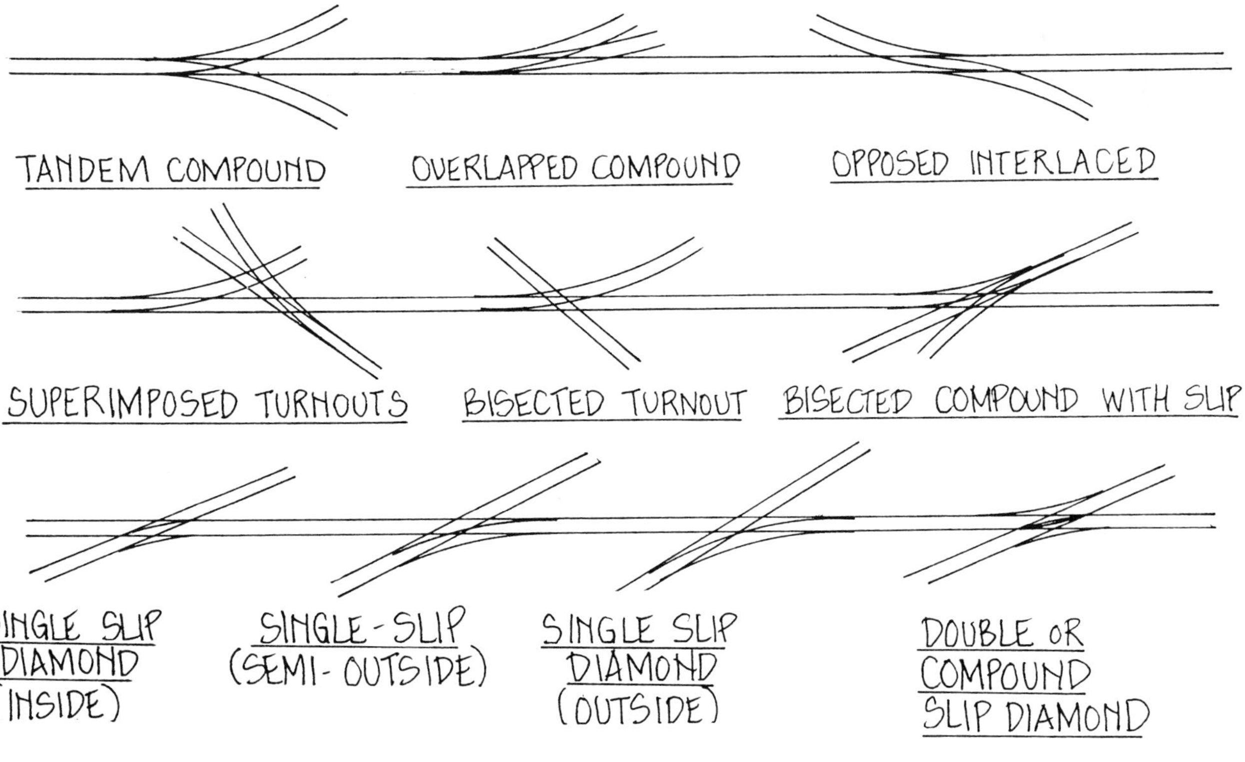

TANDEM COMPOUND

OVERLAPPED COMPOUND

OPPOSED INTERLACED

SUPERIMPOSED TURNOUTS

BISECTED TURNOUT

BISECTED COMPOUND WITH SLIP

SINGLE SLIP DIAMOND (INSIDE)

SINGLE-SLIP (SEMI-OUTSIDE)

SINGLE SLIP DIAMOND (OUTSIDE)

DOUBLE OR COMPOUND SLIP DIAMOND

A complex of crossing work trial-erected in the PW shops at Swindon. Complex, yes, but this is all common and 'K' crossings or plain rail. NATIONAL RAILWAY MUSEUM vided, to ensure that any derailed vehicle was restrained from taking a dive. The use of longitudinal timbering and bridge chairs would be extended to P & C work if this occurred on the bridge – Hungerford Bridge, outside Charing Cross station in London, has some wonderful examples.

Other special trackwork can be found at locations such as inspection or ash pits, where bridge chairs are used on 'block' sleepers, at cattle docks, where a drainage pit was incorporated, and inside sheds or other industrial buildings. Fully paved track occurs in industrial and dockside locations, or other locations where road vehicles and pedestrians must move around over the tracks; many of the big inner-city goods depots were fully paved in this way, using granite setts or wooden blocks. Concrete and tarmacadam can also be found, but less often, due to the problems involved in gaining access to the track substructure for maintenance.

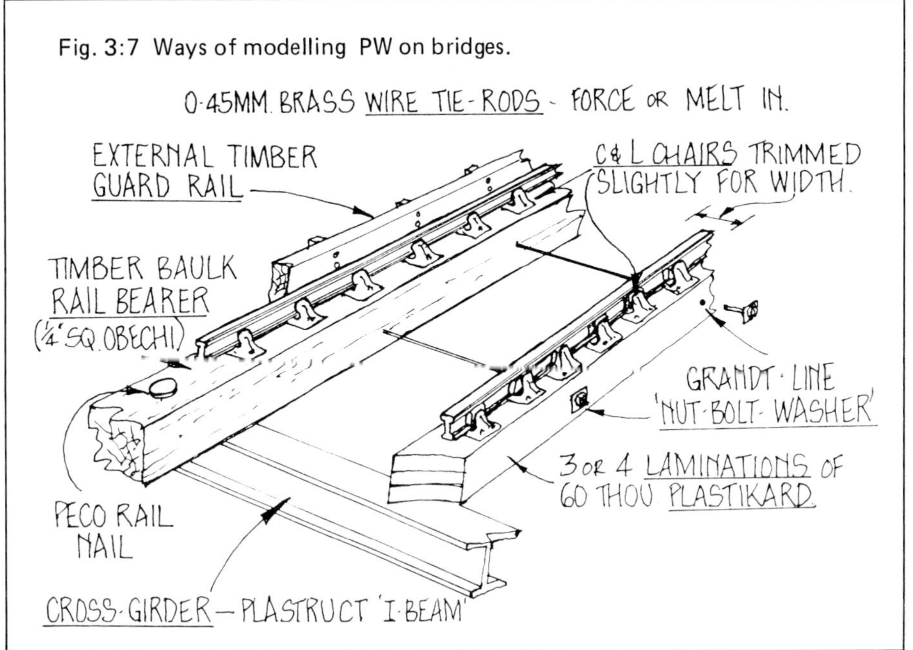

Fig. 3:7 Ways of modelling PW on bridges.

Baulks and transoms on a bridge deck on the ex-GC line from East Tinsley to Wombwell, in the West Riding of Yorkshire. LNER trackwork, May 1935. NATIONAL RAILWAY MUSEUM

SUMMARY OF PROTOTYPE CONSIDERATIONS

Long-winded though this chapter has been, it barely scratches the surface of what is a vast and engaging topic. In the context of a modelling book such as this, I'm afraid that all I can do is to generalize wildly, in an effort to paint a picture of British PW practice that can only be described as 'superficial'. There are, obviously, many more informed sources on PW matters than yours truly, and I have listed some of them in my bibliography. What I've presented here is my interpretation of what I've read and observed, and I make no claims to be any sort of authority; all I'm really concerned to do is to find out enough about the prototype to give me the chance to make a convincing stab at modelling it.

As with so many aspects of successful finescale modelling, the due study and observation of the prototype, preferably 'in the flesh', is by far the best way to get things 'right'. I've presented as many aspects of the world of 'real' track as I can in these pages, but that can never be anything more than a poor substitute for getting out with a notebook and a camera to make the acquaintance of some full-size PW – there's still plenty of 'standard bullhead' to be found on BR, while any preserved railway will have a good selection. Joining the PW gang of your local line could really complete your education in PW matters, and you can build lots of model track while you're recovering from your hernia operation!

Fig. 3:8 Track at inspection pit.

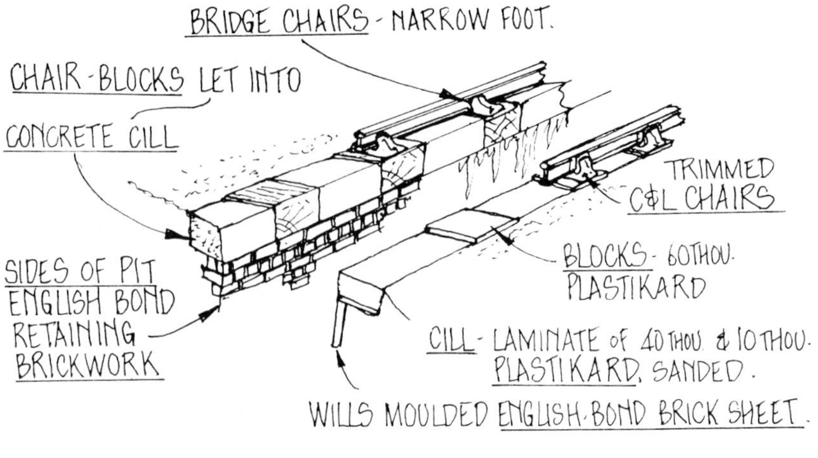

Fig. 3:9 Paved or inlaid track.

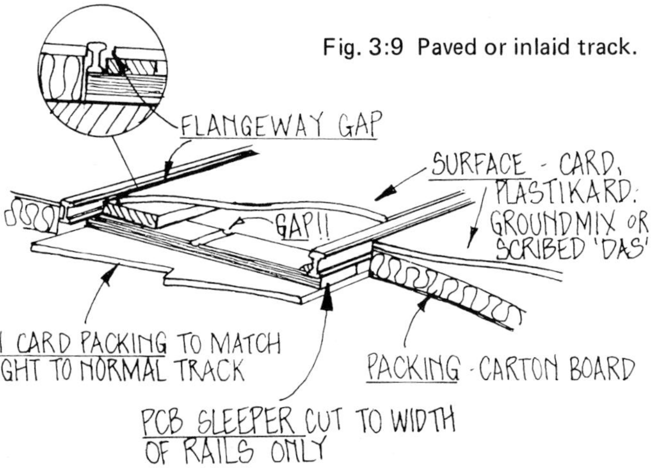

CHAPTER FOUR

TOOLS AND MATERIALS FOR TRACKMAKING

In contrast to so many areas of finescale modelling, track-making is a relatively cheap operation. By and large, the equipment required is modest in extent and cost, and most of it will figure in any reasonably comprehensive modelling tool kit. There are specialist tools of one sort or another on the market, some of which do cost quite serious money; none of them, however, is essential, any decision to purchase being based on the amount of PW you need to produce and the health (or otherwise) of your wallet. And while specialist tooling may speed up operations like sleeper-riveting, the same desirable result may be obtained by enlisting a bit of help from a modelling chum – a few beers at the end of a riveting evening come a lot cheaper than a fancy punch-and-press set!

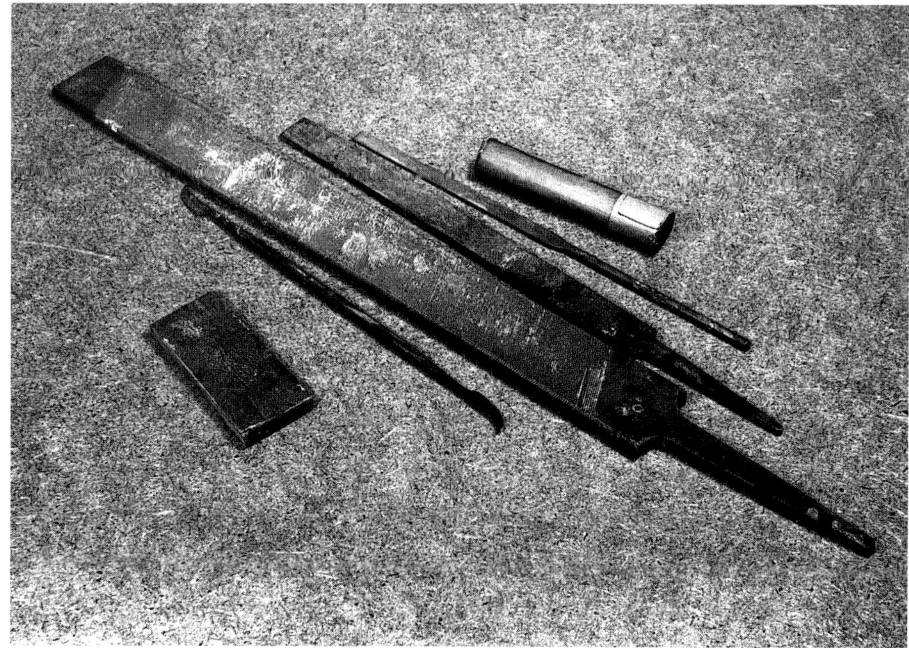

Files and abrasives. A great big file for 'roughing out', a fine (2nd cut) 6-inch flat file, and a flat Swiss file for finishing, a curved knife, jeweller's riffler for introducing 'artificial wear', and a wet-and-dry rubbing block and hard fibreglass burnishing stick for de-burring and cleaning up.

A TRACKMAKER'S TOOL-LIST

This is mercifully short, and even if composed of high-quality tools, the purchase of which I always advocate, should not cost too much to acquire. Many of the items on it do have wider applications, though do be sure that you don't thereby compromise their primary purpose. I'm thinking here particularly of files, which can so easily lose their keen edge and become clogged if used for soft metals. The ability to produce clean, accurate filed components is pretty fundamental in the production of crisp, trouble-free PW.

So I'll start with files, as these play a large part in the making of P & C components. Producing the fine planing of switch blades, or a nice, snug-fitting point-and-splice rail set, calls both for the removal of quite a lot of metal, and for accurate and high-quality finishing. This won't all be accomplished with one file – I generally find I use at least three. These are, in the order of attack, a nice big fierce bastard file – mine's about 10in, a sort of Samurai effort, being of Nipponese origin – a good second-cut flat file of about 6in, and a Swiss file, either half-round or crossing section. The big file is simply used to remove metal 'in bulk' – to rough-out a blank from which the required final shape can be produced. The accurate surface filing is mostly accomplished with the 6in flat (it can be a half-round if that's what you already have), and this does need to be a good file, and *sharp*. The best I've come across is Swiss, the UMV-Vallorbe supplied by Shestos under their catalogue number 1132. A cheaper alternative is the 6in 'Bedford' usually available from John Flack. Both addresses in the 'sources' appendix. The needle file is used for two purposes; fine finish-shaping of the switch blades and assembled crossing nose, and for introducing artificial 'wear' into the crossing, of which more in a chapter or two.

For use in conjunction with the files, I find that a nice hardwood offcut is an essential, to give you an 'edge' to file over. I'll explain this technique in Chapter 7. In the context of this list, I'll content myself with suggesting that what you're after is a nice bit of 2in × 1in close-grained oak or mahogany or, best of all, ash. Failing this, you can be prosaic and get by pretty well with some thick chipboard, of dimensions suitable for gripping in a vice. To go with the block, some short, fat screws and a couple of small fibre tap-washers will enable you to make the jig sketched in *Fig.* 7.13. These crude 'clamps' aren't essential, but they save a lot of wear to the fingertips.

For final finishing of P & C components, an abrasive paper or cloth is required. Emery cloth is the ideal, but this isn't always easy to find these days. In its absence, wet-and-dry papers of about 180 and 400 grit will serve. Also useful is a stiff fibreglass burnisher or an abrasive 'trackcleaning' block such as that sold by the EM Gauge Society.

The other operation involved in forming the components of P & C work is that of bending. This has two aspects – the gentle forming required to impart a curve to rail for curved stock-rails, closures and the diverging switch blade. For this sort of operation, fingers are all that is needed. Which leaves only the introduction of flares, sets and joggles into components like check and wing rails, knuckles and the stockrails where the switches house into them. For all these jobs, I find that a good pair of fine snipe-nosed pliers will serve, although you can form natty joggles using a vice and some rail offcuts, as we shall see. I will stress the adjective 'good' in relation to these pliers, as poor specimens will neither grip well enough to give a clean, crisp bend, nor will the tips meet and align with sufficient accuracy to form a joggle. Good snipe-nose pliers will be box-jointed and will probably be made by Lindström of Sweden. They won't come cheap, but they are of such general and vital utility that no modeller should deny himself a pair.

TOOLS FOR SLEEPERING

It is in the production of riveted sleepers that we can move into the area of specialized tooling. The original Protofour system used a modified letterhead embossing-press to both punch and rivet sleepers. A developed version of this original tool is still available (see 'sources' appendix) and it has its place in the mass-production of prepared sleeper-work. If you are faced with the production of a lot of track – and I do mean a lot – then it is a purchase worth considering, especially in a club or other group context. But, having made use of such a tool – belonging to somebody else – in my early P4 years, I can't say that I feel disadvantaged by not having one available these days. I've built my last five layouts without the benefit of this particular gadget, so I don't think that it can be considered essential.

What I do have, and use, is a small jeweller's anvil and a planishing hammer, and these form my usual rivet-closing equipment. The hammer isn't big – about a 2oz head – but it's ample for the job. I'll accept the claim that hammer-closed rivets are never as consistent as those set in a press, but I have to say that I can't see that this has had any adverse effect on my PW. I think that, provided due care is taken, then a good hard, flat surface – such as the top of a vice or a small offcut of steel plate in some decent thickness – will act as a satisfactory anvil, while any small hammer will do the closing. The usual 1½oz pin hammer that serves for so many modelling tasks will earn its keep in this role, too.

To drill holes to accept rivets in point timbers, one of the more tedious tasks in the construction of ply-and-rivet pointwork, I use a small 'Archimedean' drill with a 0.9mm metric drill, working on a chipboard offcut. The drilling of these holes is actually quite a particular sort of a job, as the ply tends to 'rag', calling for a quick rub with a small piece of garnet paper to remove the rough edges. This then tends to re-clog the drilled hole, so I also have a tapered broach handy to clean them out again. Perhaps those punching tools aren't such a luxury after all!

Soldering equipment for finescale track-building is about as basic as it could be: 145°C wire solder, cored or uncored, 12% phosphoric flux (available commercially from Martin Brent as 'Phosflux 12'), and a small iron – here, an 18W SRB type 1.

SOLDERING EQUIPMENT

I suppose that one can 'get by' with almost any type of soldering iron for track work – I built plenty of 'ERG' track with my father's monstrous old RAF-surplus Solon. However, I can't see the point of making life difficult by using equipment unsuited to the job. In the old ERG days, the idea was to end up with a 'blob' of solder between rail and tack-head to suggest the chair; these days, with superb cosmetic chair mouldings, such an accretion of solder is a dratted nuisance, as it impedes the application of the chairs. So the object is to apply the minimum quantity of solder consistent with adequate strength in the joint, best accomplished, say I, with a miniature iron and a low-melting-point solder.

There are people who tell me that I'm wrong to use my 145° free-flow solder for all the jobs for which I have found it so admirable. There is a rule of thumb, apparently, that seeks to equate melting-point with strength in the choice of solder. Well, that's as may be; I'm not going to argue that a joint made with my 145° is as strong as a silver-soldered joint, because it patently isn't. But I would certainly contend that, in the context of model work in the miniature scales, a joint made with a good 145° solder is as robust as any other soft-soldered joint. It is certainly more than strong enough for securing rails to rivets in sleepers – applying a 'destruction test' to a track sample had the rivets pulling out of the sleepers long before there was any suggestion of a soldered joint failing. And, I would argue, there is no merit whatsoever in attempting to produce a strength of joint to a factor several times that actually needed, especially when, in so doing, so many other problems and potential failures are introduced.

I'm not going to bore you with a load of soldering theory here – it's all in my previous books on loco kit construction. The essential points that affect the soldering aspect of ply-and-rivet track construction are the need to get sufficient heat into the job to ensure that the solder melts and flows freely to form a proper 'wet' joint, and to ensure that there is no heat build-up in the rail, to cause excessive expansion, leading to distortion and 'stressing' of joints when the job cools down. These two – on the face of it, incompatible – requirements are best met by using a solder that is *designed* to work at a lower temperature, rather than using a higher melting-point solder at the lower extreme of its working range.

This scaling-down of the heat-energy requirements of the soldering process has a number of side-benefits. Apart from the obvious factor of thermal expansion – or the lack of it – the low heat requirement means that a very much smaller soldering-iron, with a relatively small bit, is quite adequate. This, in turn, means that it's much easier to see what's going on at the point of joining, as well as facilitating direct soldering of joints in very confined locations. In other words, you end up with neater joints, and have less problems with complex work like slip diamonds or compound turnouts. It also makes the whole job a lot more comfortable, as you are correspondingly less likely to get a build-up of heat in things – such as the rail, or a track-gauge – that you've actually got to *hold*.

I've built most of my track with an SRB type 1 18W iron fitted with the small-diameter iron-plated bit (it stays clean!). With the withdrawal of SRB from the soldering iron business, this iron is not likely to be around much longer. I've converted to the 15W Antex iron, a very similar device to the SRB, and rather better made.

This also has a plated bit, with what looks like an iron tip, and it is very pleasant to use, being light and well-balanced. For building finescale track, I prefer the baby Antex to its bigger 25W brother, which is an amazingly potent device for its power rating, and apt to get things rather hot, rather quickly. Very good for general metalwork, but not so helpful with the small amounts of metal involved in PW work.

For flux, I use my usual solution of Phosphoric Acid, around 12% by volume in purified water. For track work, I find that you're better off without the isopropyl alcohol 'wetting agent', as the requirement is to produce a drop of flux on the rivet-head, rather than letting it run off along the sides of the rail. To apply the flux, I use a small, cheap squirrel-hair paintbrush. It really does need to be applied sparingly, so a No. 0 or even 00 brush will be plenty big enough.

There is an alternative approach to track construction, based on the use of a solder cream and a 'sweating' technique. As this involves putting heat into the rail – a situation I seek to avoid as far as possible – it will call for a rather more powerful soldering iron, and I suppose in this context the 25W Antex would come into its own. The solder cream I use for this sort of job is Carr's 188°, and I have found the approach useful in conjunction with the use of resistance soldering. Very good for the fiddlier bits of double-slips. However, I also find that the solder cream is apt to leave a burnt flux residue which can mark the sleepers if you're not careful. On the whole, I prefer to stick with my 15W iron and 'conventional' technique.

Track gauges and jigs. The vital selection – (from bottom left) crossing flangeway gauge, S4 Society square block gauge with rail clamp, old P4 point blade setting gauge/clamp (crude but effective!), ordinary Dinky grip with ends trimmed (point blade clamp), EM Gauge Society 3-point gauge, home-made (upper) and S4 Society (lower) 'roller' checkrail gauges, and, lastly, the superb old P4 '4-point' 3-legged gauge, now available once again from the S4 Society. Although these are all P4 standard gauges, the essential 3-crossing flangeway, checkrail, and 3-point, are all available for EM through the EM Gauge Society.

TRACK GAUGES

A bit of a minefield, this. There are so many types of different gauge floating about, it's a bit of a job deciding which ones you actually need. Ironically, it's in 'OO', the most popular gauge, that the choice is most limited. Remembering the need to introduce gauge-widening through curved track, it's obvious that a fairly sophisticated device is going to be needed, even in OO. In addition to the actual track gauge, we need further gauges to set such essentials as the checkrail spacing and the crossing flangeway. In many instances, the gauge must also act as a jig, to hold rails in position while they are being soldered in place.

The basic type of gauge in use for finescale work is the three-point design, which provides for automatic gauge widening. This is achieved by 'bridging' the outer curved rail with the two-legged side, effectively forming a chord to the radius of the track at that point. This effectively 'offsets' the mean datum for gauging on that side by an amount which will vary with the degree of curvature – the tighter the curve, the greater the offset. As the third leg will then gauge the inner rail at the correct distance from the datum, the actual track gauge will be gauged distance + offset; in other words, the track is widened by the offset, which varies in direct relationship to the severity of the curve; automatic gauge widening. On straight track, of course, there will be no offset, and the track will be held at the nominal gauge. The diagram will illuminate all this ...

Both the EM and Scalefour Societies supply a gauge of this type, and I would suggest the acquisition of at least a pair; I use three, two EMGS 18.83mm versions (they do both EM & 18.83) and one of the old Protofour Society ones, which is a

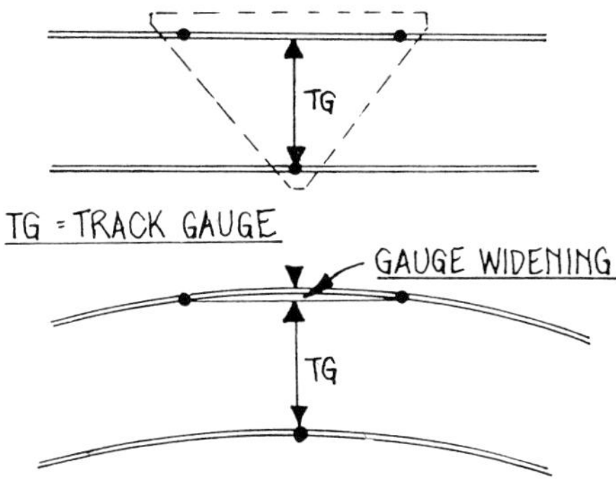

Fig. 4:1 Principle of 3-point track gauge.

beautiful thing. Of late, the Scalefour Society have been supplying an alternative type of track gauge for performing this automatic gauge-widening function, in the form of a rectangular machined steel block, fitted with a clamp to one edge, and a useful pair of 'spot test' reference ears at one end. This is designed to lie between the rails, rather than fitting over them, like the three-point gauge. It doesn't hold the rails as well, clamp or no clamp, but it does have the advantage that it can't be used the wrong way round – unlike the three-legged jobs which, if bridged on the *inner*, rather than outer, rails of the curve, will produce 'gauge narrowing' on an inverse factor! This is, to put it mildly, unhelpful.

The other two essentials are the check rail gauge and the crossing flangeway gauge. The former is usually a turned device of the old 'rollagauge' ilk, with a flange to retain the checkrail at the correct distance from the opposing rail. The latter is usually a small piece of metal of apposite thickness. You may well ask why the checkrail gauge cannot likewise be a simple spacer; the answer lies in the matter of the gauge widening on curved tracks, which, don't forget, will often need to be checkrailed. As the essential relationship in 'checking' wheels, the 'check gauge' is concerned with the *rear* of one wheel (in contact with the checkrail) and the *face* of the flange of the opposing wheel (being held clear of the inner face of the railhead) then this distance (inner face of outer curved rail to inner, bearing, face of checkrail) *cannot vary*. Hence the use of a gauge which sets the checkrail by reference to the opposing rail, rather than by setting a constant gap between the checkrail and adjacent running rail. This gap will fluctuate over a range of values, dependent upon the severity of the curve and the degree of gauge-widening applied to it.

Fortunately, when it comes to the crossing flangeway gap, life is much simpler, as in the miniature scales, and with the standards in use, this remains a constant. It can thus be set by a straightforward piece of packing, though you can get 'roller' type gauges that include this spacing in addition to the checkrail setting. I avoid these, as I find them confusing. There are one or two other 'all singing, all dancing' type track gauges, again, usually of the 'roller' pattern, that try and do everything bar making the tea in one hit. I would strongly advocate the acquisition of sets of gauges that perform each function separately – and, don't forget, no 'roller' type gauge can produce automatic gauge-widening on curves.

So, to summarize, I would regard the desirable minimum collection of track gauges as being four in number: two three-point or rectangular track gauges for automatic gauge widening; one crossing flangeway gauge; and one checkrail gauge. If I was going to expand this collection at all, I'd add a second checkrail gauge and a third three-point. Both the EMGS and S4 Societies supply these three types of gauge, in the former case in both EM (18.2mm nominal gauge) and P4 (18.83mm gauge); the Scalefour boys acknowledge only the latter standard. The Scalefour list offers a set of four gauges, which include two types not so far mentioned. The first is a 'rolling check' gauge, designed to be rolled along new-made track to ensure that the gauge has not gone 'tight' anywhere, which can easily happen, especially with three-point gauges, where there's a big gap between the 'legs' on one side. It's only relevant on straight track, of course; it should be sloppy on curves. The second 'extra' gauge is really more of a jig, being a 'clamping' gauge, with two spring-loaded bars to hold the rail firmly upright and tight to the gauging faces. Useful, but again, on straight track only.

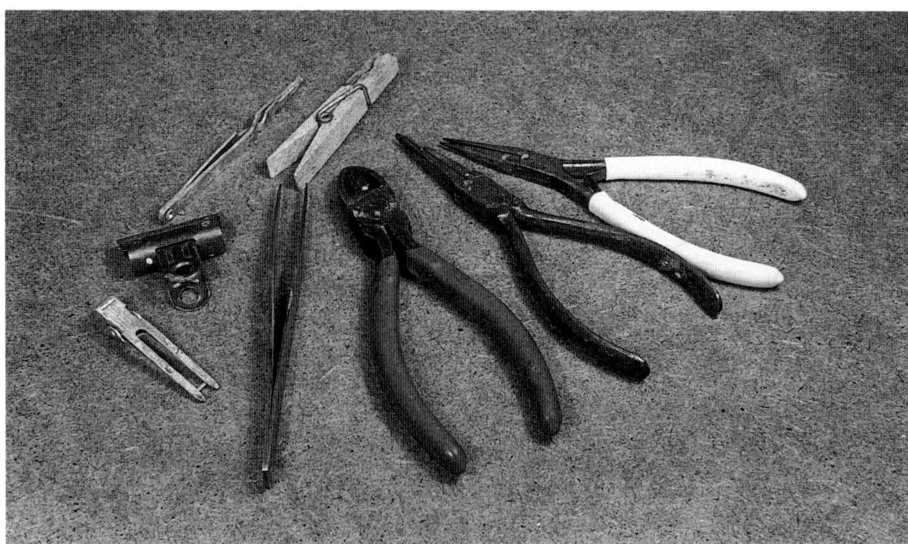

Grips and snips, snipe and flat-nose pliers, and a pair of sharp sidecutters are all you need to bend and cut rail. Fine tweezers are needed to handle C & L chairs, and clothes-pegs make good clamps. The Dinky hairgrip, Bulldog clip and Shesto purpose-made clip are all useful clamps-cum-heatsinks.

OTHER TRACKMAKING TOOLS

There are a few more general odds and bobs that can play their part in trackmaking. Some clip-on heat-sinks can be very useful in the context of complex work, or where you're anxious to avoid excessive heat build-up in rail. Shestos sell a purpose-made aluminium 'spring grip' heat-sink, but a 'Dinky' hair clip or, for serious problems, a 'Bulldog' paper clip will serve as well. The Dinky grip, with the ends cut square, is also very useful for clamping purposes. The Protofour boys used to use a pair of Dinky clips, squared up and Araldited back-to-back, as a clamp/spacing gauge for setting point blades to tiebars. I still do.

Rail needs to be cut, for which I use a sharp pair of side cutters, filing the rail-end square afterwards. A razor saw is a more 'correct', if slower, alternative. Some people go in for Dremel-type motor handpieces with abrasive cutting discs, very natty but not at all necessary. For cropping sleeper strip to length, I generally use a pair of shears, sold, ostensibly, for cutting up PCB. The sharp side-cutters also do a good job, as will a heavy craft knife such as a Stanley 199. A steel rule, small square, and a sharp 2H pencil just about completes the toolkit.

BASIC TRACK COMPONENTS

Rail, chairs and sleepers say it all, but there are a few alternatives to consider. On the rail front, there's really only one choice for bullhead, though quite a few options for flat-bottom. Chairs are starting to show more variety, while baseplates and fastenings for FB track are also starting to appear. With sleepers, it's a matter of material rather than type, with, again, more variety promised.

RAIL FOR FINESCALE

Forget Code 100 and all those other gross sections of the train-set era – for 4mm finescale we need much smaller sizes. The business of rail profiles is involved and fascinating, and it is surprising what a visual difference can exist between basically similar types even at 4mm scale. There is no argument on the Bullhead front, with the standard BS 95lb/yd being represented by the Code 75 rail originally introduced by King's Cross Models back in the late 1960s. That was nickel-silver, had a rather 'square' head, and came with some very nice stamped-brass chairs that made possible true scale 4mm BH track for the first time ('Kingsway'). The profile has been refined a bit since then, and you can now get it drawn in nickel-silver, phosphor-bronze and steel.

For flat-bottom, the picture is much more confused, with all manner of 'codes' of rail, in all sorts of sections, some of which bear no resemblance whatsoever to any known prototype. However, some of the lighter FB rails, such as Peco's Code 60 (from their 'Z' flex-track) or the American Code 55 from Railcraft (both in NS) are useful to modellers of light or industrial railways, as well as in the narrow-gauge context. The Code 60 will also make quite presentable 'bridge' rail for baulk road. Of the heavier sections, the new Code 83 FB rail accurately represents modern heavyweight FB of around 113–117lb/yd, and, used with the concrete sleeper systems now becoming available, enables a good representation of contemporary track systems to be made. This is, so far, only available drawn in nickel-silver.

As well as their Code 83 'heavyweight' flat-bottom, Peco also produce a Code 75 FB rail section – used in their 'Finescale' (*sic*) streamline, a damn fine HO track. This will also fit the 'Individulay' Pandrol-clip and concrete sleepering systems, giving a lighter FB track of the older 100lb/yd. It's not really appropriate with the concrete sleepers, but with the Pandrol clip/timber sleeper, can be used in the 'late steam age'. More on all this in the section covering the sleepering systems included in the 'Individulay' range. Code 70 FB rail is also available, from US sources, but it doesn't really coincide with any of the UK rail sections, being rather too low for its width. Other sections, such as the Peco 'N' Code 80 rail, are likewise of little use to the 4mm scale finescale modeller, as they are also not of prototype section.

THE CASE FOR STEEL

The best material for finescale rail has been the subject of some debate, and a number of alloys have been used for the purpose. I can remember building some of my 'ERG' track with brass bullhead (Bonds?) when the coffers wouldn't run to the nickel-silver that has been generally favoured. Both Peco and Wrenn used to offer steel rail that, from memory, was treated by a sherardizing process that was meant to stop it rusting. Maybe it did, but Bakers Fluid, that virulent flux so much used in those days (and which would probably have eaten through anything short of armour plate), soon did for the sherardizing, with the inevitable result. An interesting alternative to all-pervading nickel was the phosphor-bronze rail offered by Scale Model Productions, makers of the 'SMP' flexible track system. I used this on my 'Butley Mills' layout in an effort to suggest rusty rails without actually having them, but found it susceptible to dirt and rather too malleable.

C & L moulded plastic sleepers. These are the 'Dow Mac' concrete type, but timber ones come in the same format.

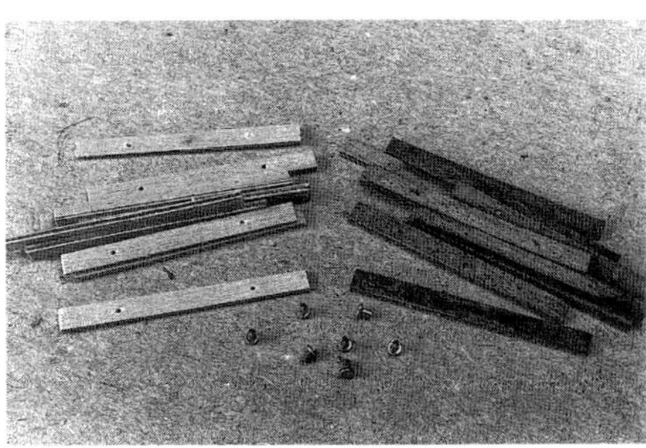

Traditional ply sleepers, raw and after staining. These are vintage EMGS samples, actually punched for the old boot-brads (smaller holes). I'm still using up my original stock, bought about 1970! (9ft pre-grouping type shown.) The rivets are S4 Society brass. The EMGS do the same thing in copper. I use either indiscriminately, after opening up the holes in my antique sleepers!

Rail sections for 4mm scale. From left to right: US 'Railcraft' Code 55 flat-bottom, Walthers US Code 70, British Peco Code 60 FB, standard 'finescale' Code 75 bullhead, and just for comparison, some old BRMSB Code 95 'scale' bullhead – the original ERG type c.1950!

So, for the last forty or so years, nickel-silver has ruled supreme. It is held to have the best electrical properties, to resist corrosion, solder well, and look the best. It is, of course, the most expensive of the materials used – but there's not much 'meat' in Code 75 bullhead, so that doesn't matter too much. What matters more, even to me, was that it doesn't look right and it doesn't stay clean. Now, this went against the conventional wisdom, but I noticed that those of my locos that had steel-tyred wheels needed less cleaning than those with nickel tyres. Might not, I wondered, the same be true of steel rail? My resolve to try steel on my next layout was boosted by a *Model Railroader* article on obtaining good running (in the context of $\frac{1}{4}$in scale inter-urbans, as it happens) that cited 'steel wheels on steel rails' as a prerequisite.

'Woolverstone', my East Anglian estuarine byway, was duly built with steel rail. It proved a great success. Not only did it run better than any of my previous essays (not hard, I know, but every little helps), but it looked, to my eye, much more convincing. The steel rail was cheap, easy to work, and, with its lower thermal conductivity, less prone to expansion during soldering and distortion on cooling. Contrary to the dire forebodings of sundry poker-faced pundits, it did not rust, even in my ancient abode. But why should it? The tyres and axles of my wheelsets, motor shafts, gears, sundry nails and other steel bits-and-bobs about the layout had never rusted.

But, best of all, it kept clean. Better than that – with running, it was burnished to a shine worthy of the down fast at Clapham Junction. Operation was a joy, for wheel and track cleaning went out of fashion chez Rice, and the layout seemed to run better as time went by. My abiding memory is of the 1990 Chatham show, held in the delightfully historic but decidedly dirty surroundings of the old Naval dockyard. By the Sunday afternoon, most layouts were in bother. The track-rubbers were being plied at ever-more-frequent intervals; trains stalled and refused to start, muffled curses filled the air. 'Woolverstone' ran on, imperturbable, the steel rail-heads agleam, burnished in two days' running to a chromium-plated perfection. I haven't used a nickel rail since.

SLEEPERING

In 4mm scale, you can have your sleepers in two basic forms; real tree-wood (albeit laminated), or fake wood, in plastic. Concrete sleepers come only in plastic – until some purist gets 'em cast in Microcrete, I daresay. Plastic sleepers come singly or combined into strips of trackbase, and in 'lop it off yourself' lengths for pointwork. The trackbase units are quick to use, as the chairs are moulded on to the sleepers – although that's not an unmitigated blessing, as we shall see.

PLY SLEEPER SYSTEMS

These are the traditional basis of 4mm finescale track, in succession to the fibre-based 'Little Western' system developed by Jim Russell. The current 'norm', using rivets, is actually the variant devised by the Model Railway Study Group in the mid-1960s, which substituted the familiar rivet for the cropped-off boot brad of Joe Brook-Smith's original design. It is a system common to both EM and P4, with the same sleeper; the rivet centres are set for P4, and EM gauge is accommodated by the use of a slightly larger rivet – head diameter 2.5mm, up from 2mm – which allows for the 0.63mm deviation between the gauges. As I've already lauded the advantages of the system, I'll say no more here. The sleepers are available in scale 10in width for both pre-grouping 9ft and post-grouping 8ft 6in, and in 12in wide lengths for producing point timbering. The 10in wide strip can also be obtained, for those who need to cut their own sleeper lengths. Both EM and Scalefour Societies supply an identical product, so far as I can tell, with EM being quite a bit cheaper, for some reason.

The rivets for use with these sleepers vary a little. The EMGS supplies a 2mm copper rivet – type 'A' – for 18.83mm, and the broader type 'B' 2.5mm in brass. These type 'B' rivets have other uses besides being used as EM chair bases – they are useful in P4 pointwork. The EMGS also supplies a special punch for closing their rivets. The Scalefour Society uses a 2mm brass rivet, and also supplies the special punch and press tool set already mentioned. I use EMGS and Scalefour components indiscriminately, and find no problem mixing them in this way. For real traditionalists, the EMGS can still supply the original Brook-Smith components, with 8ft 6in and 9ft sleepers punched for the famous boot-brads, also supplied. This way for the world's cheapest finescale track!

THE SC & LE SYSTEM

This is a recent development, designed to combine the most realistic elements of both ply and plastic systems, by using a ply sleeper with a moulded plastic chair. This is a version of the familiar C & L chair, having a pair of lugs beneath the chairbase which locate into a rectangular hole punched into the sleeper. To accommodate these lugs, a thicker 1.5mm ply is used, giving a sleeper virtually spot on for the prototype 5in thickness. This will take a bit more ballasting, which can prove a problem in some circumstances, but on the other hand, will accurately represent unballasted or very lightly ballasted track, which the skinny 1mm sleepers don't do. The chair is held onto the sleeper with a specially-formulated adhesive of formidable strength. It certainly bodes fair to be a sight more robust than any glued track system produced hitherto, and should supersede the use of plain C & L chairs Daywatted to ordinary ply sleepers. As I write this, the system is still under wraps, and I'm privileged to play with some pre-production samples.

Pointwork will use a thicker version of the usual point-timbering strip, but calls for the punching of chair-base holes with a modified version of the costly lever-action punch/riveter mentioned in the tool list. These holes take a special plastic rivet, to the head of which a standard C & L chair, sans lugs, is cemented, thus catering for the odd angles of chairs on point timbers. The standard C & L slide chairs are located in a like manner. In more critical locations – crossing nose, knuckles, check-rails – a square metal rivet is provided to fit the slots, allowing these components to be retained by the robust and proven soldering method, in a 'best of both worlds' solution of commendable pragmatism. The cosmetics are then completed by adapting and fitting standard C & L chairs as appropriate.

PLASTIC SLEEPER SYSTEMS

The first plastic sleepering system for finescale track was that designed by Dick Ganderton of the EM Gauge Society, and produced by Ratio in both EM (18.2mm gauge) and P4. This used a representation of the GWR 'Modern' 2-bolt chair on a grain-textured plastic sleeper. With the insertion of standard Code 75 bullhead rail, a very realistic 'standard bullhead' PW was produced. I used these bases for a good number of years, but found them to possess two drawbacks. The first, cosmetic, drawback was the presence of a thin but prominent plastic web linking the sleepers, which was difficult to disguise. On the last of my layouts to employ Ratio bases, 'Leintwardine', I cut these webs away altogether, which was a great improvement; normally,

Plastic sleepering systems – Ratio on the left, C & L on the right. Ratio actually has the less obtrusive joining web, but C & L's has a secondary function, as described. C & L chairs are better, and Ratio sleepers have a rather overdone 'woodgrain' texture.

With rail inserted, both systems make a nice-looking track. Ratio, on the left, has rather heftier and 'squarer' sleepers than C & L on the right. The hiding of the linking base calls for generous ballasting in either case.

Ratio bases can have their joining web cut away, as on the left, easing ballasting and giving a pleasing result; the removal of the web also eases adjustment of spacing at rail-joints. For comparison, the track on the right is my current standard, using C & L chairs on ply sleepers. No ballasting problems, and the very slight irregularity of positioning gives, in my opinion, a more 'natural' appearance to the track. The keys make a big difference, too.

they would only be cut to vary the sleeper spacing, as at track joints, or to facilitate bending of the trackbases on curved alignments.

It was curves that proved the main drawback of the Ratio base, as there was no provision for gauge widening, so necessary for the maintenance of proper running clearances. Indeed, if you weren't careful, it was possible to end up with track that was *under* gauge on curves, and that could be a disaster. So, latterly, I have restricted the use of my remaining stock of Ratio bases to straight track, mainly in sidings. Even in this situation, I find that the gauge is apt to be a touch on the tight side, although not sufficiently so to affect running.

I understand that the Ratio EM trackbase is no longer available, and that stocks of the P4 base are limited. So I mention these units in passing, for those of you – like me – who have a goodly stock of them stashed away. In the right application, they are satisfactory, but I wouldn't now contemplate basing a layout on their use.

The mantle of the plastic-based bullhead trackwork systems now rests firmly on Len Newman's shoulders, and he is certainly pushing back the frontiers. The C & L flexible track is the first such track to provide the necessary automatic gauge widening feature, which is arrived at in a most ingenious fashion. This moulded trackbase is the first model track that I'm aware of to incorporate the 1 in 20 inclination of the rails toward the centreline. As well as replicating a prototype feature (and producing a track on which vehicles run with impressive lateral stability), this inclination is then used to give gauge widening, in that, as the track base is formed to follow the curved alignment, the way the stresses in the mouldings are redistributed causes the rail to become progressively more vertical. By cancelling out the inclination, the inside faces of the railheads are moved apart, producing the necessary increase in gauge. Furthermore, this effect is proportional to the degree of curvature, so the widening is kept in the proper relationship to the severity of the curvature.

The moulded trackbase used to make the flexible track is available separately, and does everything that the Ratio bases would, but without the limitation caused by gauging anomalies. You do still have to disguise the web between the sleepers, though, so it's still not *quite* as realistic as a separate-sleeper system. And, in this case, you can't cut the web right away, or you lose the gauge-widening effect. Enter the next stage of track à la Newman, separate chairs and individual sleepers, now available in both timber and early Dow-Mac concrete patterns. The two are united using a solvent adhesive (Butanone, sold as Daywat Poly), and the result is excellent. The use of a three-point track gauge will introduce the necessary gauge widening on curves. It is quite possible to use these components for OO track, though only in the timber-sleeper version, as the concrete sleepers will have the chair 'lands' in the wrong place.

Whereas the Ratio plastic sleeper base system was designed to be used in conjunction with the established ply-and-rivet components for P & C work, C & L components extend to cover this in all-plastic format. Moulded point timbering, of graduated lengths in scale 12in width, is supplied in packs, and a slide chair is available to complement the standard running rail chair. The various 'specials' are represented by cutting and joining these two basic chairs, all assembly being carried out with the Daywat Poly. Pointwork made with these components looks very well, but there are some practical drawbacks. Firstly, it is not as strong as the soldered variety – the rail is, after all, located only by a scale-sized chair-jaw in plastic. And it also suffers from a constructional drawback, in that it is none too easy to adjust; once the Daywat Poly has done its stuff, moving a chair on its timber calls for a pound or two of Semtex!

This brings us to the last of the plastic-sleepered fine scale track systems currently available, Peco's 'Individulay', already mentioned in connection with its associated rail sections. This has been steadily developed, and now offers the modeller of the more recent scene a high-quality PW system. The two rail sections, Code 83 and Code 75, have a common foot section, and can both be used to give either a 100lb/yd or modern 110lb/yd flat-bottom track. The original components consisted of a timber sleeper and a representation of a cast steel rail base-plate with 'Pandrol' clip fastening for the rails, and 'Lockspike' retention to the sleeper. This is a form of rail support system developed by the Elastic Rail Spike Company, and first introduced in Britain around 1959. It incorporated two 'imported' inventions: the 'Pandrol' clip, designed by Per Pande Rolfsen, an engineer working for the Norwegian State Railways, and the American 'Lockspike', patented by a Pittsburg steelman with the wonderful all-American name of Arthur Corbus Jack, in about 1950. With the adoption of concrete sleepers from about 1965, the Lockspike fell by the wayside, but the Pandrol clip was a great success, being adapted to use a malleable iron shoulder insert cast into the concrete sleeper. It was adopted as the standard BR rail fixing for timber sleepers from 1965, and for the new concrete from the following year.

The Peco track, in timber-sleeper form, is thus appropriate to the steam/diesel transitional era, appearing on many renewals in the period 1961–65; I remember it going in

The current state-of-the-art in commercial trackwork. A superb standard bullhead common crossing built with the C & L all-plastic components.

on the Waverley route in 1962–3, only a few years before total closure. Point timbering and slide chairs are also available, and the resulting track is comparable with the C & L bullhead system, the methods of construction, advantages and drawbacks being very similar. Peco supply a flat-plate 'spot' track-gauge, which makes no allowance for gauge widening, but the rectangular-pattern Scalefour gauge (or similar designs for other standards) will work. Some of the three-point gauges will take the Code 83 railhead, though it's a tight fit. The only real cosmetic drawback is that the Pandrol clip is slightly oversize, which is inevitable given the compact nature of the prototype.

As well as this 'transitional' FB track, Peco have recently brought the Individulay system bang up to date by introducing the latest standard BR concrete sleeper, the Costain F40. This is a good choice, as in prototype form it has wide end lands, which can accommodate a number of different gauges. To go with this, they have come up with a fastening which, while not truly representative of any hold-down system used with the F40, suggests the right general appearance. This is a problem bedevilling any manufacturer trying to produce finescale components for the recent concrete-sleeper trackage systems from Pandrol onwards; the actual fastenings are so miniscule that they cannot be made robust enough to locate the rail, certainly at 4mm scale. It will probably call for a composite metal fastening/plastic sleeper system before this can be achieved. In the meantime, the Peco Individulay components provide a pretty reasonable compromise, and, while the fastenings are overscale, the appearance is still acceptable. It's certainly a great advance on 'Streamline', still fundamentally an HO trackage system, and is the more welcome in that it extends the scope of finescale modelling to include the contemporary scene.

OTHER PW COMPONENTS

The other basic PW component needed for both plain track and P & C work is a fishplate, and this comes in two forms. Both the EM and Scalefour Societies supply an etched brass four-bolt plate produced by Colin Waite. This is an ingenious piece of work, consisting of a pair of plates linked by a fine web, designed to be folded up into 'U' form for soldering in place. It can be used either cosmetically, or to actually join two lengths of track, by soldering. The alternative comes from C & L in the form of a plastic moulding, designed for purely cosmetic purposes, attached with a contact cement. This is also a four-bolt type, but, in common with the Waite etching, it's no problem to cut down to two-bolt where appropriate.

Fishplates, etched by Colin Waite, moulded by C & L. Both have their place and are well worth the effort.

There are various point tiebars available, usually featuring wire ends and an insulating centre sleeve. These do not really resemble the prototype very closely, but given the system of bonding switch blades to the appropriate stockrails, and the consequent need to preserve electrical separation between them, it's difficult to see any way of manufacturing a commercial alternative that is more realistic. I still use the old Protofour system for producing cosmetic tiebars, of which more in Chapter 7.

C & L list some pre-prepared P & C components, including silver-soldered crossing 'V's and planed switch blades. These are labour-intensive products, and hence costly. They are not intrinsically difficult items to produce, either, so I can't personally find much appeal in them; if you're going to build finescale track, you may as well do the whole job, gaining in satisfaction and saving quite a few bob into the bargain.

Peco produce a number of components, both cosmetic and functional, of value to the finescale modeller. They do a rail joiner for both their FB and bullhead rail sections, IL20 and 21 respectively. This is cosmetically poor, but is very functional, especially at locations where an expansion joint is required. It complements the realistic, but restricted, Waite and C & L types. For 'juice nuts', the 'Individulay' range also embraces a conductor rail system, based on the Code 60 FB 'Z' rail, and using some tough moulded plastic conductor rail chairs which are compatible in height with finescale rail sections. They also still list a product that goes back to the boot-brad days of ERG and early Brook-Smith track, the Peco brass rail nail, a more refined version of the cobbler's 'tackit'. It can still come in handy.

COMPONENT SUMMARY

I've delved a fair way down various byways in my quest for PW parts suited to the needs of the finescale platelayer in 4mm scale. I daresay there are quite a few items and products I've missed out, but they will be items unfamiliar to me. What I have described here are the components that I have used in constructing my own layouts over the past several years, or those which have come my way for assessment or review. Much though I would like to experiment further with the modern FB heavyweight systems – how do you reproduce today's yard-deep ballast beds, huge super-elevations and built-up ballast shoulders? – I have had to restrict myself to the basic 'standard bullhead' middle ground in the more practical aspects of this book. However, although the components for flat-bottom trackwork vary a bit, the theory, fundamentals and much of the practice are similar.

I have said nothing in this dissertation on ballast, sub-bases and other such aspects of PW work. This is because, before I get onto the hardware, I'd like to consider the proper functioning of these vital components of that complex entity, the permanent way. Which forms the subject of my next little homily.

CHAPTER FIVE

TRACKWORK PRELIMINARIES 1: TRACKBED AND UNDERLAY

THE RESILIENT ROADBED

Thus far, I have been discussing track, both full-sized and model, rather in isolation. Only in my 'potted history' has reference been made to the significance of that other principal constituent of the Permanent Way, the roadbed. I'm afraid it is one of the failings of we modellers that we tend to separate things into pigeonholes; certainly, no full-sized permanent way engineer would ever consider any aspect of track design without first firmly specifying that which was to lie beneath it. A railway is a 'total system', and each element of construction and design is a vital constituent of the whole. I have by me a chirpy little tome of 365 close-packed pages on *Railway Construction,* by one Willm. Hemingway Mills, M.Inst.C.E., sometime chief engineer of the GNR(I), published in 1898. It takes him until page 182 to as much as mention trackwork. ... Two-thirds of the job is done before e'er a rail is keyed to a sleeper.

Both Mills' book, and Allen's trackwork treatise aforementioned, lay great stress on the importance of providing sufficient resilience in the permanent way. Track that is inflexible beneath the traffic passing over it will be both short-lived in itself, and injurious to the rolling stock. Ills arising from too solid a road are cited as including rough riding, propensity to derailment, lack of tractive and braking power, poor steaming of locomotives (due to vibration 'shaking down' the fire, inhibiting air ingress), high incidence of broken rails and broken springs, and even more dire consequences – the failure of major components such as wheel-tyres, axles and locomotive frames.

Now, while the adoption of the chaired bullhead rail carried on timber sleepers provided a good measure of this necessary flexibility, such a track could only function on a foundation that supported and located it without inhibiting its flexure. The design of such a roadbed and ballasting system was the preoccupation of PW engineers right through the steam age for, as previously remarked, the track is the principal springing element in the suspension of the steam locomotive. With the coupling rods limiting the vertical travel of most steam locomotive axles to no more than an inch or two, the maintenance of wheel-to-rail contact was almost entirely achieved by flexure of the track, and of other elements such as the locomotive mainframes. Anyone who has had much to do with handling real BH track will be aware just how 'floppy' the rail is once the support of chairs, sleepers and sub-base is removed. Photographs of track left unsupported after wash-aways reinforce the point that, without the embrace of ballast upon the foundation of the sub-roadbed, real track can't even hold its own weight.

As for the suspension system on the locomotive – or on most steam-era rolling stock, if it comes to it – it was there to take care of secondary factors concerned with a rolling vehicle. There are short-term vertical deflections, such as rail joints, crossing gaps and other small inequalities in the rail surface, that must be accommodated. And there is the important matter of the damping of oscillations caused by all those moving parts flailing around. This is the reason that either leaf, or, less commonly, helical springs are almost universally employed for railway vehicles at this period; a leaf or helical spring, due to its internal friction, is self-damping, and, indeed, this was their principal function. If the trackwork was the resilient member of the suspension system, the loco springs were the shock-absorbers.

RINGING RAILS AND OTHER TRACK TRICKS

In accord with my usual approach, I'm now going to bore you with a touch of rather rusty theory on an aspect of model railway engineering which seems to me to have been more or less totally overlooked, and that is the small matter of harmonics. Those who prefer the wherefore to the why are excused the next page or so.

A harmonic may be described as a wave pattern, travelling in a material, that has its origins in, and in turn causes, vibration. It can amount to anything from a whisper to an earthquake, and it is defined by its frequency, that is, the speed at which the source is vibrating. Now, it is a regrettable fact that, with all model locomotives (especially mine), and to a lesser extent all rolling stock, a fair bit of vibration goes on. The sources are obvious – motor armatures revolving in their bearings, gears meshing, axles and wheels rotating, couplings coming under tension and slackening, valve gears and coupling rods going hither and thither. Good mechanical engineering can reduce such goings-on to a minimum, but in practical terms they cannot be eliminated altogether. So our rolling stock, progressing over our track, sets up all sorts of harmonics, which can interfere with the vital wheel-to-rail contact, as well as producing all manner of unseemly noises.

This is a problem which can be greatly exacerbated where the track on which the stock runs is rigid, and is thus unable to absorb these vibrations, rather as a ball dropped onto a hard surface will rebound virtually to whence it came. Drop that same ball onto a yielding surface, and it may well not bounce at all; if it does, the effect will be slight. As with balls, so with vibrating stock, which is, in effect 'bouncing' many times a second. If the surface on which it bounces is hard, the harmonic wave pattern will be reflected, and fed back into the stock, which will then change the frequency at which it vibrates in response to the new harmonic pattern set up. This is a complex business, but where we can hit major snags is when these harmonic effects become 'phased' – that is, that there is a coincidence between the original harmonic and its reflection, which has the effect of amplifying the amplitude of the wave pattern. Taken to an extreme, such a sequence of affairs can 'bounce' a wagon right off the track, which is apparently what used to happen to many real SWB 4-wheel wagons running on rigid PW.

While it will take an unfortunate extreme to derail stock through such a phenomenon, at far less dramatic amplitudes, these harmonic effects can interfere with pick-up and traction, and, as much of this activity will be taking place at the mid-to-lower end of the audible frequency spectrum, where the human ear is most sensitive, then the equally undesirable grumblings and grindings that are apt to result will also serve to impair the quality of running on a model railway. All-in-all, I feel harmonics to be a problem worth addressing where possible. Much can be accomplished in the design of the mechanical aspects of the stock, an area rather outside the brief of this book. But an awful lot can be achieved by providing a suitable track on which to run this stock.

WHITHER RESILIENCE?

I think that, by now, it will be apparent that I am advocating a degree of 'give', or resilience, in the track, or, to be specific, the track-base. But why will a resilient track help mitigate the unfortunate effects of harmonics? The answer is incredibly complex, but, by ignoring a great many factors, can be stated quite simply. When one vibrating object – our train – is in contact with another – the track and its associated track-base – the harmonic pattern emanating from the train will try to set up a complementary harmonic in the track. But, in the small scales which I am addressing here, there is very little *mass* involved in the harmonic system of the train, which is made out of small quantities of relatively lightweight material. And the mass of the material that is vibrating is a factor – a primary factor – in the effect that it will have on anything else with which it comes into contact.

Where track is rigidly glued down to a baseboard structure, it is said, in harmonic terms, to be 'coupled' to it. Thus, the track is not free to vibrate at its own harmonic frequency in response to the train, but is tied to both the frequency and the mass of the baseboard. Given the huge disparity of mass between baseboard and train, then it's pretty obvious that the low energy represented by our lightweight model doing its harmonic shimmy-shammy is going to have precious little effect on the baseboard/track structure. The result is that almost all of the energy contained in the harmonic waves is reflected back into the train, with the undesirable effects already noted. What we need to do to break this 'vicious circle' is to *absorb* this energy, not to send it back whence it came.

SOME ACOUSTIC SOLUTIONS

All these harmonic effects, whether audible or not, obey the same laws. So the design solutions adopted in acoustics (sound engineering) will have some relevance to our problem. To be more specific, we can use acoustic techniques to absorb our unwanted energy. The acoustic apparatus most relevant to our case is the hi-fi loudspeaker enclosure, in the building of which I spent long years a-dabbling before conceding that Bowers and Wilkins made a better job of it than Rice! At its most basic, a loudspeaker enclosure is a box containing a loudspeaker, more properly referred to as a 'drive unit'. The trick is to stop the whole box vibrating in sympathy with the loudspeaker, and to absorb those unwanted harmonics, emanating from the edges and rear of the cone of the drive unit, that can interfere with the acoustic signal generated by the front of the unit, which is what you want to hear. There are a number of approaches to doing this, but in the context of the problem experienced on a model railway, that which is most relevant is the sealed enclosure.

If you look at a hi-fi drive unit, you will see that it consists of the cone, driven by a magnetic coil similar in action to a solenoid. This cone is attached to a very massive cast or stamped metal frame by the 'suspension' – a ring of very flexible material surrounding the cone, and joining it to the frame. Very flexible materials vibrate at very low natural frequencies, and need a great deal of energy to make them do so. Thus, this flexible ring absorbs the harmonic energy from the edge of the (very rigid) cone, which is insufficient to excite it. That small proportion of the cone's harmonic energy that gets through the flexible material is then fed into the frame, hugely massive in relation to the lightweight cone. These two techniques, the use of a flexible (and hence inefficient) layer, then a massive one, are known respectively as 'decoupling' and 'damping'.

These principles are further applied in the design of the loudspeaker cabinet, or 'enclosure', to absorb that unwanted back-radiation. The cabinet is usually lined with a very sound-absorbent material – soft, and with a very low natural frequency. In my day, it was 'Doctor Bailey's Long-Haired Wool' or fibreglass, but these days there are more hi-tech alternatives. The cabinet itself is made of a very inert, dense material which, while not having a natural frequency beyond the audio range, is so massive compared with all the other bits of the structure, especially the vibrating bits, that it would not be excited by them at all. High-density chipboard is the usual material, which is why good loudspeakers come heavy! My B & W's weigh 56lb each, not out of the way but none too portable all the same!

DECOUPLED TRACK AND DAMPED BASEBOARDS

We can apply many of the solutions evolved by the hi-fi engineer to the design of our model railway very simply, and with the use of many of the same materials, although there are other factors we also need to consider, especially if the layout is a portable one. The first, and most helpful thing that we can do is to decouple the sources of vibration. Some of this decoupling can be done by adopting such mechanical refinements as rubber-mounted motors in our locos, but the easiest and most productive point at which to do it is between baseboard and track. Peco have been doing this for years, of course, and many a modeller will be familiar with the excellent quality of running that results from the use of foam ballast inlay with the Streamline track system. This is in stark contrast to the ultra-rigid trackage to be found on so many 'finescale' layouts, where the track is immovably bonded to the baseboard by a rock-hard concrete of PVA glue and granite chippings, with all the resilience of a Grampian boulder. Ken Northwood developed the notion of decoupled, or 'floating' track way back in the early 1950s, when his 'North Devonshire' was at the forefront of model railway design. It's still one of the best big layouts ever built, but generations of modellers have failed to learn from it (including hi-fidelity Rice, who should have known better!).

There have been reasons, of course, for the adoption of the singularly unyielding chipboard/cork glued-solid-with-granite-chips type of track system that has become so prevalent today. Initially, the glued-solid approach was advocated by those seeking the impossible grail of dead-flat track. Their efforts have been compounded by those who seek the greater realism that the use of 'scale granite chippings' supposedly endows upon

An original Ken Northwood sketch of his floating track system, which he developed from Fleetwood-Shaw's pioneering use of the then-new material 'sponge rubber' as a track underlay. This was drawn for a Model Railroader *article, hence US terminology.*

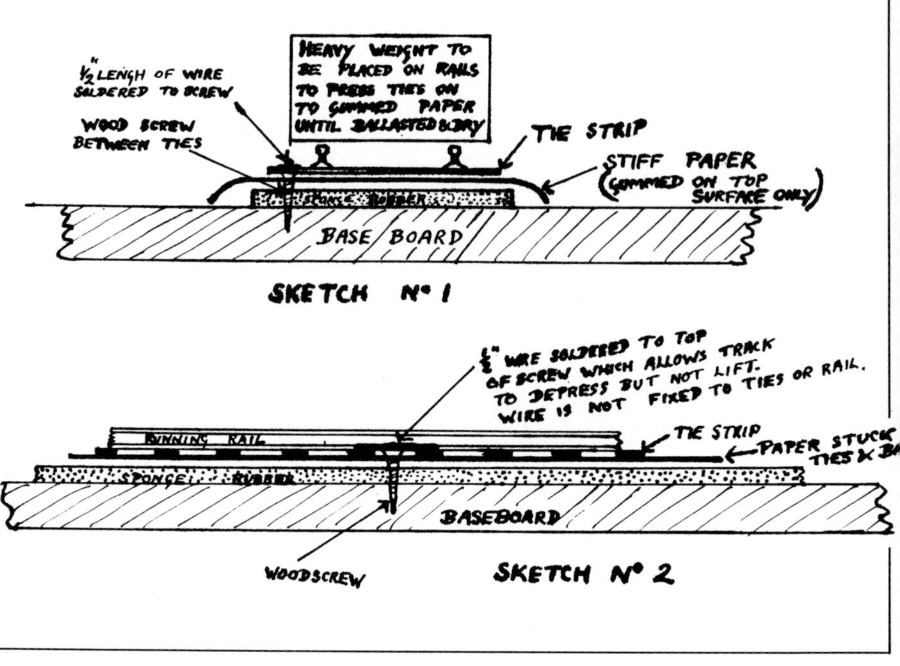

model PW. But the result, whatever the reasoning behind it, has been to hold back the quality of running that should be possible with modern motors, high-quality gears, and truly concentric wheels. Don't be misled by the words of Rice – go to any exhibition, seek out the layouts with the concreted track, and just listen and watch. Then go to Pecorama and watch a standard RTR loco gyrating on foam-bedded Streamline. Peco may not worry too much what their track looks like in a British context, but they certainly care about making it work!

A foam underlay is the most obvious and most practicable way of decoupling track from baseboard. Exactoscale have, for many years, supplied a 3mm thick skinned foam for this purpose, which I have used with some success on previous layouts. It is no thicker than 'trad' cork underlay, but a good deal more resilient. Unfortunately, it's still not quite resilient enough to form a really effective decoupling medium, although two layers laminated together with 'Photomount' spray adhesive come close. But that's an expensive solution, and rather tedious in practice. I have spent some time casting about for a better alternative, which I eventually ran to earth in our local camping and outdoor activities shop in the form of a 'camping mat'. This is a sheet of medium-density foam designed to be placed under a sleeping bag, for the dual purposes of thermal insulation and some softening of the knobblier extremities of the Earth's crust. The normal size of these mats is 1800mm × 500mm, and they come in all manner of grades and thicknesses. Mine is 8mm thick, towards the softer end of the range of resilience available,. with one smooth and one textured skin. It is a pale green-grey in colour, nearly ideal, and, at just under a fiver, not expensive; indeed, it's cheaper than traditional cork.

There is a very wide range of these mats on the market, with specifications varying from the nearly useless to the extremely sophisticated, with prices to match. There's nothing to be gained from the use of one of the better quality mats, which are often of a denser (and hence less resilient) foam, as well as being much thicker than 8mm. Some are laminations of different types of foam, and make use of some high-tech plastics. For our purposes, 8mm blown polythene is quite adequate, and I use the '3 season' mat from Total Camping and Backpacking Accessories. There are plenty of equivalents from other sources, but look for a smallish cell size in the foam, and at least one smooth skin. Oh yes, and try to avoid some of the more bilious colours – vivid lemon yellow is a less-than-ideal start for naturally coloured super-realistic PW!

We can apply the next stage of the hi-fi engineer's approach by introducing some 'inertial damping' in the trackbed beneath the resilient underlay, by making this of a dense material that is hard to excite. As most dense materials are also fairly rigid, there is no conflict of properties in the trackbed requirement. Chipboard has served well for years, but is heavy for use in a portable layout. Ply of reasonable thickness is not quite as dense and much lighter. Best of all are modern compressed fibreboards: MDFB (Medium density fibre board) or, better still if you can get it, HDFB of around 12mm thickness. These are both relatively light in weight, yet are almost immune to resonance – that property of vibrating readily to a harmonic input.

THE SOUND OF SILENCE

It will not have escaped your attention that all these measures, having their origins in the design of high-performance acoustic systems, will have a greatly beneficial effect on the 'sound' of our model railway, a factor that I have long considered worth pursuing. Decoupled track on an acoustically 'dead' baseboard (of which more anon) will eliminate the greater part of the mechanical noise that can intrude on a model railway, enabling us to hear those sounds we might want to hear, such as the odd rail-joint click. To return to the 'loudspeaker cabinet' solution, we have adopted the first two stages of the system, in decoupling our source of vibrations and allowing the track to resonate at its own frequency, thus absorbing much of the unwanted harmonic energy. We have also 'damped' this energy by feeding it into an unexcitable high-density track bed. But should we be true seekers of silence, we can take things a stage further, by interposing a further stage of decoupling between the trackbase and the baseboard proper, and by designing the baseboard itself along acoustic lines.

Now, the value of the second stage of decoupling may be a touch questionable, but the use of acoustically inert baseboards can make a big difference. One way to achieve this is to make the baseboard proper very massive – I know of one layout using kitchen worktop (1¼in thick high-density chipboard) on 8in × 6in 'L-girder' supports, which is admirably silent but bone-crushingly heavy. Having for many years now advocated a lightweight approach to baseboard construction based on very un-massive glued-ply principles, I would be loath to go back to such a neanderthal structure. However, glued-ply baseboards, with their dependence on thin panels braced in opposition, are much akin to the sound-box of a musical instrument, and are thus acoustically very 'live'. To damp out their unfortunate propensity to resonate gleefully in response to the movement of trains, the hollow spaces of the box section need filling with a closed-cell foam of some sort. Expanded polystyrene insulation blocks do quite well, as does a suitable foam rubber; I damped 'Leintwardine' with the innards of an old foam mattress, retrieved, in best Dave Rowe manner, from a skip. Best of all, though, is polyurethane foam injected 'wet' and left to expand and cure. Cavity wall insulation is the most common source of this material, though you can buy it in D-I-Y kit form from some Texas-type emporiums. For effective damping, the foam or whatever needs to be in firm contact with the panels of the ply baseboard, either by being glued to them or, preferably, by being jammed in as a good tight fit, which is what makes the expanding foam so effective.

BALLAST

I have written at some length about these sub-track matters here, as I'm quite convinced that the right trackbed can produce as great an improvement in the running qualities of model track as the use of modern finescale components produce in its appearance. Code 75 bullhead rail, though nowhere near as flexible, relatively speaking, as the real thing, will still flex sufficiently to perform a useful role in the production of a 'total sprung railway system' if it is laid on a suitable underlay, in such a way that its flexure is not adversely affected – which rules out the granite chippings and the PVA. The use of a ballast material that is, in itself, resilient, will help to ensure that the track performs in the same way as the prototype, as well as keeping things sweet on the acoustic front.

PVA glue itself is not inflexible when dry, though it's less accommodating than a latex adhesive such as 'Copydex'. It's this business of making a concrete of it with granite granules that does the damage – so if granite is out, what substitutes are there? Well, for years now I've used the oldest material in the game, granulated cork, to simulate crushed and washed stone ballast. Properly painted and weathered, it looks every bit as good as granite chips, without any of the drawbacks. My cork comes from BTA Scenics, and I generally use their 'N' version, which is nice and fine. There are other useful materials to be had, both to represent other ballasting mediums, and to do the same job as the cork. The best of these cork-alternatives I discovered quite by accident, but very good it is.

My various writings are all set down on one or other of my ancient 'Imperial' portable typewriters. The newer of these, donated by Bob Barlow (being a relic of his cub-reporter days on the *Loughton Gazette*), was apt to skate around the desk as I hammered at it one-fingeredly, a habit tamed with a small offcut of cheapo foam-backed carpet. After a bit, this foam backing, which is grey, quite dense and very soft, started to break up, leaving a residue of grey foam dust which looked for all the world like – ballast!

Eureka – a truly resilient, realistic, easily stuck granular ballast material! Putting a few chunks torn from the back of the carpet through the old 'Spong' manual coffee-grinder in the Rice kitchen soon had me a supply of this material, though the coffee started to taste a bit rubbery! It is, obviously, much akin to the scenic 'ground foams' now made by such as BTA and Carrs. If one of these admirable enterprises were to take up the manufacture of a grey 'ballast grade' foam, my cup would run over, hopefully with untainted coffee!

However, as pointed out in my brief skit around prototype trackwork, not all ballast is stone ballast, só we may need to represent ash, crushed slag, cinders and other such materials. The ground foam can, if reduced to appropriate fineness and suitably coloured, reproduce most of these, but I have used other materials, most notably ash. I find two types of ash useful – very fine flue-ash from slow-combustion anthracite stoves or central heating boilers, and sieved wood-ash. The sieve I use is a very fine-mesh tea strainer (jumble sale, 10p), the ash being pushed through with a teaspoon in best Delia Smith fashion. The fine grey granular material that results makes a good 'fine stone/coarse ash' ballast, as well as having any number of scenic/texturing uses.

Another very useful 'soft' texturing/ballasting material that has a number of uses is wood-dust, such as can be obtained by the use of an orbital sander. Some of these machines have a dust-collection system, but a bit of vigorous sanding of the odd pine offcut over a sheet of polythene will soon yield up a surprising amount to be collected. I use it 'neat' to represent ash or cinder ballast, colouring it with the airbrush once it is in place. Use of the sander on old-fashioned softboard of the 'Cellotex' variety produces a 'woolly' dust that, mixed with the ordinary variety, makes a good 'overgrown siding' mix.

The actual fixing of the track and ballast to the track underlay and trackbed I cover in some detail in Chapter 9. All that I will point out here is the necessity to bear in mind at all stages the desirability of resilience in the whole track structure. I avoid, if at all possible, any rigid track-fixing devices, although there is need of the odd pin here and there, mostly to resist the lateral thrust of point-operating mechanisms. The ideal is to locate the track to just as sufficient an extent as will keep it where it is wanted, without impairing its ability to float freely and flex in the vertical plane.

THE INDEPENDENT TRACKBED

Conventional wisdom has the trackbed as an integral part of the baseboard structure. In other words, track is laid, with or without the interposition of some decoupling resilient underlay (in which category I do *not* include cork sheet, no matter how thick) direct onto the baseboard. This approach seems to me to have a number of practical disadvantages to add to the acoustic and harmonic hang-ups I've already discussed at such wearisome length. Baseboards, even relatively modest portable ones, are still apt to be bulky and awkward to handle in the 'workbench' context, which is why most of us have built the track 'off the layout', on which it is then laid, wired, ballasted, finished off cosmetically and hooked up to whatever point-operating system takes our fancy. Which means that, once laid, the track on the baseboard is once again bulky and awkward to handle. And as for such jolly japes as wiring up or installing point linkages whilst upside down on the Axminster, or crouched in cramped confinement beneath the baseboard – they are not for Rice. I prefer to build my track as far as possible upon the workbench, in comfort, with good light, and without blobs of solder burning holes in my best pullover.

I have already introduced the notion of a trackbed of dense, inert material designed to act as a damper for spurious harmonics. I have mentioned the possibility of decoupling this from the baseboard structure proper. Well, I take the notion of decoupling to its logical extreme, by making my trackbed a completely separate entity which is installed, replete with track, ballast, underlay, wiring and point actuators, to the baseboard only when completed, tested and passed. And I further take this opportunity to inveigle a spot more of the ever-desirable decoupling into the system, by sitting the trackbed on blocks of the foam camping mat, and attaching it by screws which are not tightened down. The trackbed itself I now cut from MDFB, in units of a convenient size to handle on the workbench, and of a shape appropriate to the trackwork they are to carry. The various units of trackbed are joined one to another by the use of splice plates, also of MDFB, and chipboard screws.

This isn't a new idea, of course. But like so many of the good ideas that have been around for years, it seems to have gone out of fashion these days. Again, this is probably due to that paranoid search for the great myth of totally flat track that demanded a surface braced to utter rigidity – difficult with a self-contained trackbed. There was also the spectre of warped soft board to haunt the memory, but modern materials like the MDFB are far less inclined to do that sort of thing. Even if they do move a bit, the 'top' can soon be restored if required by adjusting the hold-down screws, although at some slight loss of the decoupling effect. Anyway, in the context of contemporary finescale, flat track is not an issue, as the suspension systems we now incorporate into our models are more than capable of coping with any slight waywardness in the vertical plane. So I'm a firm believer in building my PW in bite-sized chunks on the bench, although I will always lay it out as a whole, usually before cutting the trackbed out in the first place.

The actual baseboard structure to which this independent trackbed will be tenuously attached can take a number of forms. I discussed several of these in my book on layout design, but really, it's not that relevant at this point. I've already remarked on the desirability of making the baseboard acoustically inert, but other than that, so long as it can support the trackbed adequately, its down to preference and the materials and facilities to hand.

THE IDEAL SUBSTRUCTURE

So, to recap all of this, let me set out the properties that I think will serve to get the best out of modern finescale trackage systems, ply or plastic-based. Firstly, a resilient underlay thick enough and soft enough to absorb and otherwise damp out both audible and subsonic harmonic effects, in the form of 8mm skinned foam sheet, this to be used in conjunction with adhesives and ballast materials that will not impair this resilience and thus adversely affect the decoupling of track and trackbase. The trackbase itself to be independent of the baseboard, and fashioned from relatively dense, acoustically inert material such as MDFB. Ideally, this trackbase to be further isolated from the baseboard structure by use of more foam blocks and a non-rigid retaining system. And finally, the baseboard itself to be 'damped' as far as possible by the use of sound-absorbing materials such as foam rubber, expanded polystyrene blocks, tight-packed fibreglass insulation or polyurethane foam in all voids. Quite a tall order, I know, but worth the effort if you want the running of your finescale layout to match the appearance. I would certainly say that you need at least the underlay and the dense trackbed if you're not going to impair and compromise the performance of the track. Either that, or it's down to building frictionless, vibration-free mechanisms, fitting all the stock with truly concentric wheels, and reducing all tolerances to a level that would make a watch-maker blanch! I happen to think that a bit of foam mat and some wobbly glue is a *lot* easier to cope with.

SUPER-ELEVATION OF CURVES

You only have to look at photographs of prototype running lines to spot that most curves are laid out with super-elevation – that is, the outer rail is raised slightly above the inner, twisting or 'canting' the entire track to incline vehicles towards the inside of the curve. This was originally done to resist the supposed 'spreading load' imposed by centrifugal force as the train rounded the corner, although in later years this was of

Modellers are a lot fonder of built-up ballast shoulders than the prototype ever was, especially within station limits. This is Haverhill, on the dear old Stour Valley line – no problem to reproduce this entirely typical situation with an overall foam underlay.

less importance than a reduction of rail and wheel wear and greater passenger comfort. The amount of super-elevation applied is determined by the radius of the curve and the speed of trains passing over it. A given degree of super-elevation is strictly speaking correct only for a particular speed, but in point of fact the maximum line speed is generally the value used for the calculation. In fact, at low speeds, the effects of centrifugal force are minimal, and thus only a very small amount of cant, or often, no cant at all, would be applied to branch and mineral railways. In his book, Mills gives the formula

$$\frac{V^2 \times g}{r \times 1.25} = S$$

where V is the velocity in MPH, g is the track gauge in feet, r = radius of the curve, also in feet, and S is the super-elevation of the outer rail in inches. Applying this little equation in a couple of instances is quite revealing. Taking a reasonably prototypical case, with a line speed of 40 mph on a curve of 20 chains radius, we would get

$$\frac{40^2 \times 4.75}{1320 \times 1.25} \text{ or } \frac{7600}{1650} = 4.606''$$

not a huge amount, then – almost exactly 1.5mm at 4mm scale.

Take a far more typical model case, though, and things get a bit more out of hand. It's our tighter-than-scale curves that do it, as in this example, which takes a line speed of 25 mph on a curve of 5 chains (4′ 4″) radius, giving an answer, according to my Casio fx-7 all-singing scientific calculator, of 7.2″, or near enough 2.5mm at 4mm scale which, I'm afraid, makes our modest 4′ 4″ curve look like the big dipper at Butlins. It also begs the question of whether a real train would stay on a 5 chain curve at even 25 mph. Put that speed up to the 40 or so that a lot of model trains run at, and you're looking at an impossible situation, calling for some 18″ of super-elevation by Mills' formula, inclining the track at an angle of nearly 20°, which is more like the wall of death on a bobsleigh run!

All this is highly suspect, of course, as it might be said to devolve around the long-vexed question of scale speed. And while it is undoubtedly true that a real train encountering a 5-chain curve at 40 mph would be destined for a spectacular pile-up, super-elevation notwithstanding, it is equally true that our models will sail round happily in those same circumstances, reduced to scale. We don't actually *need* super-elevation in the working context of a scale model railway, other than in a cosmetic sense. And when it comes to cosmetics, we can deceive the eye, which is happy to accept our 5-chain curve as reasonable and our speed as likewise. And, of course, real railways don't go in for bobsleigh super-elevations, the usual limit being 6in, which is actually quite pronounced. So, to go back to my first example, I regard 1.5mm as about right in most instances; not too obvious, but enough to be seen. The EM gauge manual has a pithy page or so on super-elevation, which includes a table relating it to speed and curve radius. With a radius of 1320mm (virtually spot on 4ft 4in or 5 chains), 1.5mm of super-elevation gives a line speed of exactly 40 mph. That should do most of us, methinks.

In actually applying the super-elevation, I prefer to produce the necessary cant in the actual MDFB trackbase, by angling the supports by which it locates to the baseboard crossmembers. Do ensure that you introduce this cant gradually, as any sudden twists in the track are not likely to promote smooth running, although they may allow you to emulate the spectacular pile-up aforementioned! It should be introduced over the length of the easement, or transition curve, as evenly as possible. The MDFB trackbase helps here, but solid rather than resilient mounting is needed to ensure accuracy; thin packings between baseboard and trackbase may well be necessary. Thank goodness my mineral lines, by and large, do without such fripperies!

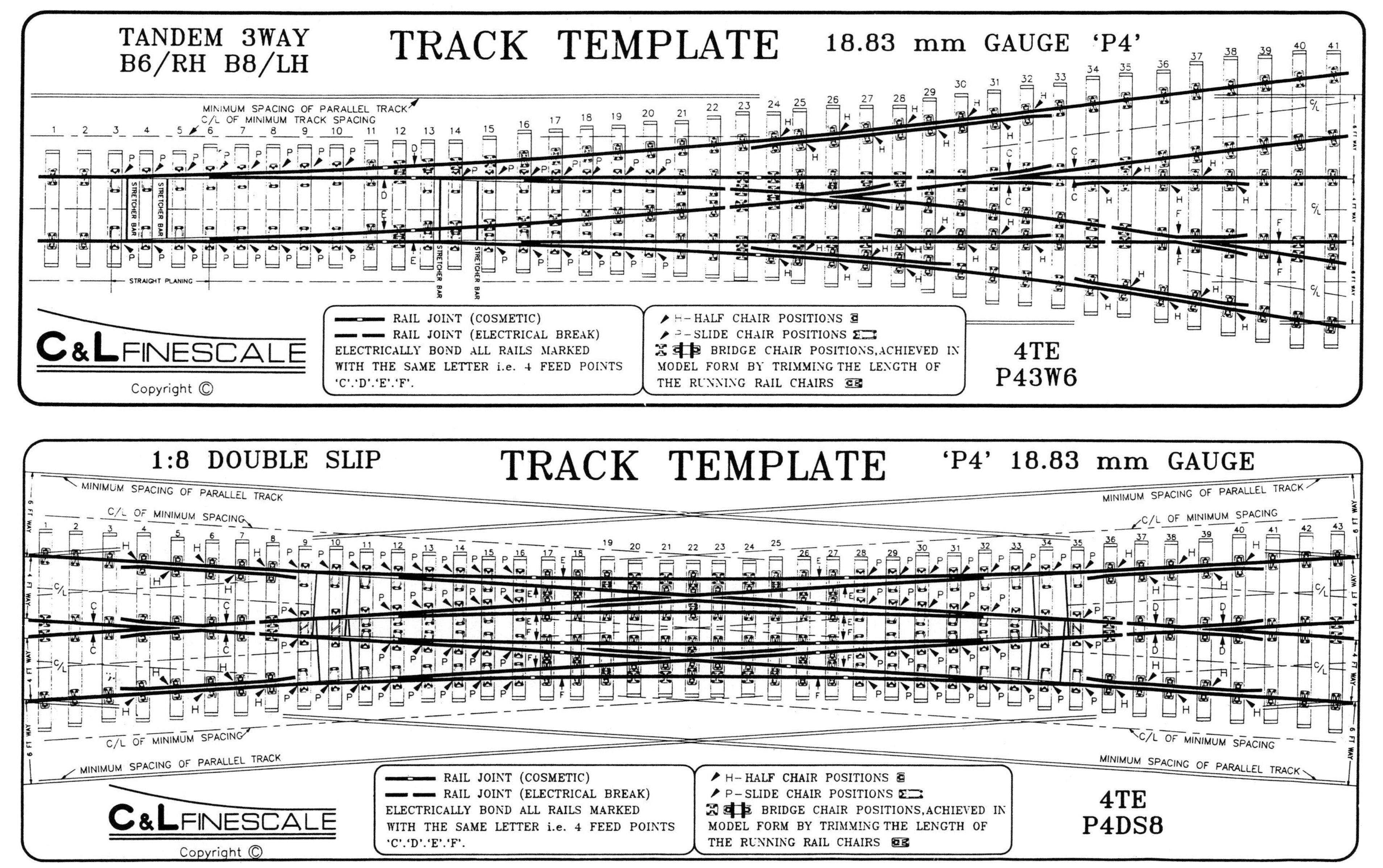
TANDEM 3WAY
B6/RH B8/LH
TRACK TEMPLATE
18.83 mm GAUGE 'P4'
MINIMUM SPACING OF PARALLEL TRACK
C/L OF MINIMUM TRACK SPACING
STRETCHER BAR
STRAIGHT PLANING
RAIL JOINT (COSMETIC)
RAIL JOINT (ELECTRICAL BREAK)
ELECTRICALLY BOND ALL RAILS MARKED
WITH THE SAME LETTER i.e. 4 FEED POINTS
'C'.'D'.'E'.'F'.
H-HALF CHAIR POSITIONS
P-SLIDE CHAIR POSITIONS
BRIDGE CHAIR POSITIONS,ACHIEVED IN
MODEL FORM BY TRIMMING THE LENGTH OF
THE RUNNING RAIL CHAIRS
4TE
P43W6
C&L FINESCALE
Copyright ©
1:8 DOUBLE SLIP
TRACK TEMPLATE
'P4' 18.83 mm GAUGE
MINIMUM SPACING OF PARALLEL TRACK
C/L OF MINIMUM SPACING
6 FT WAY
4 FT WAY
RAIL JOINT (COSMETIC)
RAIL JOINT (ELECTRICAL BREAK)
ELECTRICALLY BOND ALL RAILS MARKED
WITH THE SAME LETTER i.e. 4 FEED POINTS
'C'.'D'.'E'.'F'.
H-HALF CHAIR POSITIONS
P-SLIDE CHAIR POSITIONS
BRIDGE CHAIR POSITIONS,ACHIEVED IN
MODEL FORM BY TRIMMING THE LENGTH OF
THE RUNNING RAIL CHAIRS
4TE
P4DS8
C&L FINESCALE
Copyright ©

CHAPTER SIX

TRACKWORK PRELIMINARIES 2: SETTING OUT AND TEMPLATES

PLANNING

It never ceases to amaze me how many modellers set out gaily on the tricky business of laying out and building a complex of model PW with nothing more to guide them than a scribble on a beermat. I'm afraid that PW that is designed 'on the hoof' usually looks like it, with all manner of awkwardnesses and compromises forced on the builder. The result, in my experience, rarely works well, so I deem the time and effort that goes into refining the track design as a *scale* drawing well worthwhile. Apart from all other considerations, it's a lot easier to rub out and re-draw a few lines on a sheet of paper than it is to lift and relay finescale track.

With scale drawing work, the bigger the scale, the greater the accuracy. The ultimate conclusion of that logic is a scale of 1:1, and there's much to be said for drawing out at full size. However, it's a pretty unwieldy process, so I start off with 1/12 scale, or one-inch-to-the-foot, which is big enough to get things pretty accurate. Nowadays, I've become so used to working at this scale that I can draw by eye and know that I'm there or thereabouts. But if you're not certain of things like track centres, turnout leads, formation lengths and so on, then equip yourself with the necessary point templates, and measure them. If you use a larger scale – say, 3 inches to the foot – then it's quite possible to reduce actual templates on a modern photocopier, and to 'paste-up' the design using these.

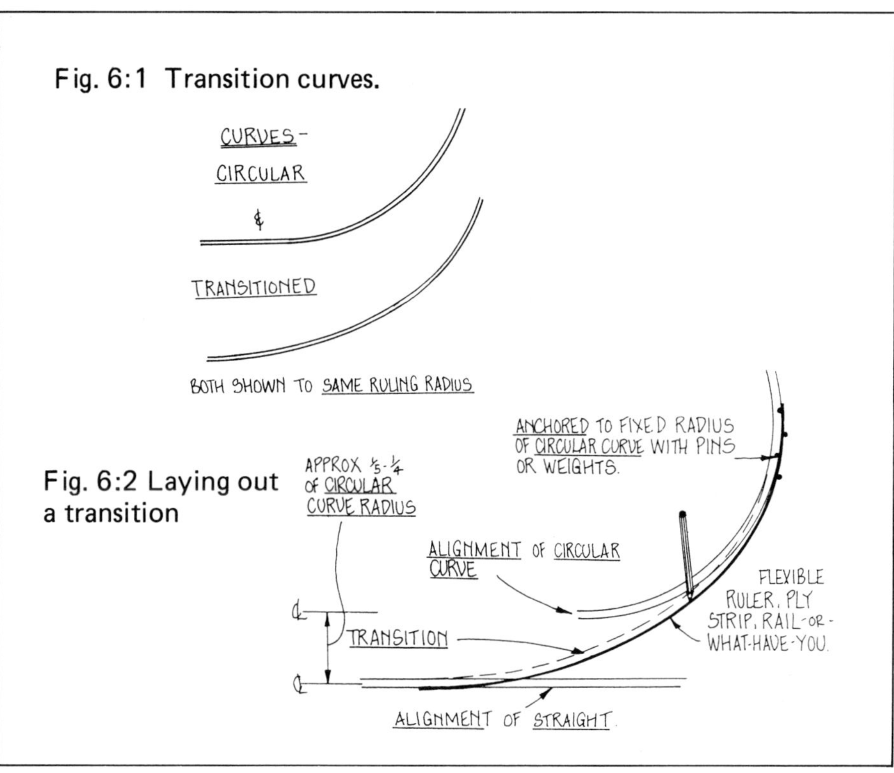

Fig. 6:1 Transition curves.

Fig. 6:2 Laying out a transition

CURVES

Probably the trickiest aspect of track design is the accurate assessment and laying out of curves. As mentioned a while back, real PW curves are complex animals indeed, and are calculated and laid out by formulae going something like:

$$T_e = \frac{B^2 - W^2}{8R}$$

(just one of a daunting selection extracted at random from *Scalefour Digest* 21:0 – 'Curves, Prototype Considerations', by Derek Genzel, who *knows*, being a real full-size PW engineer). If you can play chess, do Rubik's cube and the Times crossword, and are generally adept at theoretic abstractions, you might well apply prototype methods to determine curvatures. Me, I just do it by eye.

Before the mathematicians among you hound me down with slide rules, let me take shelter in the slit-trench of pragmatism. Unless you are very fortunate in the space at your disposal, then virtually all the curves you will be laying are well below prototypical minima. In reality, any curve on a running line below 10 chains (660ft) radius will be check-railed and subject to speed restrictions. To save you working that out, it's an 8ft 8in radius at 4mm scale, not allowing for easements. Few running lines in open country get down anywhere near this sort of curvature, though. Most of the examples in Mill's textbook talk of 60 chains radius as desirable; and I can't recall too many 4mm layouts with 52ft radius curves . . .

I think that this unfortunate aspect of real railways has placed a great, if unnecessary, inhibition on a lot of finescale layouts. The ethos of 'dead to scale, or bust' precludes all but dead-straight formations, any idea of going round in circles being quite outlawed. These days, I'm glad to report, this puritanical approach has lost favour, and the curve – exaggerated, underscale and restricting as it must be – is staging a comeback. Indeed, there are now layouts, such as Steve Lee's 'Grafton', which are virtually 100% curved, on radii getting down towards 3ft – or a tad under 3½ chains, which is the tightest curve I've so far located on a running line (Boyces Bridge on the Wisbech and Upwell Tramway). Mineral and industrial lines got down to about 1½ chains (1ft 4in radius at 4mm), but a normal minimum would have been 5 chains (4ft 4in), and this seems to me a pretty good 'ruling radius' for model railway applications.

EASEMENTS

In real life, a railway curve is of basically parabolic form, with the radius getting progressively tighter as the curve progresses, down to a minimum, or 'ruling' value, from which point it gradually eases out back to the next section of straight track. As Mr Genzel demonstrates in his text for the 'Digest', calculating these varying curves is a pretty sort of a business, but the essential point about them is that they incorporate an easement. That is, the curve proper is linked to the preceding straight by a section of track whose gently-tightening radius is designed to minimize the abruptness with which a train passing over the line is required to change direction. And I have found that, so long as this feature of the prototype is reproduced in the model, then the result both looks realistic and functions correctly. The fact that the easement does not follow the mathematical path that the calculations would define, and is of an improbably tight mean radius, seems to have but scant effect on the result.

The simple rule-of-thumb way to produce a workable easement in both plan-drawing and track-setting forms are illustrated in my diagram. A set of French curves are invaluable in producing the scale drawing, and a whippy bit of wood, such as a narrow offcut of 3mm ply, will serve at full size. The eye is the ultimate arbiter of this process, which I describe in detail in a page or so. But, with both scale and full-sized drawings, I have found that this is one of those happy cases where something that pleases the eye also seems to work well.

LAYING OUT AT FULL SIZE

Having exorcised, the bugs and entrapped the inspiration to produce what looks like a workable track layout to answer the aesthetic and practical criteria of your design brief, the next stage is to set it all out at full size, to check the practicality of the design in the first instance, but finally to produce a definitive blueprint to which the track can actually be built. Rather than use the templates supplied for track building individually, I aim to combine them into one giant template for the entire layout.

Strictly speaking, I suppose that one is bound to buy a sufficient stock of templates for the purpose. Like most people, though, I long ago equipped myself with a complete set to use as originals for photocopying (purely for my own use), when I can readily and simply run off the 'sacrificial' templates used to build the track. I prepare the templates for laying by cutting them out at 'sleeper-end'.

I never lay out direct onto a baseboard or sub-base, but always onto paper of appropriate dimensions. If I'm only setting out a 'rough', to check that what I've drawn will work at full size, then I use the back of some cheap wallpaper. If I'm actually setting out the final layout, then I use a good-grade paper, cut into strips or sheets sufficient to encompass the trackwork with a goodish margin at the edges. As we'll see in the next chapter, I actually build the track onto this paper, which not only serves as a template for the entire track formation and for the cutting out of the MDFB sub-base and foam underlay materials, but also forms a vital part of the track substructure in itself.

Whatever the paper, it needs locating before it can be used to make an accurate full-sized drawing. By this stage, I've usually come by the sheets of ply and MDFB I'm going to use in baseboard or trackbed construction, so I tack the paper in place on these, usually late at night on the kitchen

Wot, no templates? But this chunk of GWR P & C work being laid in will have started out as a very detailed scale drawing. Accurate positioning is here achieved by crowbars and sweat. Have to get a move on or the PVA will go off! NATIONAL RAILWAY MUSEUM

floor, this being the biggest room at Rice Towers. I retain the paper with Pelikan 'Roll-fix', a film dispenser adhesive system that has all manner of modelling uses. The film can be obtained in 'temporary' or 'permanent' grades – the former is just the job in this instance.

With my paper assembled into a size and shape adequate to enable me to set out the entire trackwork and any associated features, I start by marking as many 'datum' points as I can; joints, fixed features, clearance points, baseboard cross-members (if fixed at this stage) and other structural considerations, basic track centres, distances in from front and rear baseboard edges, and so on. Only when I have thus determined the 'envelope' into which I've got to fit my track do I start juggling with templates and straightedge. I find that most track layouts have a fairly obvious 'focal point' about which everything naturally aligns, so I start with this and work outwards to the extremities. At this stage, I'm only positioning 'standard' point or crossing templates, not plain track or curved or 'special' point templates. It may not be possible to locate all of the standard templates without setting out a few curves first, so this is the next job to consider. I don't stick any templates down permanently at this stage – I tack them in place with little dobs of the 'Roll-fix'; however careful you may be, and however clever you think you are, they always seem to need a bit of adjustment at some stage!

Fig. 6:3 Trammel.

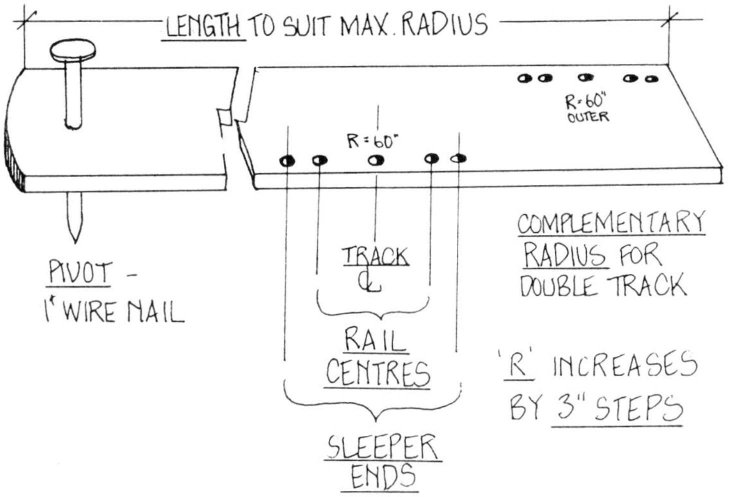

Fig. 6:4 String compass.

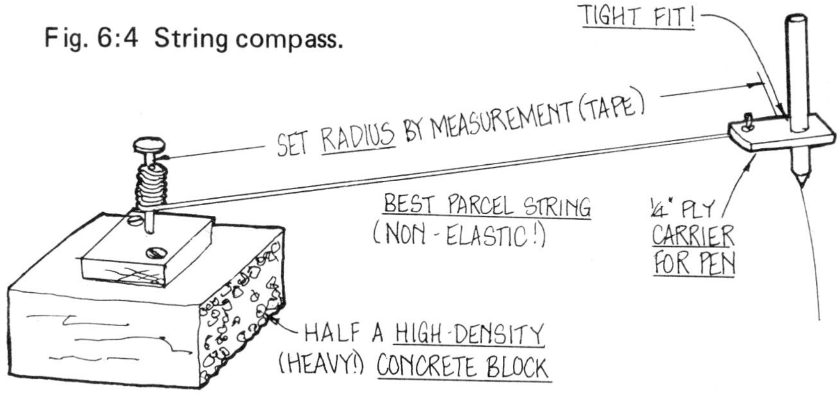

SETTING OUT CURVES

Before curved plain track or curved turnouts can be laid out, it is necessary to draw the curves that they need to follow. Curves, so far as we are concerned in this exercise, come in two varieties; circular, and transitional. Circular curves are a simple enough proposition, calling for some sort of compass. Up to a bit over 5ft radius, I use the simple trammel illustrated in the diagram. This is made out of a bit of 6mm ply about 1¼in wide, 5ft 6in long overall. At one end is a pivot, a 1in round wire nail whopped through to stick out beneath the trammel. For each radius of curve I wish to draw, there are no less than five holes, just big enough to take the point of a felt-tip or pencil. As well as the track centreline, my trammel provides for a line 9mm either side of this – to give rail positions – and a further line 18mm each side of centre, giving sleeper ends for 9ft sleepers. These holes are set out down the right-hand edge of the trammel. Along the left edge are a further set of holes at the radii appropriate to the second line of a double track outside the 'prime' or inner curve radius.

In use, the pivot end of the trammel is whacked into a good heavy block of wood, which is then propped up on some makeshift support in the appropriate position relative to the job to enable the curve or curves to be drawn. To avoid confusion, I draw centrelines and sleeper-ends with a red felt pen, and rail positions in pencil. As will have been noted from the 'easement' diagram a page or so back, the circular part of the curve does not meet the ensuing straight or whatever; rather, it is offset to the inside, and stopped some way short, being linked by the transitional curve of the easement. This must be born in mind when trammelling happily away. Also bear in mind that this circular part of the curve is the 'ruling radius' of the track, which will have to observe a minimum value dictated by the locomotives to be worked over it. So – if, when you draw your curve, you find that there's not enough room for the easement, think carefully before drawing a curve of tighter radius to overcome the problem; it may be better to move the curve centre or the alignment of the straight track. This is the sort of pretty problem often thrown up when laying out the full-size 'rough', and is in itself a sufficient justification for that exercise.

For curves greater than the 5ft 2.086in radius that is the maximum my trammel will accommodate, I use that old favourite of geometry teachers through the ages, the string compass. You can make longer trammels, of course, but they are a mite unwieldy, and the string works very well. I usually enlist some aid to hold the pivot still, and to assist with the measuring tape when the thing is being set up. I only set the centreline; when this is drawn, I mark the rail centres off of it, and adjust the string to suit. I hope my sketch will reveal all.

SETTING OUT TRANSITIONS

This is the potentially tricky nub of laying out curved trackage. As I've already described, the transitionally-curved easements are, in reality, governed by subtle and complex mathematical considerations. But, fortunately, they can be effectively and simply reproduced by using the natural flexure of a thin strip of material of suitable resilience. If you hold a ruler on the edge of a table and flex it in best schoolboy ink-pellet-launching manner, it will not take up a curve of fixed radius, but will take up a form whose radius relaxes gradually from the table-edge outwards. This is the principle by which I lay out easements, aligning the 'fixed' or 'table' end of my 'ruler' with the last part of the circular curve, and flexing it until it meets the alignment of the ensuing straight.

The implement I actually use generally is a 25in draughtsman's rule, of thick clear plastic with just the right degree of 'spring'. But a piece of thin ply or a yard of Peco Code 125 'O' rail serve as well. On the rough, I enlist help to align the rule, but for the final setting-out on the trackbase, I maintain alignment with pins whacked into the trackbed, which enable me to keep fiddling and adjusting, sighting along the rule until my eye is satisfied that I've come to the smoothest and most satisfying union of the circular curve and straight track. The expression 'flowing' is often used to describe well laid-out easemented curves, and very apt it is too; the transitional parabolic curve is a predominant occurrence in nature and is very pleasing to the eye. It is one of those features of the railway which enable it to exist in harmony with the landscape.

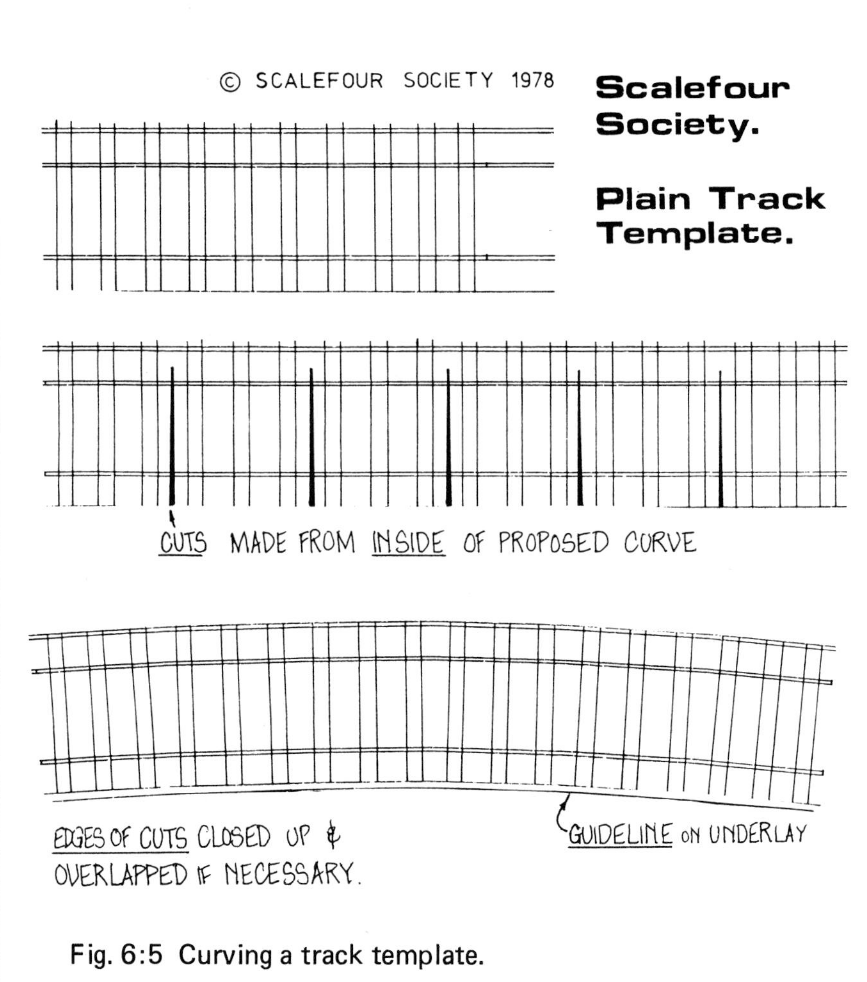

Fig. 6:5 Curving a track template.

CURVING TEMPLATES

Templates, as supplied by the various societies and commercial firms like C & L, cover only straight plain track, turnouts with a single curved road, and diamonds, slip diamonds and compound turnouts of like rectitude. If our design calls for sinuous trackage and for P & C work of curvilinear disposition, then we need to bend these linear patterns to our requirement. That requirement is defined by the curved lines trammelled, strung and flexed onto the trackbase, so it comes down to making the templates conform to these curves.

The basic technique for curving templates is to 'fan' them – that is, they are slit across from the inside edge of the would-be curve to a point just outside the opposing rail, and then closed-up so that the inner edges of the template sections overlap slightly. The smoothness of the resulting curve depends on the radius, and the number of cross-cuts made. More cuts are needed for tight curves than for wide ones. The main difficulty arising is the alignment of the template with the drawn curve, given that, once in place, the template conceals the drawn lines. With photocopies, I find that the red centreline still shows through, and my 'sleeper end' lines give a reasonably accurate location for the edges of the template, which I always cut off at that point. I also lay curved templates in short lengths, so that I've a frequent check on alignment. The templates are stuck to the paper strips on which the curves were drawn.

With curved turnouts, it may be necessary to start with a template of longer 'lead' than you aim to finish up with, as curving the 'straight' point template will shorten the lead and tighten the radius of the curved road if that lies to the inside of the line of the curve. Conversely, if the point is to be curved on the opposite hand to the existing curved road – that is, into 'Y' form – then start with a shorter-lead template, as curving in this case will ease the curve. I arrive at the best template to use for curved turnouts by trial-and-error at the 'rough' stage, keeping the minimum-curve requirement ever in mind.

Don't get too obsessed with making a 100% perfect job of curving templates – they are, after all, only a guide. Their main function is to enable you to prepare and position the sleepering. Given the adjustment provisions inherent in the actual track constructional process, such imperfections as slight doglegging of the rails on a 'fanned' template is irrelevant. When the actual rail is laid, it will take up a smoothly-curved alignment, rather than being dictated by what the template shows. Your eye and the gauges are the determiners of rail positioning.

NON-STANDARD TEMPLATES

From time to time, there arise instances where no standard template, no matter how curved, chopped up, 'cut and shut' or otherwise mutilated, will serve your purposes. With my propensity for modelling light railways, mineral lines and other rather 'non standard' bits of the prototype, this is a situation that I've often come up against. After all, I can't see a minor industrial line employing a fully-fledged PW engineer to design and lay out their P & C work for them. An experienced platelayer and rule-of-thumb are nearer the mark in such circumstances, and I have successfully employed the 4mm scale equivalent of such techniques in building some of my more 'offbeat' layouts, merely working off an accurately-marked centreline and constructing pointwork to suit as I went along. Such an approach does not, however, preclude the need for careful planning and scale drawing. It still has to fit the site!

There are certain rules to obey, of course, such as the timbering arrangements necessary to properly support and locate the crossing and switches. These same rules can be brought into play to simply design and produce 'custom' point templates. These are usually required to unite trackwork elements already positioned and determined by other considerations, so the basis of the template is arrived at by reference to these existing alignments. I start with a sheet of thin paper – typewriting copy paper is fine – laid over the site of the formation. The centrelines of the tracks are picked up and projected – as straight lines – onto the paper, which should be sufficiently transparent for this to be possible.

To reduce the possibility of error, I always bring the 'standard' track as close as I can to the limits of the non-standard formation. The projected centrelines will cross, suggesting the position of the actual common crossing of the point. This will, more than likely, be at an 'odd' angle, as it often was on the prototype. We modellers may stick with a limited selection of 'whole number' crossing angles, but real PW included fractional crossing angles on a routine basis. Don't overlook that, unless unavoidable, the line through the actual common crossing will be straight, so any necessary curvature should be introduced on either side of the crossing. I lay these curved lines out in the same way as a transitional curve, using my 'flexible friend' to obtain as smooth and progressive an alignment as possible. With pointwork, I anchor my 'flex' at the heel end, so that the curve tightens progressively from the tips of the switchblades into the crossing.

With the track centrelines thus drawn in, I can then mark off either side to obtain rail positions. There's no need to get these exactly at gauge – I content myself with an 18mm spacing for both EM and P4. The offset required to bring the rails into correct gauge is minimal and well within construction tolerances. I don't usually bother with niceties like check rails and wing rails either, as the various gauges will serve to position these in relation to the stock rails and crossing nose.

This then gives a 'skeleton' template, needing only the sleepering drawn in to make it usable. The rule here is to attend to those critical timbers relating to the crossing and switch, starting with that actually situated beneath the crossing nose. This is set so that the tip of the 'V' is about 1mm back from the toe edge. Next to this timber come two others, that supporting the knuckle, where the bends imparting the 'set' to the wing rails come just over the heel edge, and that supporting the wing rails, which is

Fig. 6:6 Drawing a point template.

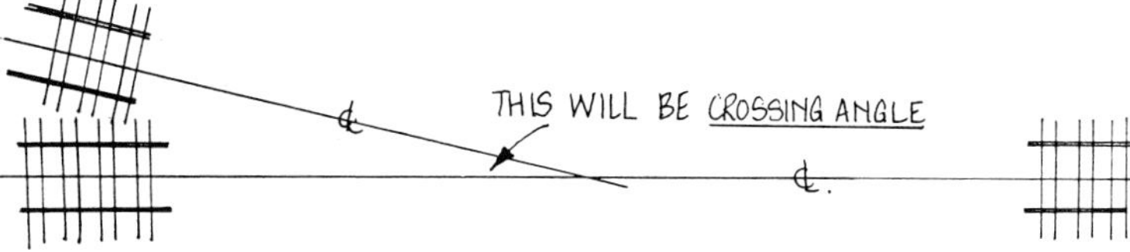

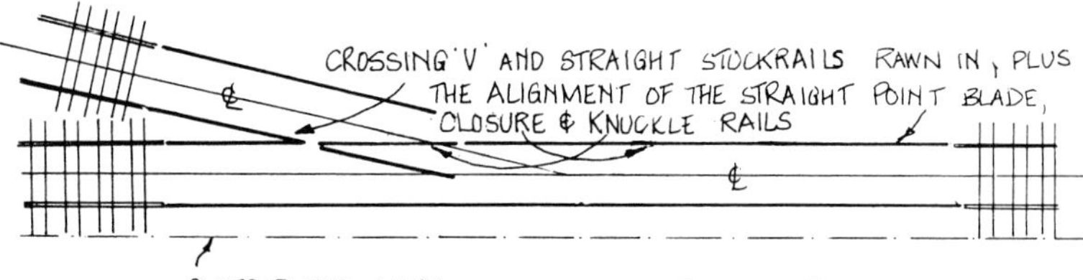

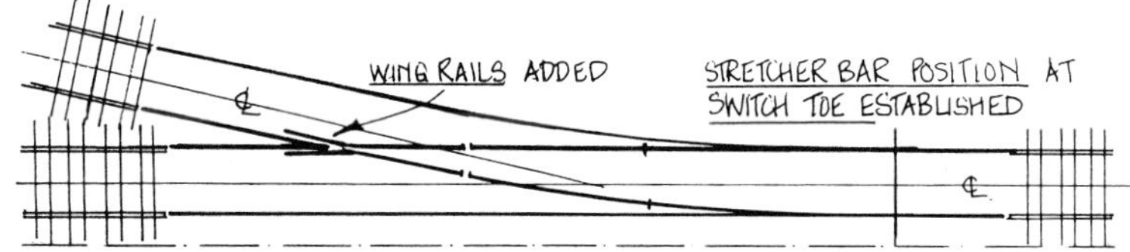

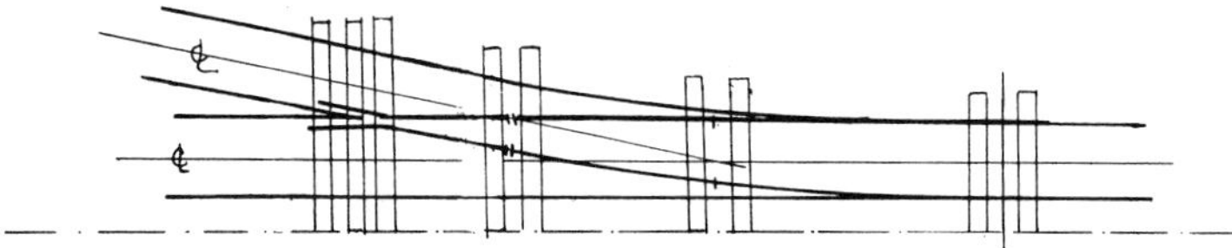

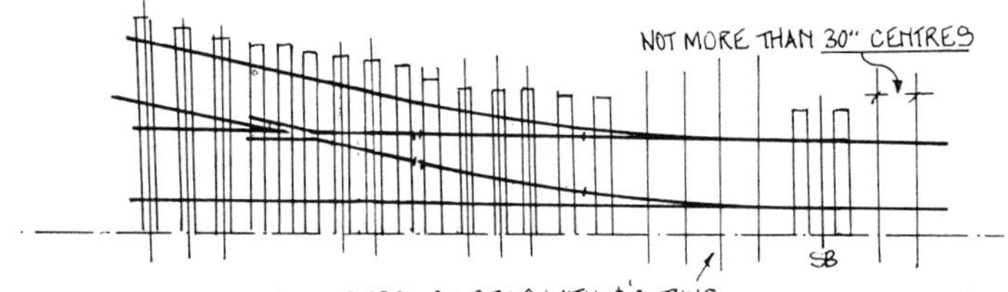

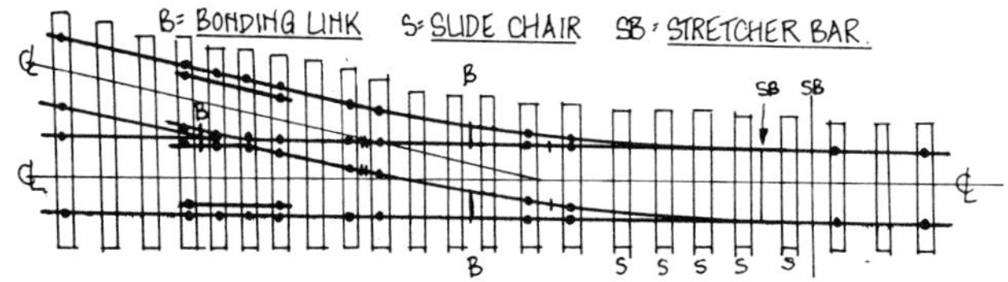

usually centred under the point at which the wing rails are flared out.

The next two critical sleeper locations are those either side of the joint between the knuckle rails and the closures. Note that, in common with all sleepers adjacent to joints, these are on close centres. Attention is then turned to the switches, which will need equally-spaced timbers appropriate to bear the number of slide chairs dictated by their length; 5 for an 'A', 6 for a 'B', 7 for a 'C' and so on. The correct length of switch is generally pretty apparent – a useful rule-of-thumb is $\frac{1}{3}$ of the total 'lead'. Once these timbers have been positioned, add one further timber at the same spacing (generally the standard 30in centres) at the toe end, and a pair either side of the joint between the heel of the switch and the closure rails, set at the 'joint' centres, usually 1ft 9in or thereabouts.

The rest of the timbers are then fitted in, at centres of 30in or less, depending on circumstances. Normally, sufficient timbers to give the below-30in centring will be used, evenly spaced out between the predetermined positions of the 'critical' sleepers. Occasionally, the centres are kept on 30in, and the discrepancy taken up with a single out-of-position sleeper which is often virtually touching those adjacent to it. I ink the template in with a Rotring pen and flexible drawing curves, ruler and so on, to make an original for photocopying. Why not build on the original? In case you make a mess of things and need to 'start over', that's why. I've yet to meet the template that can be used twice!

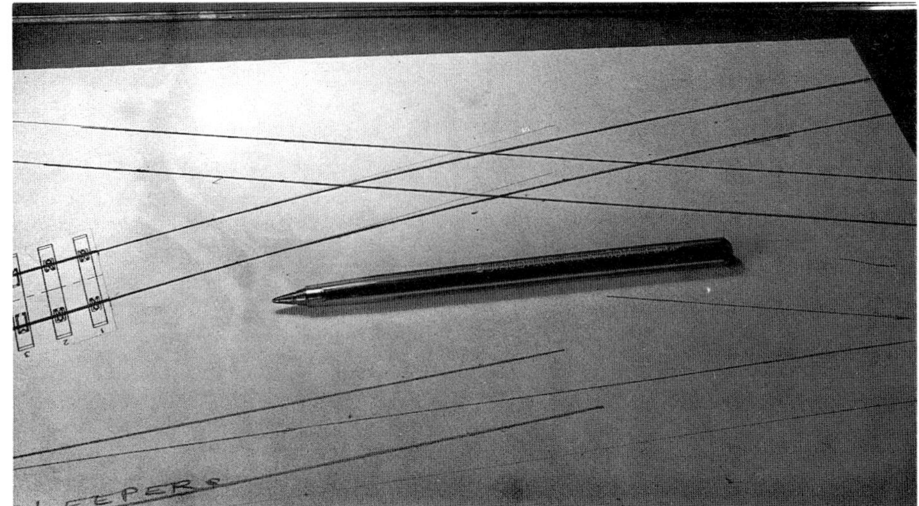

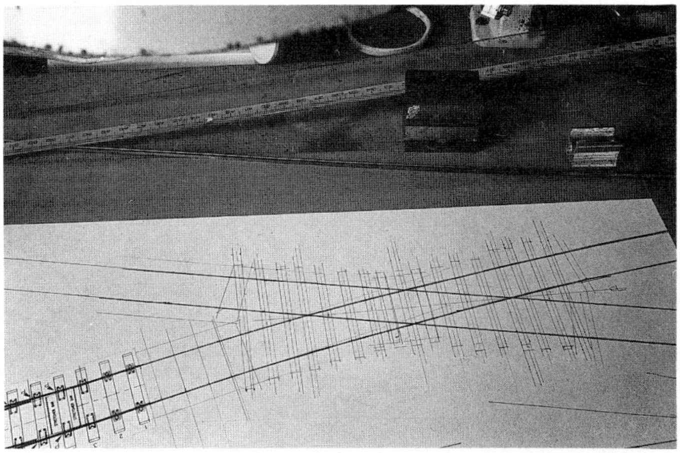

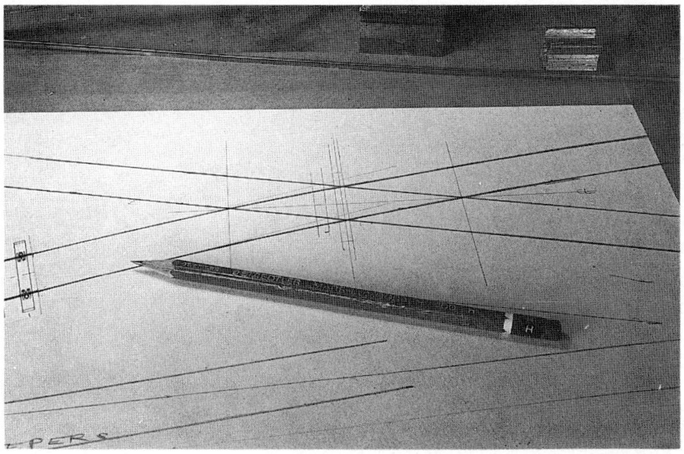

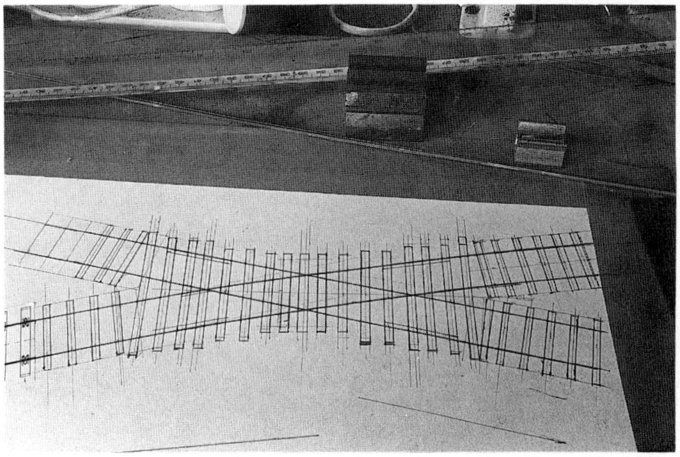

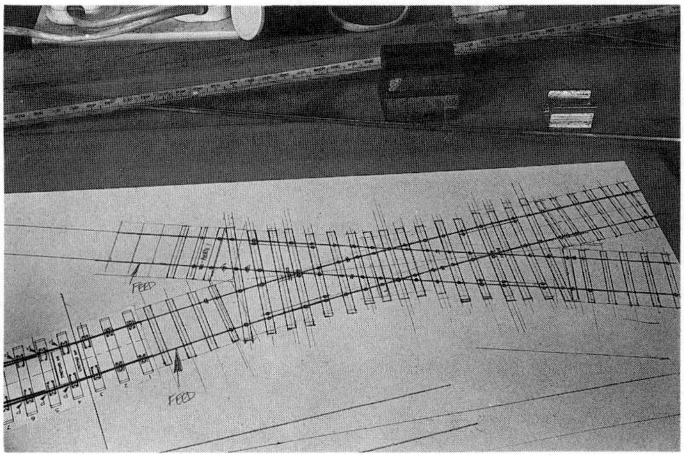

The diamond crossing at 'Trerice' is a good example of a 'drawn in situ' template – in this case, straight onto the paper track underlay (see next chapter). Starting with the adjoining template, the first job is to establish the rail alignments. Usually, I do this off the track centrelines, but here I've used a combination of measurement (off the layout plan) and projection of existing rail alignments. With rail positions established, the sleepering is marked out, starting with the crucial timbers beneath the obtuse crossings. The timbering of the common crossings was then added, and the remaining timbers inserted by the '30in centres or less' rule. I establish sleeper centres first, then draw the outline to facilitate sleeper positioning. All this preliminary drawing is in pencil. Once I'm happy, I ink it all in with a biro (immune to paint and glue). Last job is to mark the rivet positions and any rail-breaks. The prudent amongst you will then photocopy the result!

CHAPTER SEVEN

TRACK TECHNIQUES AND PLAIN POINTS

A PW PROGRAMME

As I hope will have become apparent during the course of this windy narrative, I am averse to considering track in isolation. This is never more true than in the building, for before track can be built, some thought must be given to the manner in which it is to be laid. At the very least, such considerations will dictate the order of doing things, if not that which is done. The convention has it that the track is built remote from the layout, on templates fixed to a workboard, from which templates it will be separated before being laid upon some prepared roadbed. Nothing wrong with that, is there?

Well, no. Not wrong, exactly. It's just that, having carefully combined all my templates into a smooth-flowing, accurately aligned, unified whole, then I'm loath to reduce this once more to component parts, built discretely in the hope that they will all fit together when they're done. My experience is that, due to accumulated error, they don't, well not for me anyway! The results range from unwanted doglegs or awkward 'not quite' alignments to the loss of vital clearance at fouling points. I much prefer to build my PW *in situ* on the full-sized 'layout template', in as large a unit size as I can manage. However, such an approach has repercussions on the tracklaying front – you won't lay a chunk of PW several feet long into a wet-glue carpet if that be the intended approach; the glue 'goes off' too fast, even on a damp day. Large units of PW are also fragile and difficult to handle if they must be 'lifted and laid'. The choice comes down to sawing the formation up into manageable chunks, to be reunited at the tracklaying stage, or to not having to lift and lay it at all, by building it where it is to go, and ballasting it where it lies.

Regarding the templates on which the track is built as part of the track structure, and simply ballasting right over them, seems to be frowned upon in 'proper' circles, although I can't really see why. I know I've done more damage to PW trying to get it off the template that at any other stage in the trackbuilding process, for all that I retained the sleepers in place with 'Cow Gum' or some other low-tack glue. (Usually, this fails to keep everything in place while you're trying to build the track, then flat refuses to let go once you *have* built it!) How much easier to stick the sleepers down with a good manly glue in the knowledge that you haven't got to hoick them all up again. If you can accept that the purpose of the template is to enable you to prepare and position the sleepering, then the possibility of laying sleepers and ballast simultaneously opens up, for with the rivets in place, the rail locations are apparent, and the template is therefore largely redundant; the fact that it's buried in ballast will be of little account.

THE BEARING OF BALLAST

Ballast is awkward stuff, and ballasting model PW is never easy – at least, not if the track is to look and function optimally.

The method by which the track is to be ballasted is, in fact, a pretty fundamental decision with repercussions throughout the building and laying stages. When the possibility of a resilient underlay is being considered, then ballasting becomes even more of a problem, as the adhesive used must not 'clog up' the underlay, thereby stiffening it and greatly reducing its effectiveness. Ken Northwood had an ingenious solution to that one way back in 1953 – he didn't fasten the track to the underlay at all, but stuck both track and ballast to a paper 'underlay overlay', as in the sketch. Now, this is a very sound idea indeed, as it effectively increases the degree of 'decoupling' between track and trackbase very considerably, without in any way impairing the flexibility of the actual track itself.

Adhesives for tracklaying. The PVA glue is used for the actual constructional/ballasting stage, and the carpet adhesive for attaching to the foam underlay. Double-sided carpet tape then holds underlay to trackbase.

The nature of the ballast also has a bearing on the matter. If you're using stone chips, then they can either be laid into wet glue, or they can be laid 'dry', then impregnated with a PVA glue/water/wetting agent mix later – much the currently favoured method. But you can't play that trick with cork or foam granules – they just float away on the glue/water mix and you end up with the most almighty mess! Buoyant ballast materials can only be laid 'wet' – into a carpet of glue – with the problems already noted if that glue carpet needs to be any sort of size.

There are various solutions to this particular problem, depending upon the stage in the tracklaying/building process at which the ballasting is actually carried out. If you want to lay completed track straight onto the foam underlay, then it's possible to use one of the spray adhesives sold for sticking down carpet. This stuff is what I use for actually gluing the foam underlay to the trackbase, for which it's ideal. But, for retaining track, it's a bit on the 'fierce' side; there's absolutely no scope for adjustment – once the sleepers come into contact with this glue, it'll 'grab' them, and you'll be lucky to get the track up again without considerable damage. It will also only retain a layer of ballast material one granule thick, a bit on the mean side for a lot of trackage.

The alternative to this is to do a Northwood, and stick the completed track and the ballast to a paper overlay, and then stick this to the foam. It's a lot easier to position ready-ballasted track onto foam with the carpet glue, as the whole job is considerably less critical than trying to align individual units of track. I have used this approach myself, without too much of a problem. I stuck the track to the paper overlay, the overlay to the foam, and, lastly, the foam to the trackbed. Any slight discrepancies at the end of each section of trackbed can be adjusted when the trackbed itself is installed.

A variation on the paper-overlay approach is to lay sleepers and ballast as a single continuous operation onto templates previously stuck to the overlay. This is what I now prefer to do, as I find it a very great deal easier to make a really good, realistic job if ballasting is undertaken before the rails get in the way. One is always working with the glue at an ideal consistency, as only a very small area is tackled at once. I use PVA 'School Glue', from the Educational Supply Association, which is only about £1 a litre – it comes in 5 litre cans. Art shops stock a similar PVA if you can't get round

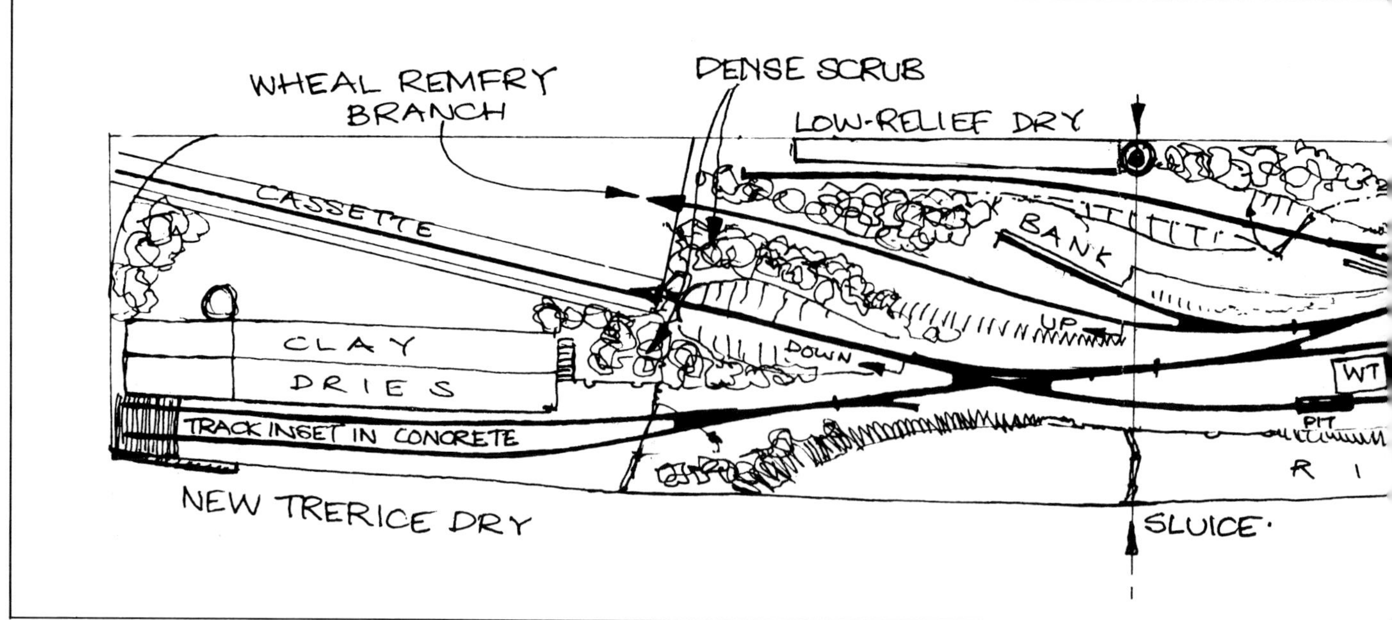

Fig. 7:2 North Devonshire track. Ken Northwood's development of a Fleetwood-Shaw original idea, c.1953.

your local headmaster or evening institute tutor, although not, I fear, at an ESA price.

PAPER TRACKBED OVERLAYS

The use of a paper membrane between track and underlay does present one or two problems. Using water-based adhesives such as PVA can cause the paper to cockle, whilst paper impregnated with PVA can become quite stiff and acoustically 'lively'. Indeed, quite a lot of loudspeaker cones are made from PVA-impregnated paper! Ken Northwood used a relatively 'soft' type of black photographic paper; his adhesive was 'gum arabic', which apparently neither caused cockling nor stiffened the paper. I've experimented with a variety of papers, including some watercolour art papers – relatively immune to cockling, but too stiff.

In the event, I've found that ordinary cartridge paper does the job as well as anything, especially if you 'stretch' it. I buy it in 'imperial' sheets (approx. 30in × 20in), usually big enough for most chunks of PW, though it's no problem to join sheets if needed – I just use a splice of paper over the rear of the joint. This paper is 'stretched' onto MDFB boards – I generally use the sheets of 12mm from which I'm going to cut the trackbase. 'Stretching' simply involves wetting the paper, and taping it down to the board with gummed parcels strip while it's still wet. It'll cockle like billyo, but dry it out and it'll be as flat as you like. An old hairdryer is a useful aid to speeding this process, while either a wet sponge or an atomiser spray will do the wetting. I stretch enough paper onto the MDFB bases to enable me to lay out all the trackwork in one go, as advocated a page or so ago.

The templates are stuck in place on this stretched paper with yet more PVA – again, any slight cockling that appears will vanish under the warming blast of the hairdryer. Non-templated track is simply drawn in place on the paper, and I also find I end up with fixed features, wiring runs and all manner of cryptic notes and reminders dotted on what has, in effect, become a 'whole layout template'. All the trackwork is built *in situ* on this paper, complete with ballast and all manner of track details. Only when it is completed, tested, painted and weathered do I cut it free for installation on the layout.

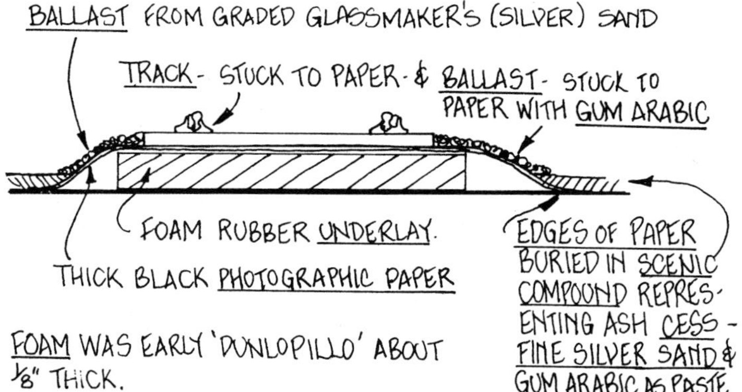

Ken Northwood's track was completely 'floating'; that is, it was not attached directly to the underlay – the edges of the paper were restrained, and the track held down by wires, bearing on adjacent sleeper-ends, as in one of Ken's original sketches (prepared for, but not used by, *Model Railroader,* hence the 'ties' rather than sleepers) reproduced alongside. I tried this system, but found it to be noisy as the paper tended to resonate under the trains. This, I think, is due to the low mass of my small engines and plastic rolling stock – Ken's engines are good and heavy, and think nothing of sixteen Exleys! So I stick my paper to the foam underlay, which seems better. I'm sure that I haven't yet arrived at the optimum system of resilient restrain for track, but it seems to work well enough in practice.

A TRACKBUILDER'S AGENDA

At the end of all this debate and exposition, I can identify three sequences of track construction. Firstly, individual units, combined at the tracklaying stage after being built on templates. The main drawback to this approach is that each item of PW is built in isolation, rather than as an integrated part of the whole. This, as noted, can lead to alignment problems and, due to accumulated minor errors, to the whole formation 'drifting' from its intended location – not necessarily a problem if you've got plenty of space, but potentially disastrous if you haven't!

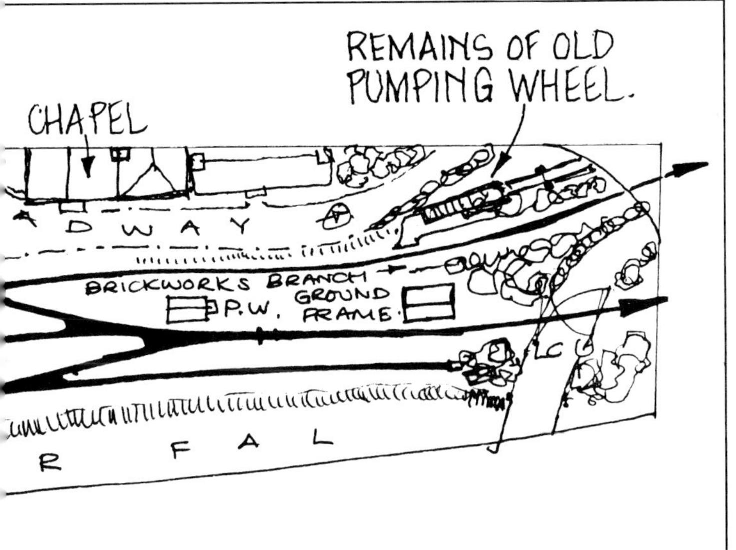

Fig. 7:1

'Trerice', the Cornish china-clay model, slowly and painfully emerging from the usual chaos of skip-looted ply offcuts and junk currently cluttering up the workshop. A design aimed at maximum shunting potential in a minimal space, it crams in a semi-outside slip, five plain turnouts, a tandem and a diamond crossing – all in eleven feet. Track illustrated in this book was built for this layout.

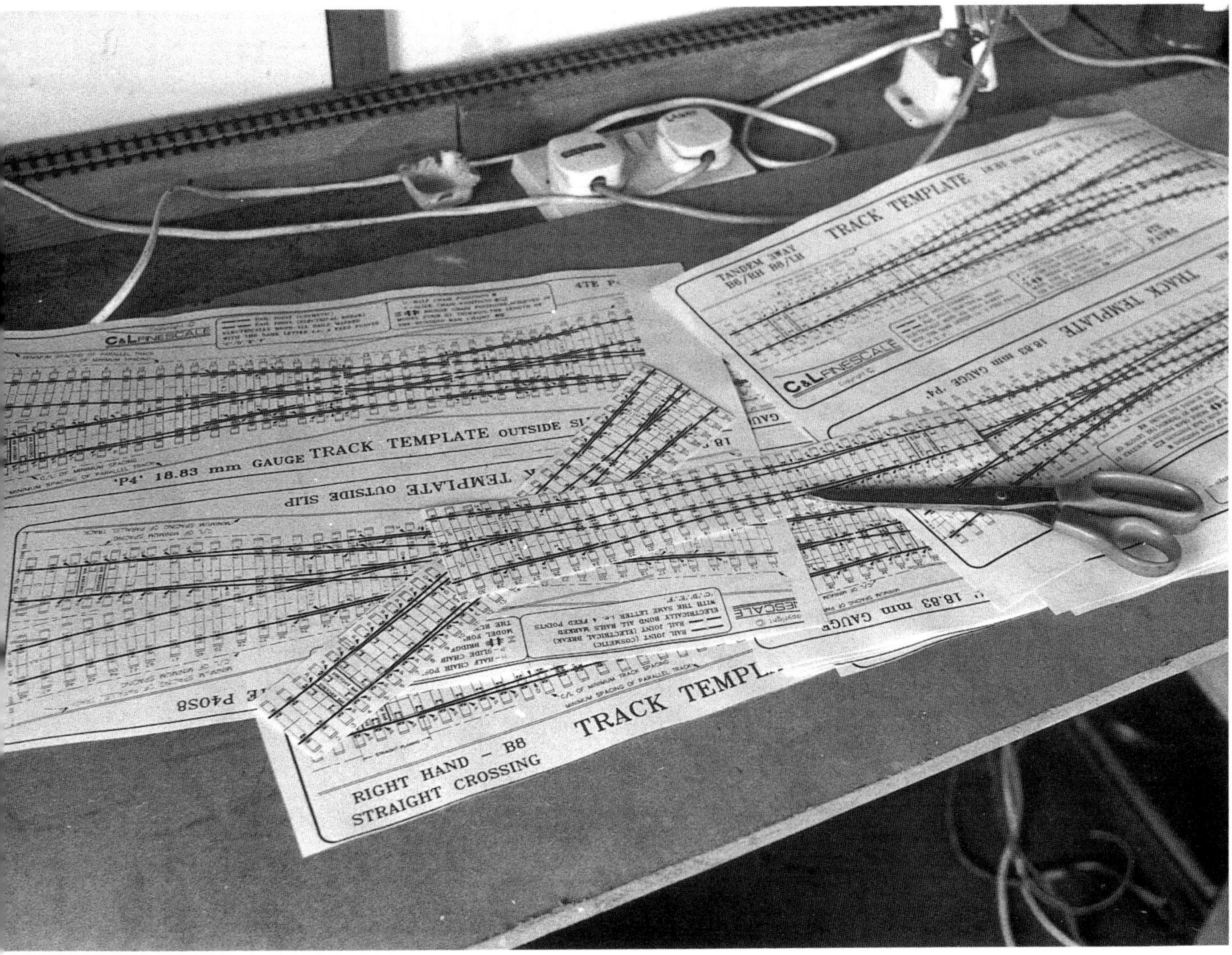

It all starts with templates, here being cut out to the sleeper-edges prior to being incorporated in the 'layout template'.

Stretching down the paper track-base. A suitable-sized piece of paper is wetted using a plant spray atomiser. The wet paper is then taped down to an MDFB workboard with 'Butterfly' brand gummed brown parcels tape – the old-fashioned stuff you used to hate licking because it tastes foul! I use a wet sponge to moisten the gum. At this stage, the paper is horribly cockled, but drying will cure this. I speed things up by using an old hairdryer.

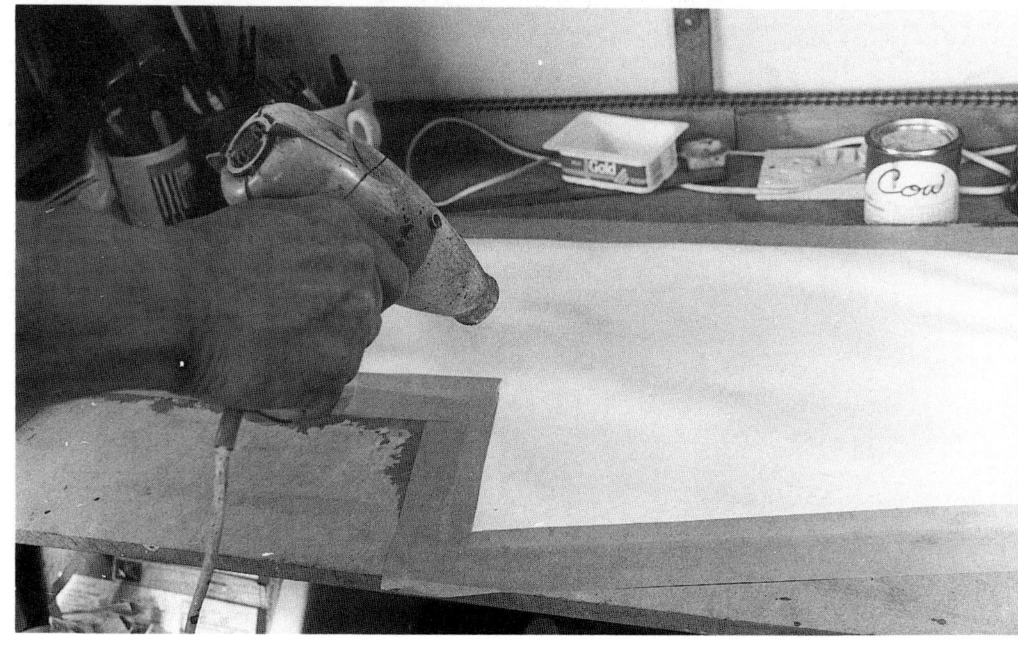

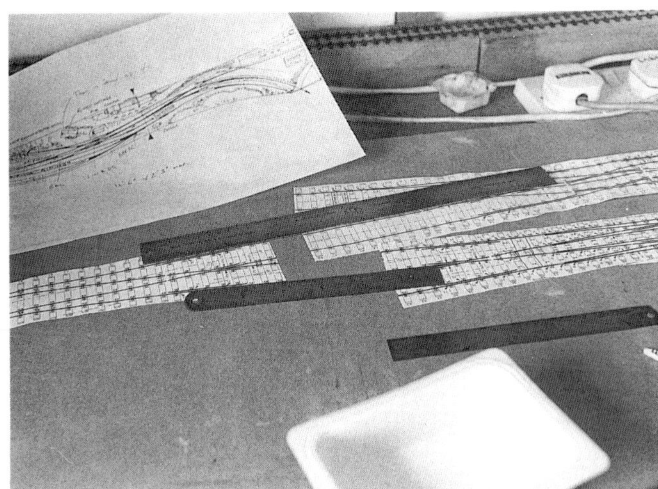

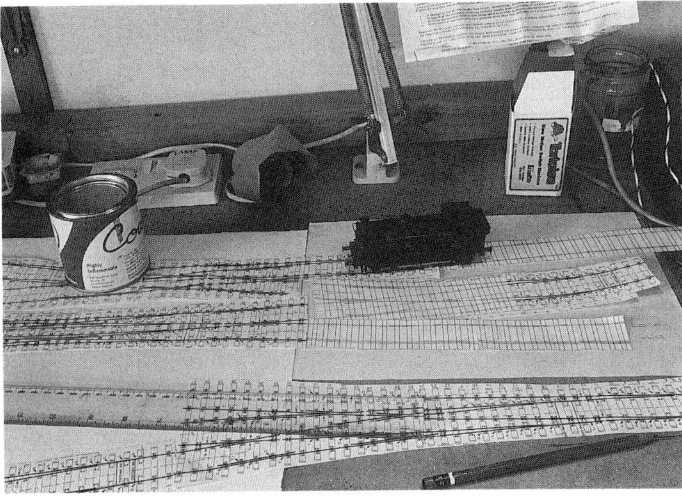

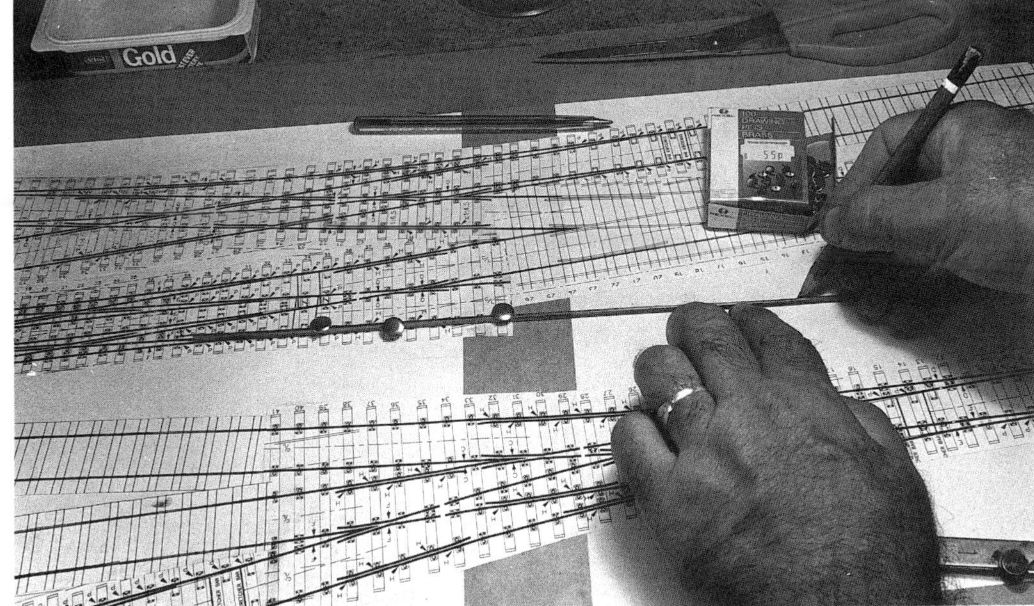

Laying out templates onto the pre-stretched paper is a complex and time-consuming business. I use every ruler I can find to ensure that everything lines up, but it comes down to fiddling, sighting, measuring and constant checking. Parts of the formation whose relationship is predetermined, such as the semi-outside slip and turnout in the photos, are joined as units and moved as such in relation to the rest of the formation. Note that the point template is itself a composite – a C & L 'B' switch spliced onto a Scalefour Society 1 in 5 crossing to give a B5R.

As the formation is built up, some track alignments are drawn in. Here I'm drawing in a curve using Peco Code 125 'O' gauge rail as a 'Flexi-curve', held in place with drawing pins. Note the parcels tape covering a join between two sheets of underlay paper; there is a splicing-piece glued under the join with PVA. The tape just keeps it all in line during 'stretching' and while the glue dries.

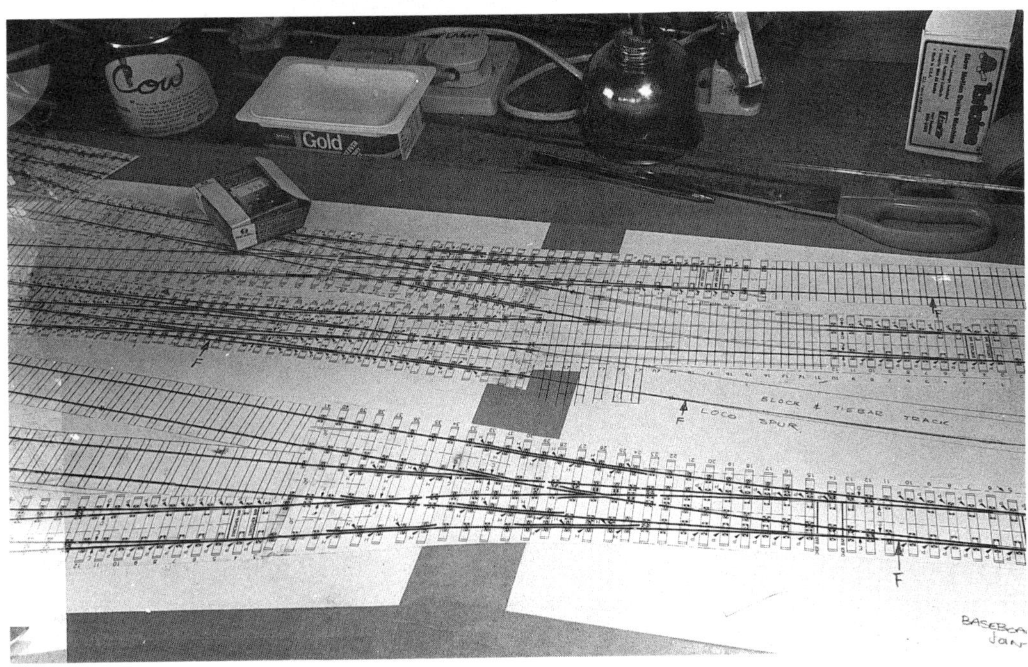

The finished result – all you gotta do now is build it! I used a rather simpler example for this book, which is why you're reading this in the twentieth rather than twenty-first century.

The second alternative is to build quite a large chunk of PW – a whole formation of P & C work and the associated plain track – onto the carefully aligned templates, which chunk is lifted as a unit when complete for laying. As I've already remarked, trying to lay a biggish complex in one hit by the wet-ballasting method is a bit of a non-starter, due to the tendency of the wet part of the equation to dry out before it's done its stuff. If you intend to stick with dry-ballasting, then there's no problem. Alternatively, the formation can be chopped up into more manageable units, safe in the knowledge that the correct alignment and relative positioning of the various units has already been 'built in'. It is then possible to re-assemble the original complex without significant scope for error. The amount of track that can be wet-laid in this way is really determined by the consistency of the glue, and the ambient temperature and humidity; you'll get away with more on a cool wet day than on a hot, dry one. For the record, the biggest formation I ever attempted to lay 'wet' in one hit consisted of three turnouts and a diamond, on Don Leeper's 'Pistyll'; on a warm May day, we made it by the skin of our teeth, and with a good deal of patching of bald spots in the ballast.

This brings me to a third, less fashionable alternative, one which goes right back to the days of the ERG track I mentioned in my introduction. The prepared sleepering and the ballast are laid together, working on a small area at a time – no more than half-a-dozen sleepers. These are fully treated – stained, dried, drilled and riveted – before being laid into a small area of wet PVA, and immediately ballasted. The part of the photo-sequence covering this operation should show how the glue is laid, to ensure that each fresh section starts against the edge of a sleeper. The chief drawback of this approach is, of course, that as you lay the sleepering and ballast it, your template progressively disappears. As I've claimed a page or so ago, this shouldn't matter too much anyway, as the main purpose of the template is to give sleeper length and positioning, plus the locations for the rivets needed for P & C work. I generally prepare *all* the components of the formation before I lay the sleepers and ballast, so that it's just a case of soldering/sticking down the rail and chairs. Any queries as to positioning can, after all, be resolved by reference to a spare template! In practice, I find that, once I've located one stockrail, I can work even the most complex piece of pointwork off this, using the gauges. The rail positions on templates – especially photocopied templates, which will distort very slightly – are only intended as general guides. The use of gauges is always essential.

There is, of course, no limit to the amount of track you can build and lay at one 'hit' using this technique, though I limit myself to the convenient 'workbench' size already noted. If you're so inclined, you can apply further painting and weathering techniques to the ballast and sleepers before the rails are laid. There's also less tendency for ballast to get where it's not wanted, or to clog up tiebars and other moving parts, if it is in place before the real 'engineering' starts. In my hands, this is the technique which produces the best-looking, most reliable trackwork. But it's all really a matter of personal choice, and experiment. I'm not going to claim that other approaches produce inferior results.

PREPARING SLEEPERS

Throughout this section of the book, I'm assuming the use of the traditional ply sleeper, in conjunction with a modicum of rivets and a multitude of C & L chairs. For the all-plastic systems, C & L or Peco, you can skip this section; you can't stain a plastic sleeper, and it'll get painted once it's laid. But raw ply sleepers do need staining, and that's best done at the outset. This does at least give us the chance to make them a realistic colour, as a basis for a little subtle weathering later on. Real sleepers start off a fairly intense brown-black, but rapidly fade through brown-grey to a pale, warm silvery shade. Most model sleepers are far, far too dark.

In America, you can buy cans of 'tie stain', a wood dye of supposedly suitable shade. From the colour pictures in the *Model Railroader,* I'm not convinced, and prefer the alternative approach of brewing my own stain using India ink and alcohol. The Americans use 'rubbing alcohol' – whatever that is; I use isopropyl, obtained from the chemist. I mix it with about twenty times its own volume of water, and drop in a little ink – black India and sepia or nut-brown drawing ink. The aim is for a weak brew, as the ply absorbs the dye very readily, and it's easy to end up with it stained far too dark. I decant a little of the dye into an old tobacco tin, and drop in a couple of trial sleepers.

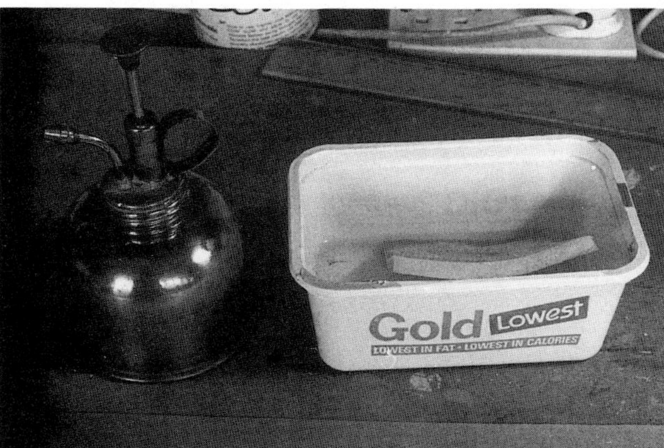

Wetting agents – an atomiser spray, and a piece of sponge and a tub of water.

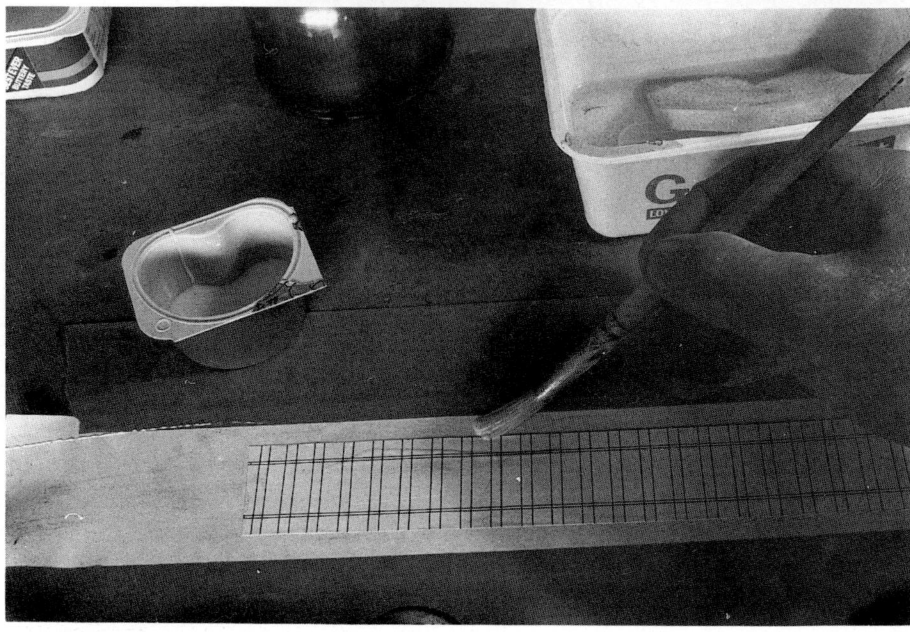

Templates are stuck down with PVA glue, taking special care to ensure that the edges are firmly secured.

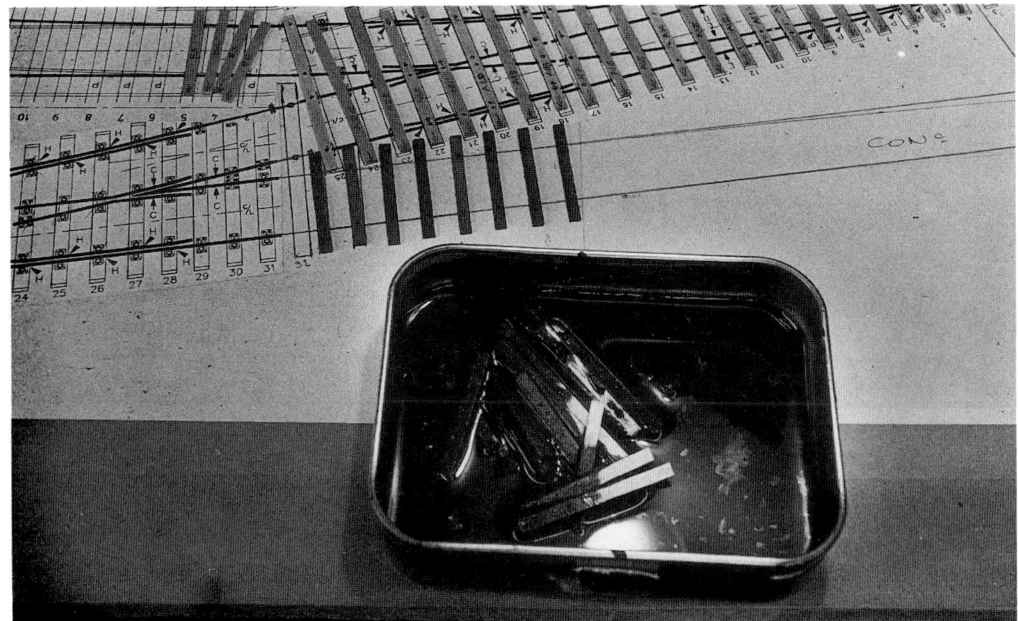

Turnout timbers are stained as a batch, prior to riveting and laying. Never do more than one turnout's worth at once!

Put the tin lid on, give it a shake, extract sleepers, dry (hairdryer!), and examine the result. I aim for a fairly feeble, slightly brownish grey, with the grain of the ply showing just a shade darker. Get this right and it's mighty effective. Actually, it's not so much the colour as the shade that's critical. So long as the result is somewhere on the brown side of grey, the exact tint's not important. It's achieving the right degree of lightness and transparency that makes the difference. Usually, I find that I'm adjusting the dilution of the stain, not its colour.

Once you've arrived at a satisfactory brew, its simply a matter of dunking a sufficiency of sleepers. I keep my stain in a 1-litre ice cream tub with a good, tight-sealing lid. The sleepers are simply hurled in, sloshed around for a moment, hooked out with an old tea-strainer and drained, then spread on newspaper to dry. I usually have a bulk sleeper-staining session, and prepare as many as I'm ever likely to need for a particular layout at one hit. Don't, for goodness sake, mix up 8ft 6in and 9ft sleepers in one dyeing – keep them apart or you'll run out of bad language when it comes to sorting them out for laying.

Point timbers are a slightly different case, as they really need to be cut and drilled, if not riveted, before they are stained. I do a turnout at a time, numbering the sleepers to correspond with the sequence on the template. Once drilled and checked, they are dyed as a single small batch, using the tobacco tin, and kept and dried separately. I generally lay them as soon as they're dry; that way I stand a better chance of neither muddling them up nor losing them.

The only snag that I have so far discovered with ink-and-alcohol sleeper stain is that it sometimes changes colour under the action of excess phosphoric acid flux, when it can go a fetching shade of pale mauve, or even a ripe purple if your phosphoric's a touch on the strong side. I suspect that there's potassium in the ink somewhere. There are alternative dyes that will avoid this problem; a mixture of Colron 'Jacobean Dark Oak' woodstain with a dash of 'Walnut', suitably diluted with white spirit, seems to work well (if rather hard on the nasal orifice during the mixing and dyeing; a job for the great outdoors, methinks). 'Humbrol' type enamels, thinned with white spirit, will also serve, though I've found it hard to get as subtle a result as is possible with the ink stains when using these alternatives. More recently, I've had success with Humbrol Acrylics diluted with water – a brew also immune to phosphoric acid flux.

For plain track, the pre-staining of the sleepers is 75% of the job, given that I only rivet one sleeper in every four. Bernard Weller reckons this is generous, and that one in six would do. Using his super new glue to stick the chairs down, I suspect that even this is excessive. The SC & LE system, with it's lug-and-slot chair fixing, is probably as strong as a fully riveted track.

Turnout timbers, of course, need drilling or punching to take the rivets, whether traditional roundheads or SC & LE square or plastic 'specials'.

Marking out rivet positions on point timbers calls for care and accuracy. Obviously, it pays to use a template drawn for the gauge in which you're working – although I have built many a P4 point on an EM template, and occasionally vice-versa, merely offsetting the rivet centre fractionally in the desired direction. These days, the C & L templates are the standard, considerably better than the older alternatives, and available in OO, EM and P4. I mark out my sleepers for rivet position and final length in one operation, using a sharp 'H' pencil and always marking from the same relative end – preferably the 'straight' stockrail side. I mark the underside of each timber with its number, also marked on the template, and with a little arrow to show me the 'datum' end. It's surprisingly easy to turn a timber 'end for end', which tends to throw the rivet positions out somewhat!

As I don't employ a full complement of rivets, even on turnouts, it's necessary to work out where they're needed and where you can do without. Obviously, any rail end will need a rivet as close as possible, as will the crossing nose, knuckles, wing rails and the heel end of both crossing 'V' and switches. Checkrails will call for double rivets on the 'check' side, and a single rivet under the opposing rail to maintain the check gauge; depending on the length of the checkrail, you may need two such timbers – one each end – or possibly three if it goes on a bit. I've marked up a template to show the rivet positions I normally use, and study of the pictures in the photo sequences will show how I've tackled more complex formations. If you've got any doubts, shove an extra rivet or two in, and don't in any case leave more than three or four unriveted sleepers in a row, as on plain track. The exception to this is the switches, where there may be anything up to eleven slide chairs. With the sort of points I build, seven is about the limit. One of the advantages of my 'lay the sleepers and ballast before you build' approach is that the sleepers carrying the slide chairs are located and held other than by the chairs, as is the case when you build and lift. I find it worth attaching the slide chairs – after the stockrails are in place – with epoxy adhesive or Evo-Stik, sticking them to both rail and sleepers to reinforce a potentially weak area of the track.

A boxful of stained 8ft 6in sleepers are seen at stage left. Also seen are the essentials of riveting – the rivets themselves (Scalefour Society 2mm brass, in this instance), a suitable object (such as my little jeweller's anvil) on which to close the rivets, and something to hit them with. I use a wide-faced jeweller's planishing hammer, which will close pairs of close-spaced rivets in one go. It also allows a touch of inaccuracy induced by the consumption of the Uisge Beatha which helps relieve the monotony, while a spot of Bach does ensure that rivets are closed in triple time with counterpoint!

RIVETING SLEEPERS

Not exactly a thrilling pursuit, but one calling for a little care and a lot of persistence! It's important to make sure that the hole in your sleeper or crossing timber is big enough to accept the shank of the rivet without the need for force to fit it – chances are, you'll bust the sleeper. So open them out with the taper broach if need be, and give them a rub on a bit of fine garnet paper to get rid of any 'rag' around the holes. I scatter a few rivets onto the anvil, where at least some of them will land head down. The sleeper is placed over the shank, and pressed onto the rivet, when a moderate tap with the hammer or quick 'kerchunk' of the press should close it home. Don't overdo the hammering or the pressing – the likely result is a split or broken sleeper.

Drilling point timbers for their rivets calls for little comment – so long as you mark and drill accurately, there's not a lot to go wrong. The worst problem is the setting of double rivets for check rails – if you try and put them too close, it's quite likely the sleeper will split when the second rivet is closed. I mark the centres at 2.5mm apart, which gives a theoretical $\frac{1}{2}$mm margin between rivet heads. Alternatively, ease these holes out a touch oversize, and close both rivets together so that they 'self adjust' rather than getting on top of each other. The

Riveting. (Not very, really!) Clear holes in sleepers with taper broach, removing any 'rag' with a rub on a bit of abrasive paper.

I scatter a few rivets head down on the anvil, locate sleeper over the shanks, and – bop! – close rivet. Don't hit too hard, or you'll split the sleeper. I give a couple of gentle taps, just letting the weight of the hammer do most of the work.

With a supply of both plain and riveted sleepers to hand, track-laying can commence. A small area of trackbed overlay is coated with a good dose of PVA glue – here, over the length of 7 sleepers, ensuring that the edge of the glued area aligns with the outer edge of the last sleeper at each end. The glue hardly obscures the template at all, so it's no problem to locate the sleepers in their correct alignments. Note the close-spaced sleepers and twinned riveted sleepers adjacent to the rail joint.

With the PVA still wet and sticky (the sleeper-laying takes only a few seconds), ballast is poured on and tamped down. Here, I'm using BTA Scenics' fine cork granules. The surplus ballast can be removed almost immediately, using a soft brush, and catching the material in a suitable clean receptacle. I use a cheapo plastic dustpan held under the edge of the workboard. Voila! Ballasted sleepering.

same goes for the triple rivets sometimes needed at crossing noses.

All-in-all, riveting sleepers is far from riveting, if you'll pardon the appalling pun. If you're not careful, you end up with the brain in neutral, which is when a lot of rejects get produced! Some convivial company helps, as does musical accompaniment. Or, as Mr Karau suggests, pick a night when there's something interesting on the wireless. It's not a job I relish, hence my predilection for eschewing rivets in favour of chairs. The fact that it results in a better-looking track is just a welcome bonus!

Occasionally, the PVA 'goes off' before the ballast hits it, resulting in a 'bald patch'. This is simply patched by puddling some dilute PVA onto it using a small brush. Add more ballast, tamp down, and remove surplus. All a lot easier with no rails or chairs to get in the way.

PREPARING RAIL

There's a fashion about these days for building track in scale 60ft panels – a fashion to which I don't subscribe, as it's at odds with my 'big units, not little bits joined together' approach. The less rail joints needing alignment, the better, so far as I'm concerned. This isn't to say that I'm advocating that the prototype's 60ft (or whatever) panel length should be ignored – far from it. I just prefer to represent it cosmetically rather than lumbering myself with a lot of potentially troublesome rail joints that I don't really need. In other words, I'm espousing the philosophy that led the prototype to CWR in half-mile lengths. My regret is that, these days, it's hard to buy rail in anything more than the ½-metre lengths that postal considerations have dictated.

For cutting rail to length – for whatever reason – I use a sharp pair of side-cutters, filing the ends square. As with all fitting work, I cut over-length by a fraction, and file back to the final finished size. While I've got the file handy, I also put a slight taper on the sides and base of the rail-foot, to ease the sliding-on of the C & L chairs. I know that this is strictly non-prototypical, but the fishplates at the rail-ends disguise it.

Fig. 7:3 Filing rail end to ease chair entry.

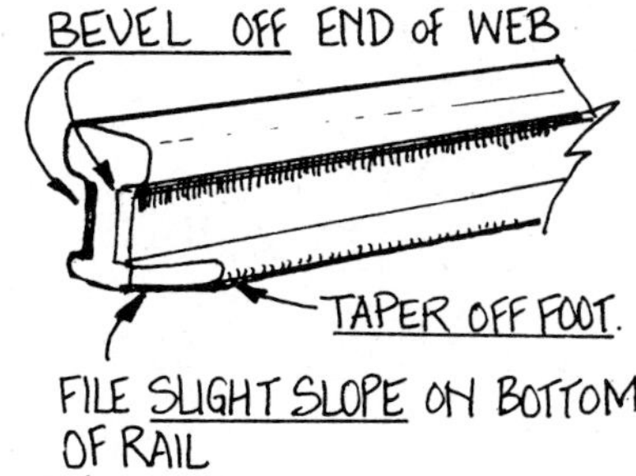

To simulate joints where the prototype should have them and Rice won't have them, I simply cut through the rail-head with a razor saw, and sweat on the Colin Waite etched fishplate to complete the subterfuge. I mark the position of such dummy joints by reference to the template and the sleeper positions, rather than by measuring off into the correct panel lengths willy-nilly. It's far more important that the joint should bear the correct relationship to the sleepering than it is to have a rail-length that is 'spot-on'. Apart from anything else, the rail length is only nominal, and rails would be cropped to suit their situation. Really, all that the 'correct' rail length tells you is the permitted *maximum* possible in that particular design of PW. To mark rails for cutting, I wipe on a splodge of permanent felt marker in the right general area, and make an accurate cutting guide with a scriber. Cutting rail is essentially a fitting operation, and I always prefer to offer up and mark direct, rather than relying on any form of measurement.

COMMON CROSSING COMPONENTS

For some reason that I'm unable to divine, a lot of people seem to regard the production of the main component of the common crossing – the 'V' – as a bit of a problem.

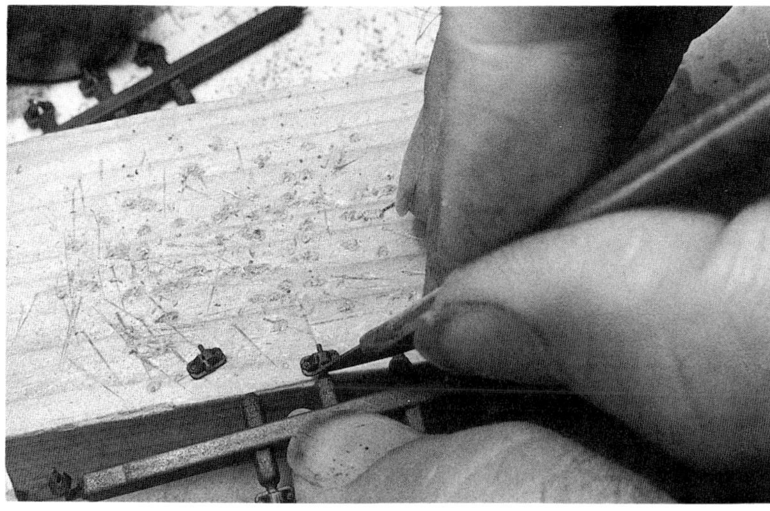

With the C & L chairs threaded onto the rail, they are shunted into appropriate groups to correspond with the non-riveted sleepers in the formation. The rail is then soldered to the rivet heads in the normal way, keeping the chairs as far away from the soldering iron as possible. Using an 18W SRB type 1 iron, a blob of phosphoric acid flux on the rivet head, and 145°C solder, I have yet to melt or distort a chair; if you're worried, clip on a heat-sink (aluminium Dinky hair curler) between soldering iron and chairs. Keep the amount of solder to a minimum, and, obviously, don't linger. If the joint doesn't flow immediately (it should), remove heat, re-flux and try again.

Cutting off and threading C & L chairs. Cut over the edge of a block of scrap wood, and support the rear (non-keyed) edge of the chair while the rail, prepared as in Fig. 7:4, is fed in from the 'key end'. Do not force! These tiny mouldings are fragile.

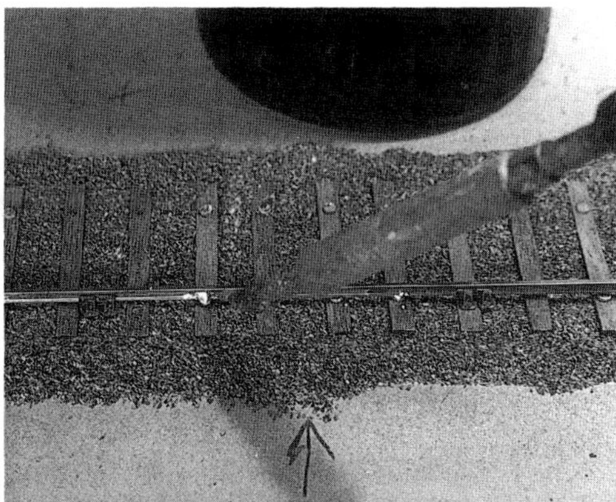

The C & L chairs can now be positioned on their appropriate sleepers. I use fine tweezers to push them along, with the knife used to lift the rail slightly so that the chair-base doesn't catch on the sleeper edge. The chairs are then retained by flooding the chair/sleeper joint with Daywat Poly. This disolves the ABS plastic, which leeches into the grain of the ply and then hardens when the solvent evaporates, gluing a surprisingly strong bond.

Locating the second rail is simple enough. I use a pair of 3-point gauges thus for straight track. On curves, lay the outer rail first, and use the gauges to 'bridge' the curve. Otherwise, soldering and chair locating is identical to first rail. The rectangular block gauge also shown is not really suitable for use on chaired track – the chairs prevent it from 'seating' properly.

Simulating a rail joint. The rail-head is nicked with a fine razor saw, with firm rail support (hence extra rivets even at dummy joints). The Colin Waite etched fishplates are my preference. These came from Scalefour stores, but the EMGS also supply. They are cropped off into 'H' form, and folded to lie either side of the rail. Note that the square (nutted) fishplate goes to the outside of the track. They are soldered in place with a minimum of solder. The cryptic numbers on the baseboard indicate chair positions and numbers.

Adding chairs to the riveted sleepers. These are cut in half and 'Daywatted' in place. If the rivet is not quite central beneath the rail, the chair may not fit properly. It can be persuaded by placing the soldering iron on the rail and pushing the chair into place as the plastic softens. End result – no rivets!

Last job before painting – running trials! Power leads are clipped to rail-ends and a loco run up and down to check for displaced chairs or other ills. Here, the duty is being performed by 14xx 1434, veteran of Model Railway Journal No. 1, still going strong on a new P4 chassis.

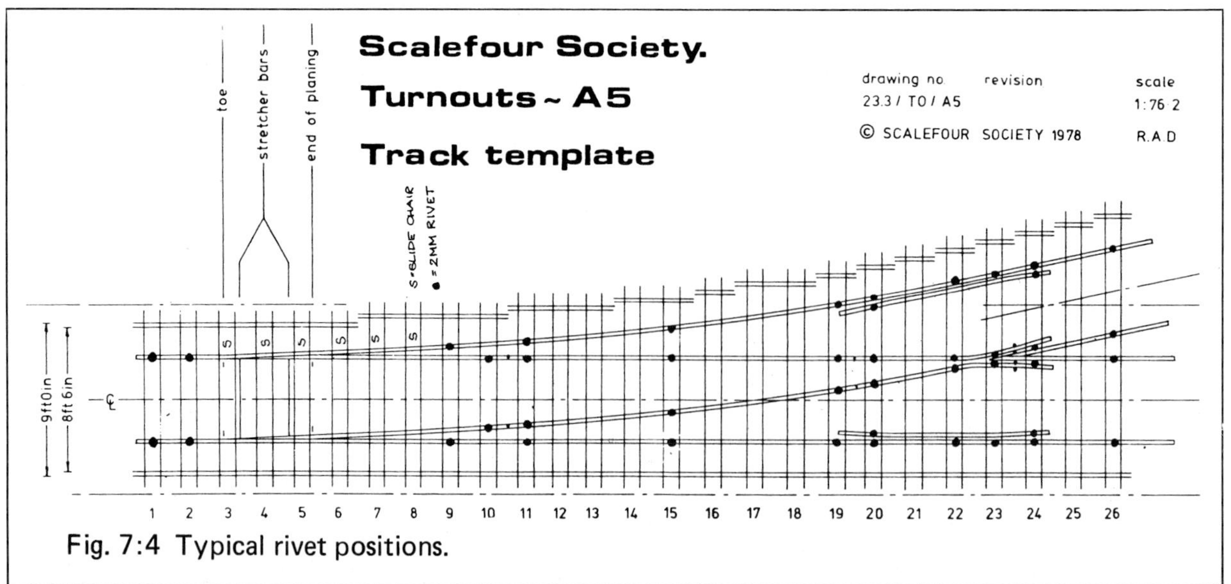

Fig. 7:4 Typical rivet positions.

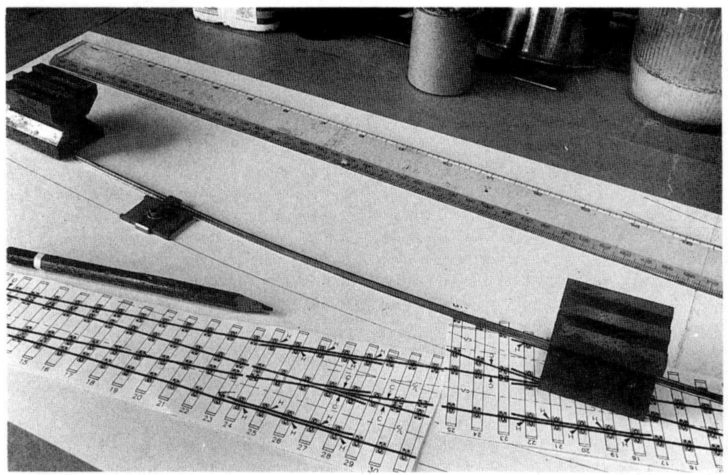

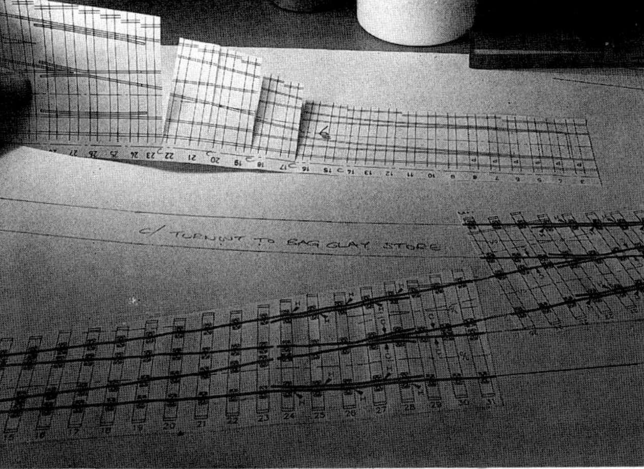

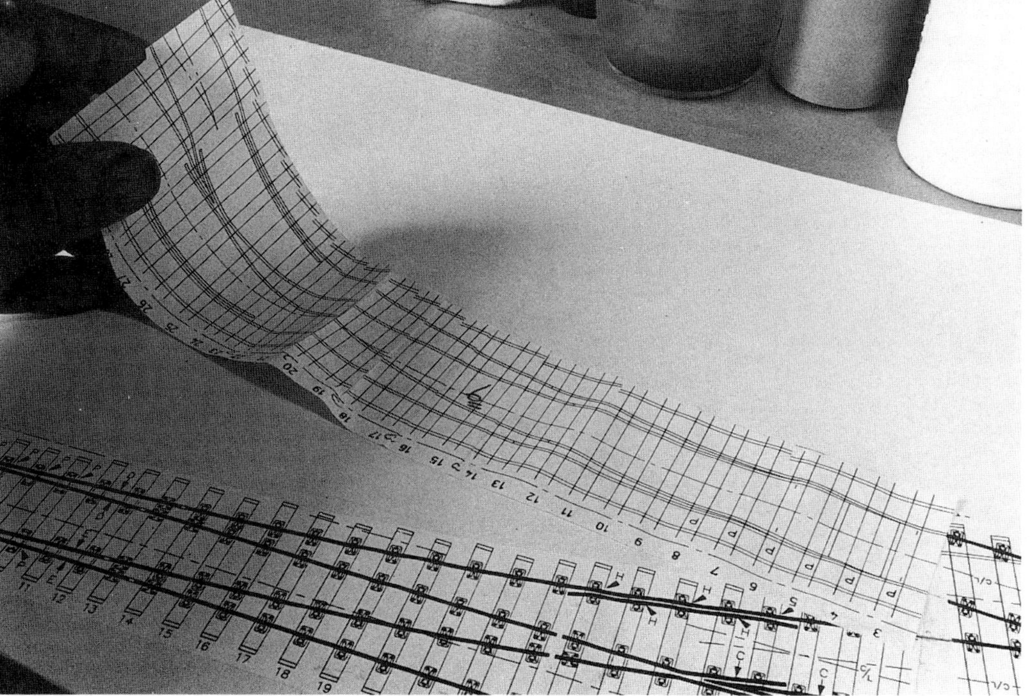

Positioning the templates for the pointwork at the south (Meledor Mill) end of 'Trerice'. The loop entry, bottom left, is a B6L, while the lead into Wheal Remfry Sidings is an A4R – both standard C & L templates. The sidings split immediately beyond this '4', involving a turnout on a sharpish curve. I first drew the curve of the 'through' road, using my Peco Code 125 rail and the rectangular track gauge. A Scalefour Society B6R template formed the basis of the curved turnout, cut almost through as in the second photo. This is then coated with fairly dilute PVA on the rear, and eased into place following the drawn curve.

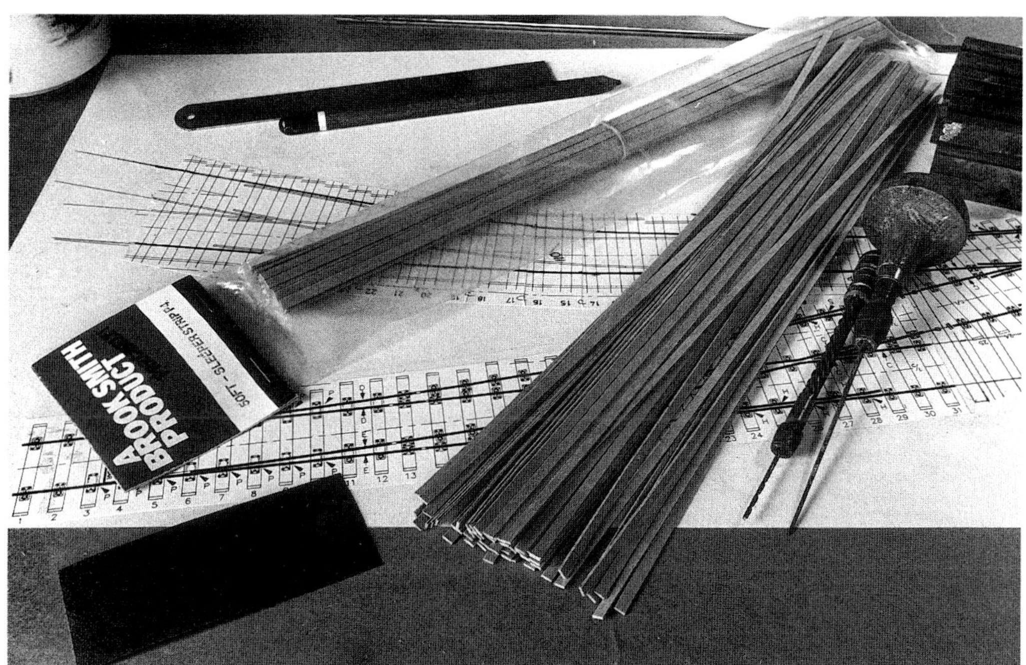

Preparing point sleepering, stage 1. The ply sleeper strip, which comes in packs of 50 x 300mm lengths, needs to be marked and cut, then drilled as necessary for rivets. The photo below shows how I mark. Note the orientation arrows to identify the ends. The timbers are numbered to correspond with their positions on the template. Mark rivet positions as accurately as possible. A sharp 'H' pencil is best. Rivet holes are drilled with archimedean drill and scrap wooden block. Sorry about the horrid blackened fingernail – it got in the way of a piece of granite during a dry-stone walling exercise. Ouch!

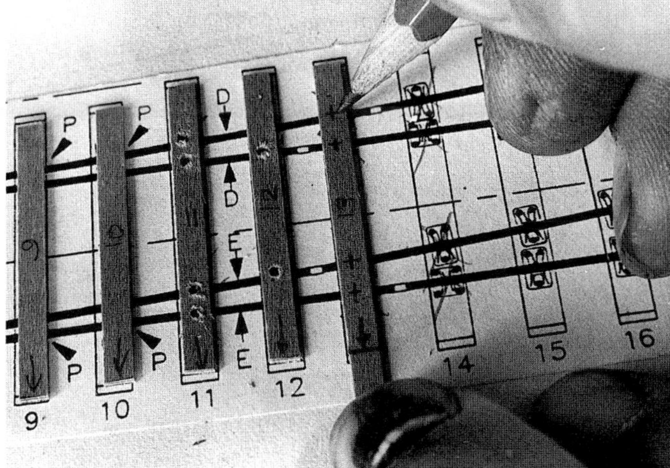

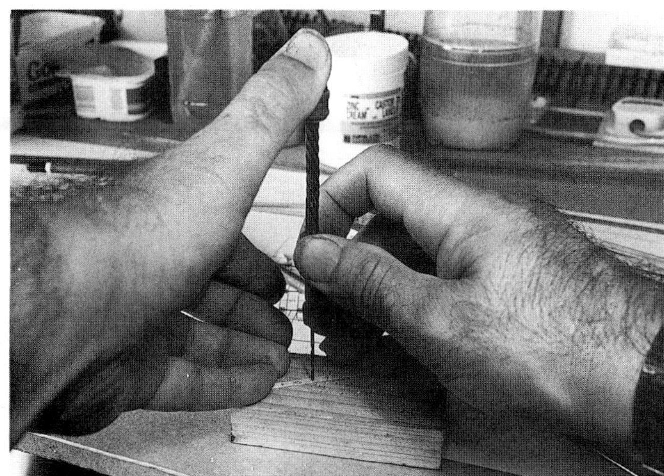

Here is a complete set of turnout timbering ready for staining and riveting. In fact, there is rather more than one set of timbering, as this turnout is in close proximity to the siding entry point, and the ballasting will need to embrace both sets of timbers plus a few on the curved turnout as well. Being able to sort all this timbering out and align and lay it in one go is a prime benefit of building large formations 'of a piece'. The sleepers of the plain track adjoining the turnout have likewise been positioned.

Sleeper staining. The tin contains the dye. In this case I used dilute matt acrylic paint in water, which worked well. One turnout's worth of timbers is 'dunked', and given a good shake (lid on!). I then push the timbers up to one end, and incline the tin to drain off surplus dye. The sleepers are then spread out on old newspaper to dry. The hairdryer can, once again, speed things up a bit.

Setting the rivets. I close paired rivets together, working from the 'right' side. This is so I can see what's going on, and avoid the situation shown in the photo where the heads of adjoining rivets have overlapped each other. This calls for a new timber – aggravating!

Laying sleepers and ballast. A worthwhile refinement is to wash over the trackbed area with an approximation of the final track colour so that bald patches in the ballast are less obtrusive. Tea-time obviously!

The ballast itself, on this freight-only minor line (a Cornish china-clay branch, remember?) is ash-based, so I used a mix of sieved wood-ash, as here, BTA fine cork, and talcum powder. I used a liberal coating of PVA to hold sleepers and ballast, causing a bit of cockling of the paper underlay in spite of pre-stretching. No matter – a bit of weight and a quick blast with the indispensable hairdryer soon had it all back to rights, giving the result shown at the bottom of this page.

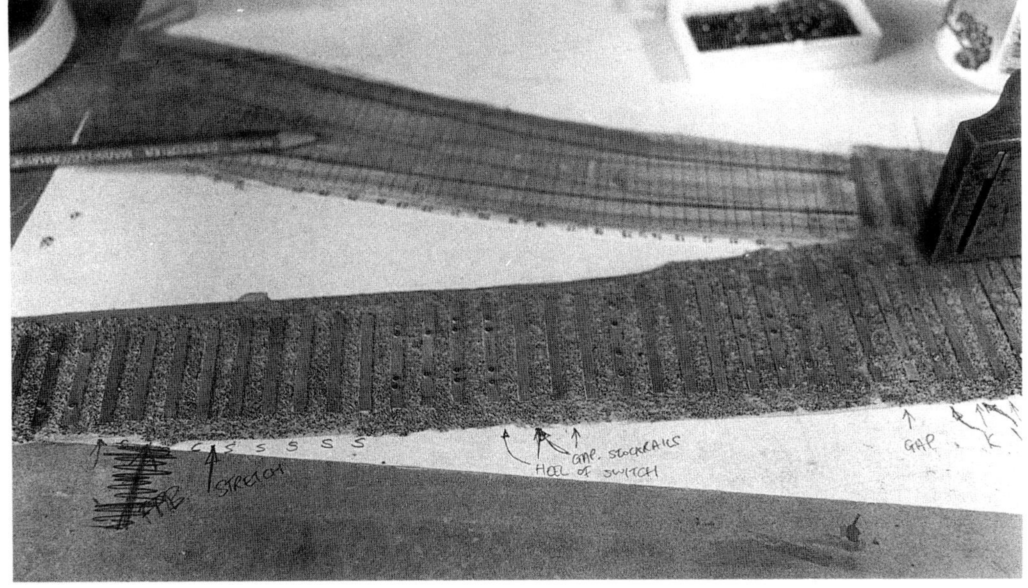

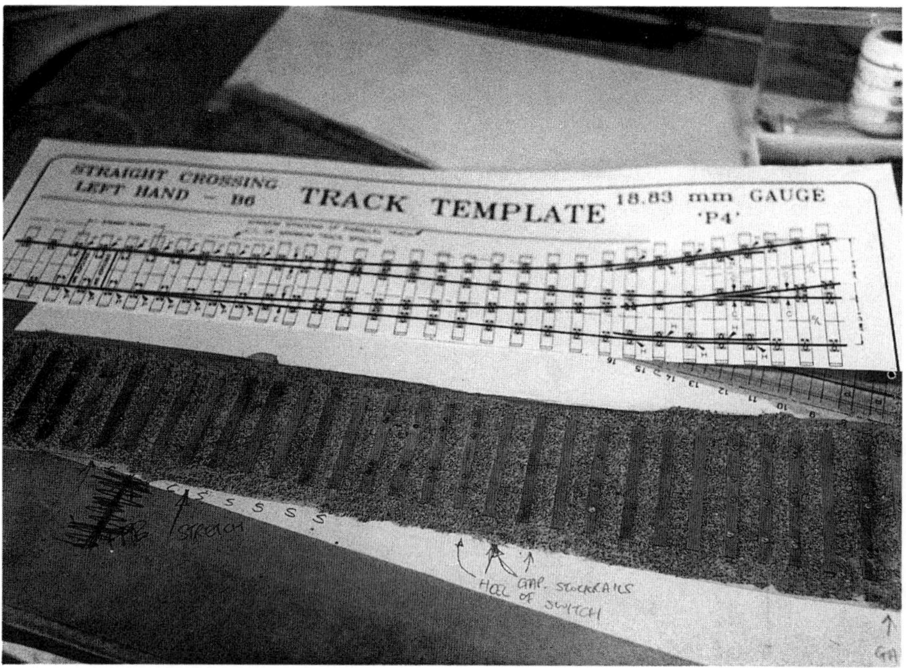

With the ballast obscuring the template, some details need transferring from a spare template. Here, I've noted (not always correctly!) the positions of joints, stretcher bars, etc. on the underlay margin. I do this by counting sleepers to obtain locations, not by holding the template up and trying to mark off.

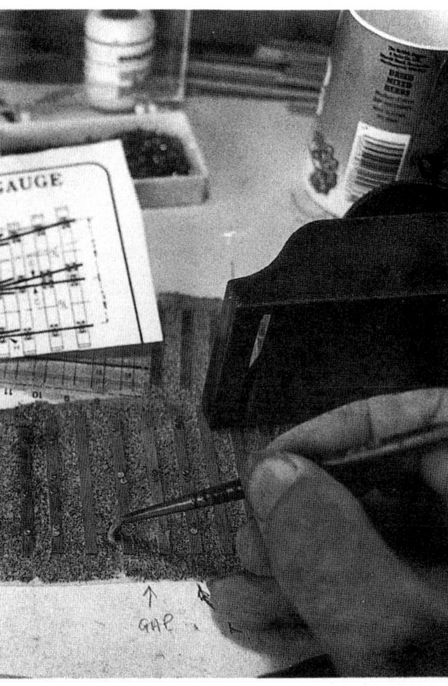

Now is the time to do any required patching of the ballast, as for plain track.

The first stock-rail is now laid. I start with the straight (or, on a curved turnout, the widest radius). As for straight, plain track, the chairs are threaded on and grouped as appropriate before the rail is soldered in place. Slide chairs, though, have to go on later.

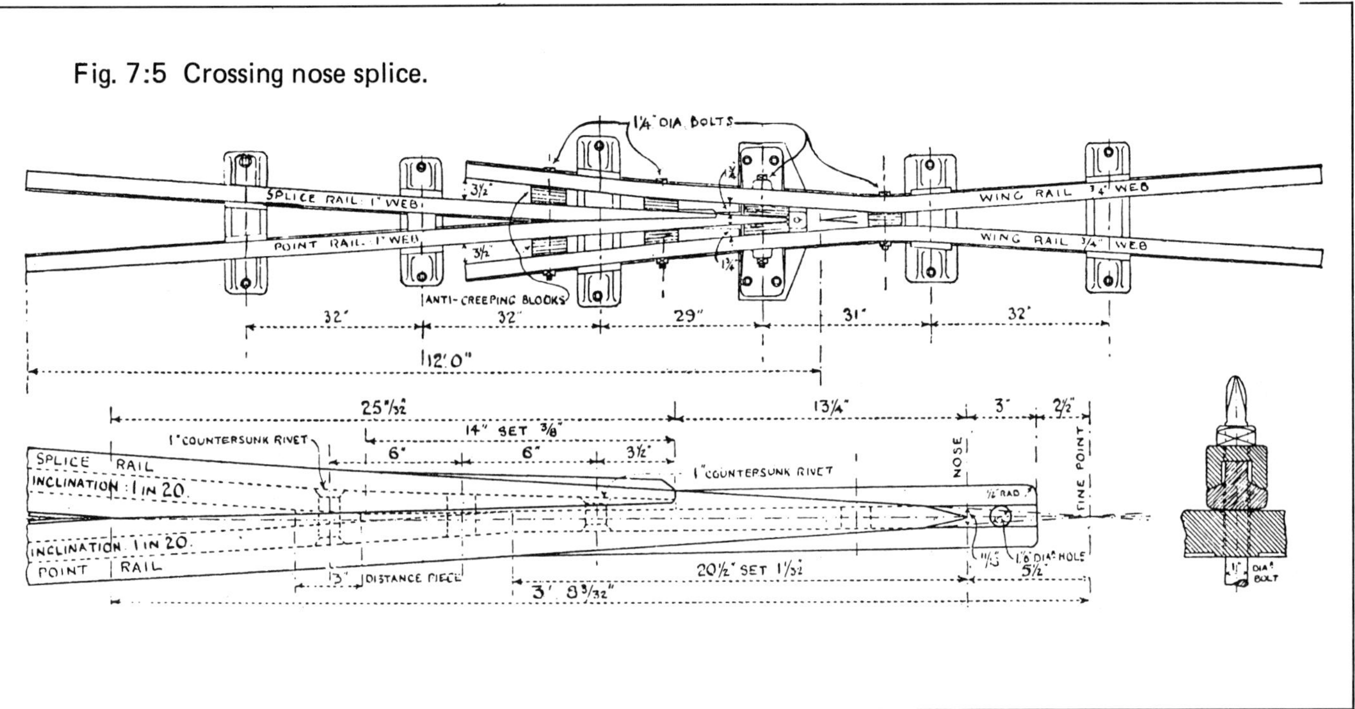

Fig. 7:5 Crossing nose splice.

A rumour seems abroad that unless your crossing 'V' is silver-soldered, then nought but ruin and disaster will ensue. Well, I've lost count of the number of turnouts that I've built over the years, and I've never silver-soldered a 'V' yet. As I use steel rail, I expect some 'expert' will tell me I ought to weld it! All I do, of course, is to soft-solder it like any other bit of fabricated model metalwork. I suspect that the idea of using silver solder to assemble crossing 'Vs' is to ensure that they won't come unsoldered while being fixed in place. Not being that clever, I find that the facility of being able to unsolder (and hence 'tweak') a crossing 'V' is a boon, rather than an impediment.

The crossing 'V' consists of two components, the point rail and the splice rail, arranged as in the diagram. Properly, the splice rail is slightly 'housed in' to the point rail, and I expect some meticulous modeller somewhere does just that. Me, I just file off as close to the correct angle as I can get, and solder in place with a good blob of 145° to fill up any slight gap. So long as you file your angle to be on the acute side of correct, you won't have a problem. What will cause difficulty is too obtuse an angle, which results in the situation shown in my sketch. Obviously, I aim to get the angle of both my point and splice rails as accurate as I can, but to get them absolutely precise would call for some sort of jig and a grinding wheel.

I do use a jig – of sorts – to build 'Vs', as illustrated. This both serves to hold rails in alignment while the 'V' is assembled, and also to act as a filing guide. Using this simple device (mine are made from small offcuts of Formica-faced chipboard with alignment

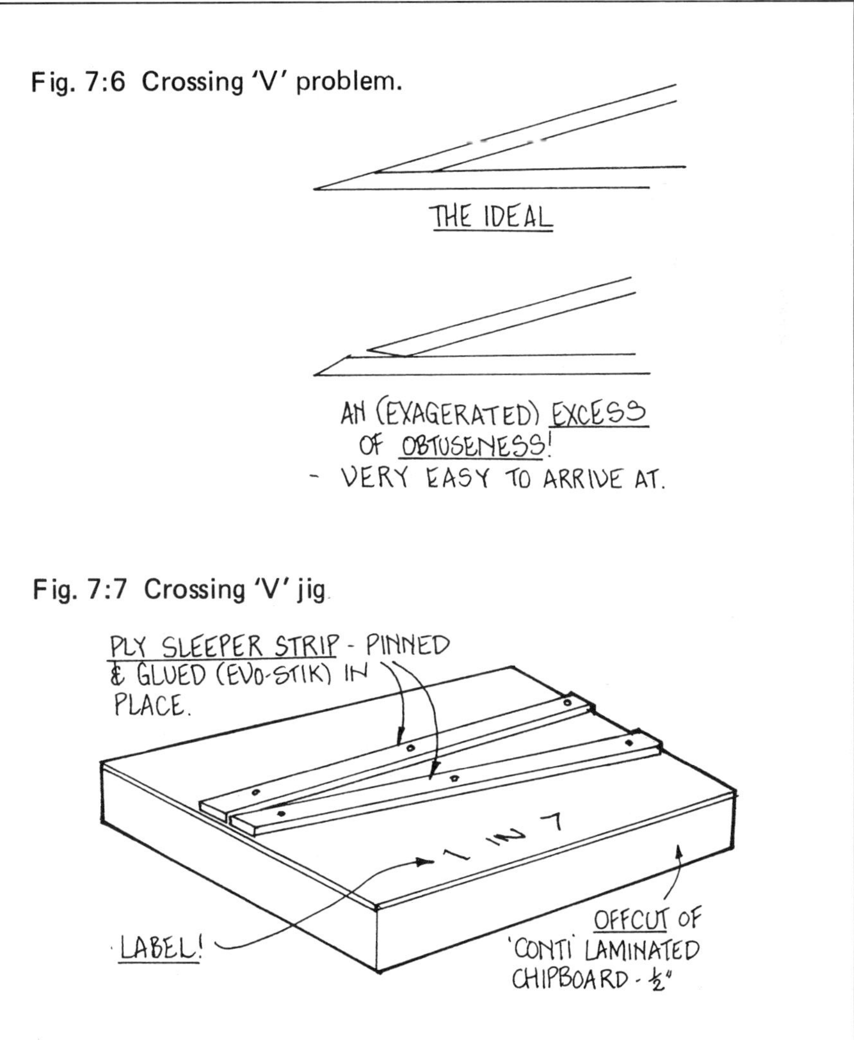

Fig. 7:6 Crossing 'V' problem.

Fig. 7:7 Crossing 'V' jig.

Next job in the sequence is the fabrication and installation of the crossing 'V' – filing point and splice rails over the edge of a hardwood block clamped in the vice.

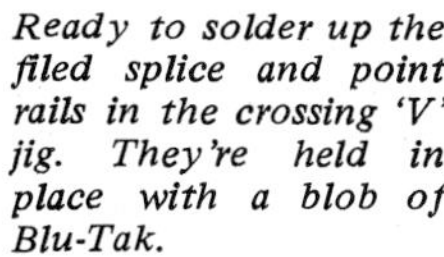

Ready to solder up the filed splice and point rails in the crossing 'V' jig. They're held in place with a blob of Blu-Tak.

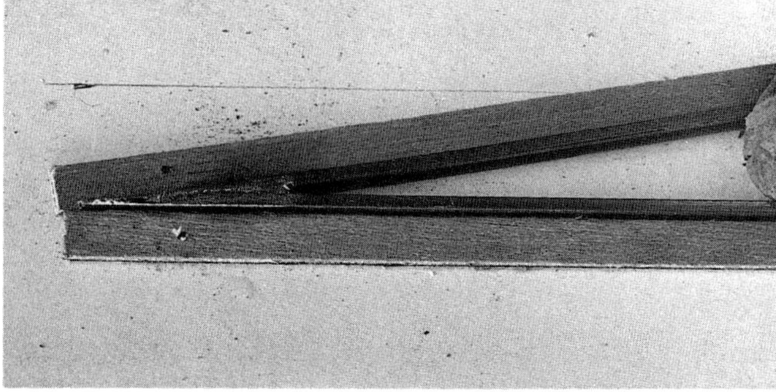

Close-up of the 'V'. The slightly too acute angle of the splice rail has been filled with solder. Next stage is to clean up and finish-file the 'V' as in Fig. 7:10.

Fig. 7:8 The bodger's crossing 'V'.

FILE OFF EXCESS AFTER SOLDERING 'V' TOGETHER

THIS GAP GETS FILLED WITH SOLDER.

BOTH RAILS FILED TO AN OVER-ACUTE ANGLE!

edges made from ply sleeper strip stuck on with Evo-Stik), I find that I can make a pretty fair job of filing up and assembling the rails. By filing the rails to be a shade on the 'too acute' side, I end up with the situation shown in *Fig. 7:8*, which can then be simply dressed into the correct form by filing back to the dotted line. This is done by laying the big flat file on the bench, and rubbing the splice rail along it until the offending portion of the point rail has been removed. I finish off the 'V' by soldering a piece of flat strip (waste from an etched kit, like as not) across the bottom of it, far enough back from the nose to clear the timber beneath at this point. This strip has a number of functions – it reinforces the 'V', gives a useful anchoring point to the wing rails, and bonds the crossing into a single electrical unit.

The last job I undertake on a crossing 'V' is to do a little subtle shaping with a fine Swiss file. The end of the nose is rounded-off slightly in elevation, and the sides of the 'V' back from the nose are given a slight 'planing' at about 45° for some way back along the rails; this simulates the wear which real crossings suffer at this point, and which actually assists in the smooth negotiation of real P & C work. After all, the 80-odd tons of the average latterday steam loco is going to win any argument with the track, and real PW distorts to accommodate vehicles passing over it. Likewise, any obstructive edges soon get eroded to suit the stock. Model track is, comparatively speaking, far stronger and more wear-resistant than the real thing, so a bit of artificial 'wear' with a file has to compensate.

Fig. 7:9 Reinforcing and bonding crossing 'V'.

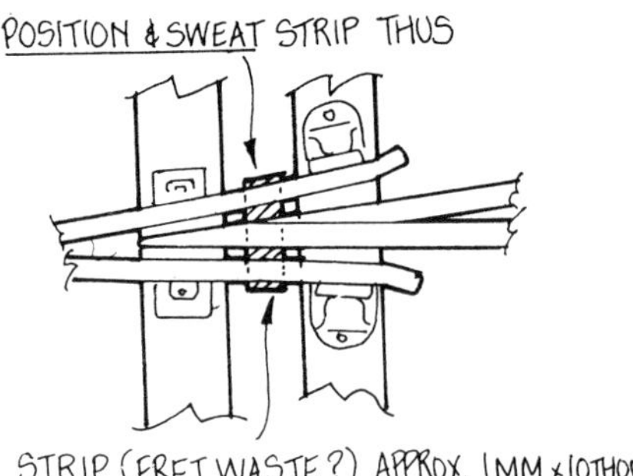

Fig. 7:10 Shaping crossing nose.

ROUND OFF TIP OF NOSE IN PLAN & ELEVATION.

CHAMFER OFF SIDES OF NOSE AT ABOUT 45° & SLIGHTLY ROUNDED FOR APPROX. 15MM.

Installing the completed crossing 'V' on the turnout. It is gauged from the straight stock-rail.

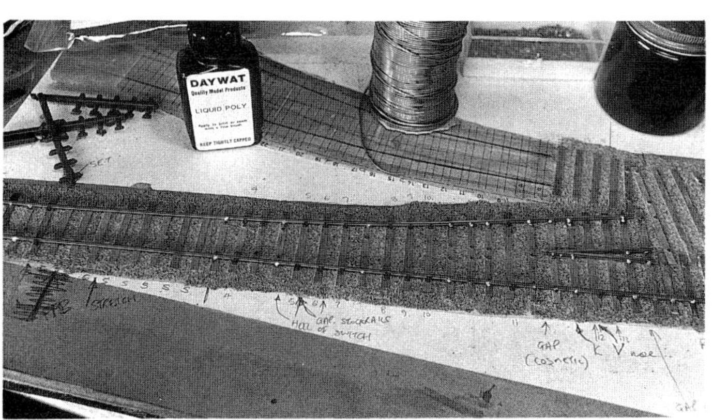

At this stage, the curved stock-rail is only tacked in place. This was, in turn, gauged from the crossing 'V' once this was in place, only I forgot to take a picture! Still, here is the finished result.

Installing the knuckle rails – straight road first. The rectangular block gauge with its rail clamp is ideal for this. Note the aluminium strip crossing flangeway gauge in situ. Note strip beneath 'V' for bonding of wing rails.

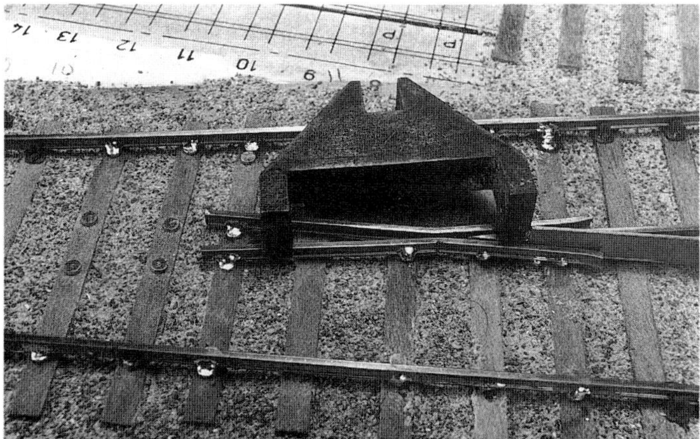

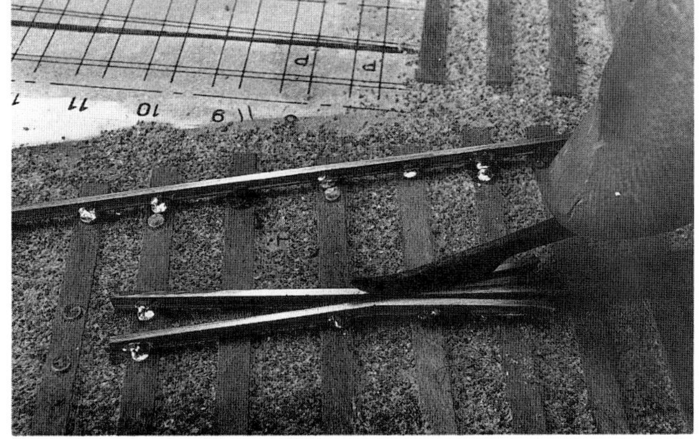

Left: *No one really makes the ideal track gauge for this job. I use my old Protofour 3-point, with one 'leg' sitting over the crossing nose. It seems to work OK.* Right: *A bit of 'artificial wear' is introduced to the knuckle rails with the fine riffling file – just made for this particular bodge!*

With the crossing and stock-rails located, next job is to install the switches. I start by fitting the slide chairs, glued to both stock-rail and sleepers with either epoxy or Evo-stik. I work the adhesive into the jaw of the chair with the tip of a cocktail stick, as here, and tweezer the chairs into place.

POINT BLADES

After the knuckle-to-crossing nose traverse, the other likely cause of bother in finescale pointwork is a poorly shaped or ill-housed point blade. Real point blades are quite subtle in their form, so there's a bit more to it than simply filing a taper onto a piece of rail. Making point blades is tedious rather than difficult, as there's rather a lot of metal to remove – which is where my big meaty file comes in so handy. I start by using this to 'rough out' a blank, taking metal off one side of a length of rail until I just start to break through the web of the rail. The angle at which this metal is removed is obviously dependent on the type of switch for which the blade is being made – the longer the switch, the shallower the angle. As with the filing of point and splice rails, no trouble will arise if you err on the acute side – *Fig. 7:11* should show the critical factors.

I actually undertake this filing with the rail sitting on top of a small offcut of hardwood, as specified way back in Chapter 4. As my sketch shows, this keeps the rail supported while allowing the file to attack at the desired angle. I generally keep the rail in place simply by pressing down with the fingertips of my left hand, although it has to be said this is a mite hard on the pinkies, and is not an option for female PW fabricators with cultured nails! The alternative is some form of simple clamp, and my effort in this direction is illustrated in yet another sketch, using ordinary wood screws and hard rubber tap washers.

Once the blade is roughed-out in this manner, the donkey work is over. I take a final few passes on the taper side with my fine-cut 6in flat file, just to get rid of the worst of the tool-marks left by the big bastard file, then turn the blade over and start my attack on the inner side. Here, the 'planing-off' is far less severe, being mainly confined to the rail-head over a shorter distance. I start by filing a gentle 'flat' taper along the head, starting at a point roughly three-quarters of the way along the heel-end of the main taper on the other side, and finishing up with about half the residual thickness of rail head left at the tongue (see diagram). The file is then canted over at about 45°, and a mitre cut made along the railhead, gradually fading out to zero about two-thirds of the way along the main taper. (This is the 'head planing' noted on some turnout templates, and as a rough guide, it usually extends over the length of the blade carried on slide chairs.) This mitred planing should produce a virtual knife-point at the tip of the blade, which is then finished by being 'rounded off', as in the last sketch in *Fig. 7:14*.

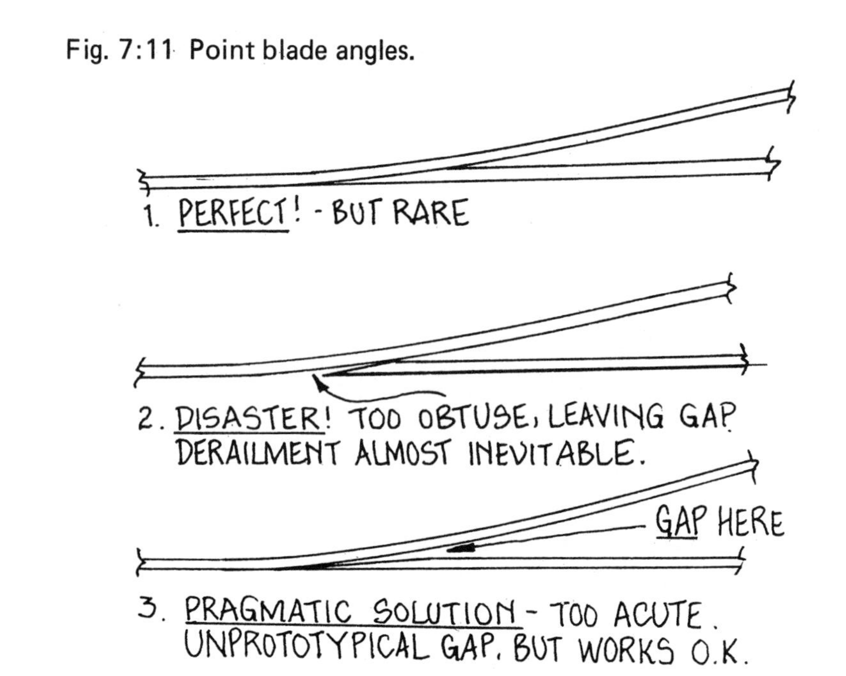

Fig. 7:11 Point blade angles.

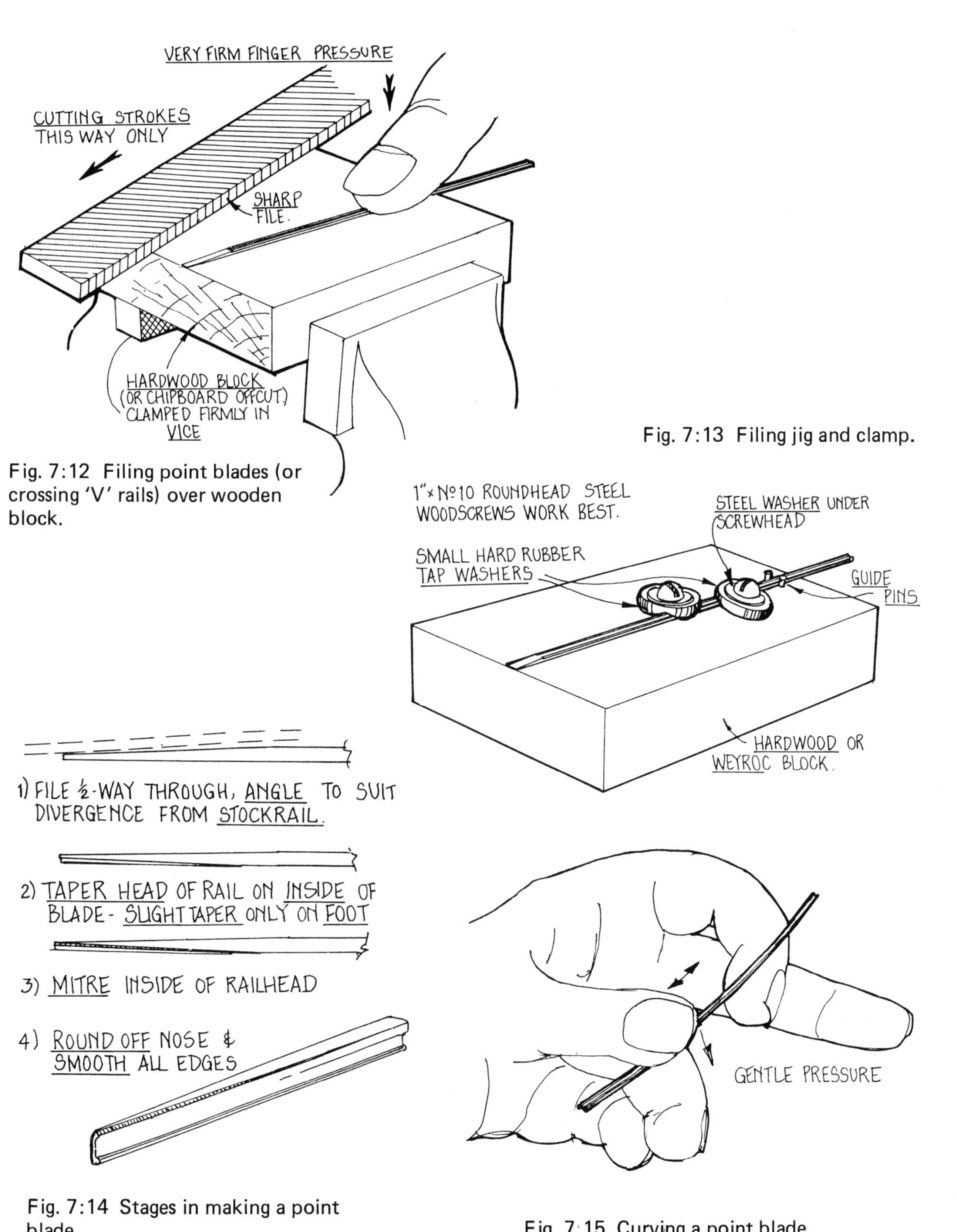

Fig. 7:12 Filing point blades (or crossing 'V' rails) over wooden block.

Fig. 7:13 Filing jig and clamp.

Fig. 7:14 Stages in making a point blade.

Fig. 7:15 Curving a point blade.

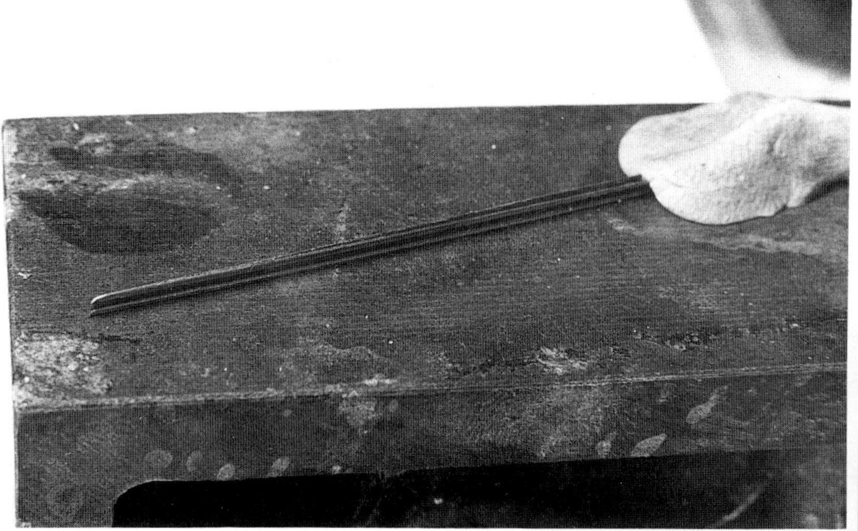

Point blades – persistance with a file! These are produced as described and drawn in Fig. 7:14. The first picture has a completed blade, viewed from the 'inside'. Note the rounded nose and the mitred planing on the rail-head. The second picture shows the insulation sleeves for the stretcher rods inserted in holes drilled in the blade. More on these in Chapter 10.

The last job I find worthwhile on a point blade is to go over it thoroughly with some fine (320 grit) wet-and-dry to eradicate all tool-marks and burred edges, and, once again, to impart a modicum of 'artificial wear' to the component which helps it function more smoothly. It may also be necessary to drill holes for dummy tie or stretcher bars, if you're using the old Protofour system of representing these – of which more in Chapter 10. The blades can now be trimmed to length (with a small 'finish-fit' allowance), labelled as to intended location, and stored away ready for installation. This is the stage at which I usually find I've carefully made two blades of the same hand, instead of a pair!

STOCKRAILS

At the preparatory stage, the only work that may need to be undertaken on stockrails is the introduction of some form of rebate where the blades 'house in' to the rail. Now, the use of either machined rebates or 'joggles' in stockrails was by no means universal, so the first thing to check is whether it would be appropriate in the context of the trackwork you are modelling. The idea of 'housing-in' point blades to stockrails was to prevent hammer-blow and wear to the blade; by making a cut-out, the tip could be brought inside the line of the inner edge of the stockrail, which thus guided wheelsets to a point beyond the tongue. The snag was that the stockrail itself was weakened at this critical location, and the old companies seem fairly well divided as to which was the lesser evil. In the case of some lines, like the old GER, the use of rebates was probably prudent, given some rather ropey track and at least one good derailment due to a wheel-

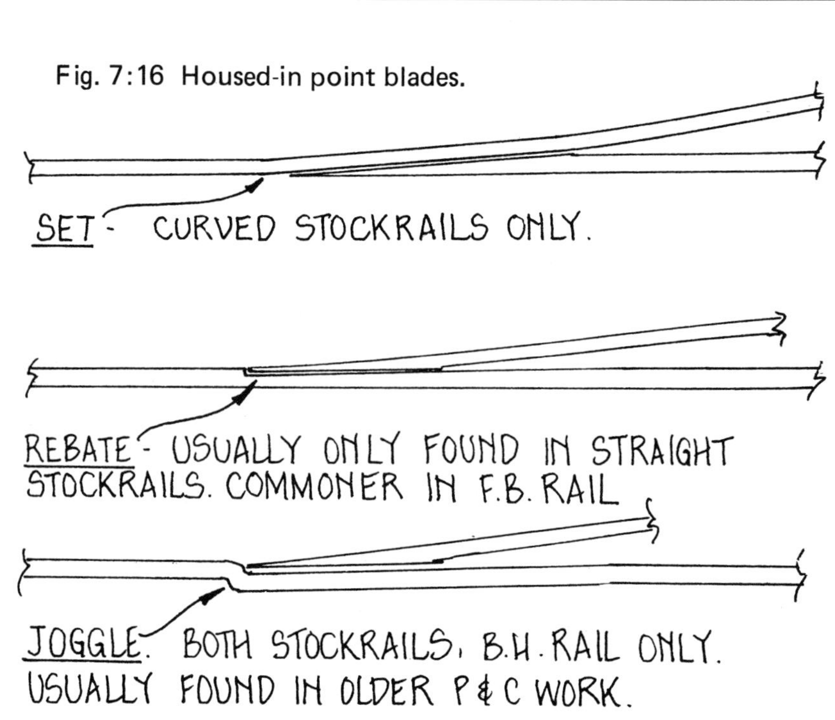

Fig. 7:16 Housed-in point blades.

flange striking the end of a poorly-housed point blade.

The GWR used a 'joggled' rebate on the straight road, and a 'set' in the opposite stockrail, as in the diagram; the NER would have none of it, with no joggles or rebates at all, whilst the GE went in for quite generous joggling. Generally, with improving steel quality – and hence wear resistance – as time went by, plus better, more accurate machining and a more sophisticated point tongue profile, the practice has tended to die out, and most post-grouping 'standard bullhead' is free of any notches or joggles, the switch tongues being machined to an accurate fit against the stockrail. Which means that most of us won't need to bother about forming these rebates; for those that do, I've sketched the needful in *Fig. 7:17*.

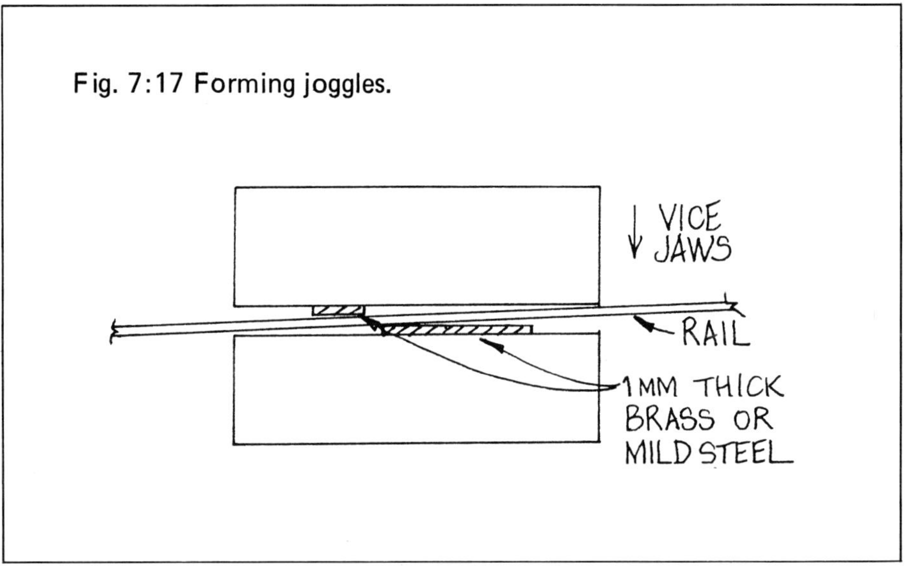

Fig. 7:17 Forming joggles.

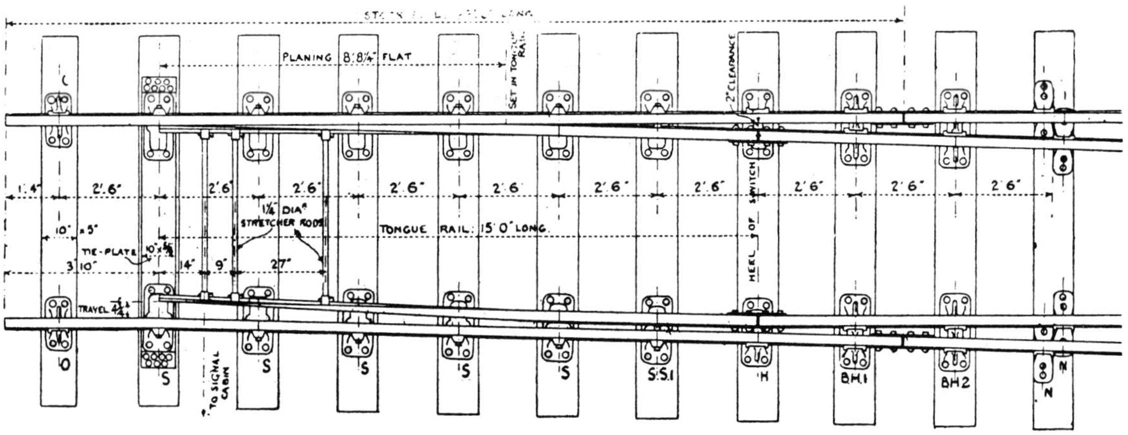

NER switch.

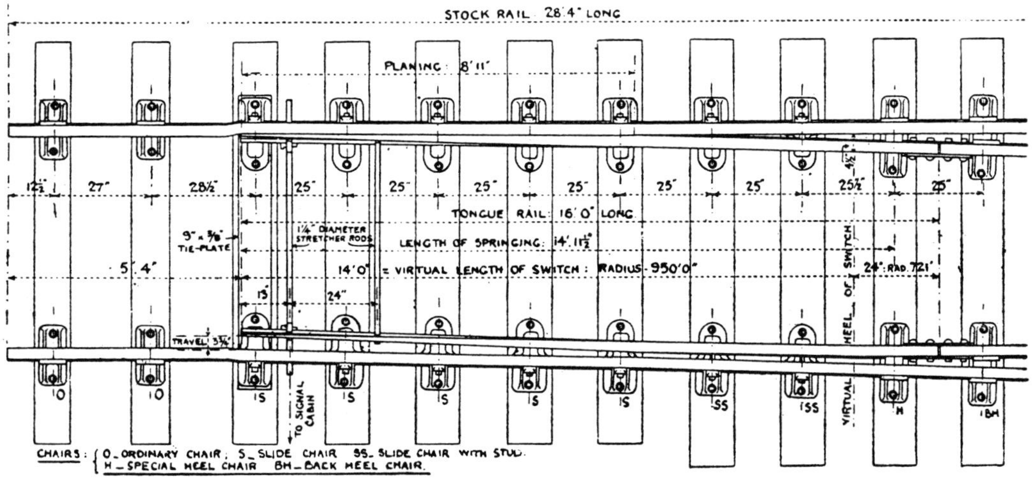

GWR switch.

Installing the switch blades (on a sunny day!). I fix the straight blade first, clamping it to the stock-rail with a 'Dinky' curler modified by cutting the tips off. The rectangular track gauge with clamp is ideal for this job. The second, curved, switch blade is added in the same way, using the three-point track gauge. The blade was pre-curved as in Fig. 7:15. Sorry about the shadow of the curler in these pictures – couldn't turn sun off (and, in such a poor summer, didn't want to!)

The installed switch, awaiting only connection to the turnout actuator (Chapter 9), and installation of stretcher rods and cosmetic tiebar – of which more in Chapter 10.

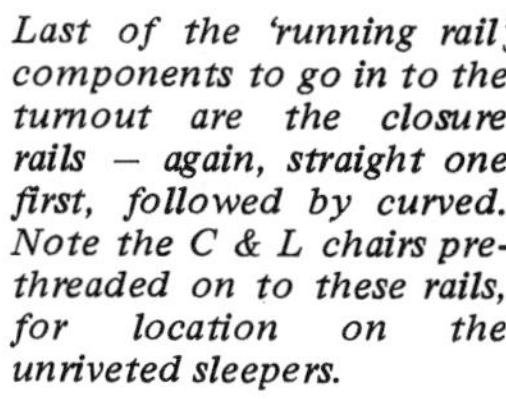

Last of the 'running rail' components to go in to the turnout are the closure rails – again, straight one first, followed by curved. Note the C & L chairs pre-threaded on to these rails, for location on the unriveted sleepers.

Locating curved closure rails can be a mite tricky, calling for a pair of 3-point gauges, with, more often than not, a spot of eyeballed 'tweaking' at the ends, to get good alignment with switch and crossing.

Chairs, cut in half and generally carved around as needed, are added cosmetically to the riveted sleepers, as shown on the right, where a chair-half is being 'helped home' with the soldering iron. A small piece of 60-thou square Plastikard Microstrip has been installed to represent the spacer block of the knuckle chairs.

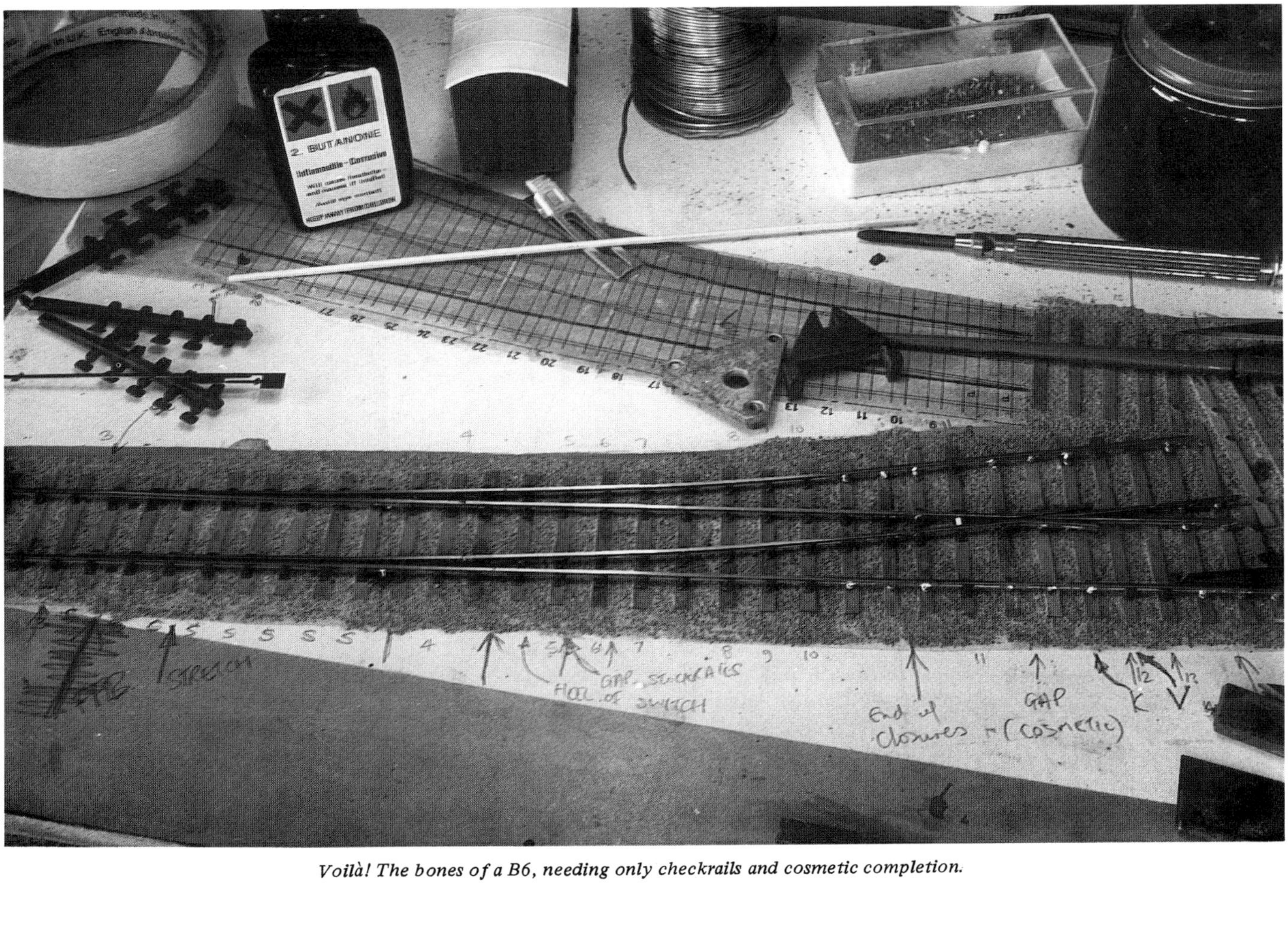

Voilà! The bones of a B6, needing only checkrails and cosmetic completion.

BENT BITS

Firstly, with the exception of 'short' curved point blades or closure rails, I find that there is no need to pre-form curved rails; the rail itself has sufficient 'spring' to take up virtually any curve likely to be found on a finescale layout simply by being flexed as it is laid. Where I do need to curve a point blade or closure, I do this between my fingers, as in the sketch. The steel rail is very easy to form like this, the harder nickel-silver a little more difficult. Try annealing it very slightly – heat to a dull purple-brown in a gas flame, and drop into cold water. The one thing to avoid is a 'kinked' curve (unless you're modelling a light railway, mineral or industrial line, when such things as kinks were not unknown!).

The other bends we need to make are the much sharper variety encountered at knuckles, wing rails and checkrails – where the rail is turned through a sharp angle, more properly known as a 'set'. It is important for both the appearance and proper functioning of the track that such bends are cleanly and accurately made. Nothing looks worse than a turnout whose knuckles are not quite opposite one another or whose wing rails have flares at different angles, starting in different places. To make a crisp bend, file a small V-nick in the side of the rail to the inside of the bend, preferably with a 'knife edge' Swiss file. I mark the bend positions by my felt-pen and scriber method, and always make such bends *before* trimming the rail to length. You can produce items such as checkrails and knuckles/wing rails by reference to the template – either the one that you're building onto or, more simply, a spare copy of the same thing.

The basic turnout completed, and here being tested by running a suitable vehicle (in this case the unmotored chassis of my GWR 1366 class pannier tank, conveniently under construction at this juncture) through the uncheckrailed crossing. This is to check for 'tight spots' before the influence of the check-rails complicates matters.

Installing the check-rails. This is my home-brewed check-rail gauge – the 'official' item is basically similar. These gauges clamp the check-rail tightly, and set it by reference to the opposing running rail. The check-rail of the diverging road has had its dummy chairs added. This job now requires completing for the rest of the turnout. Fig. 7.18 shows the various 'special' chairs the prototype employs in the crossing area while Fig. 7.19 shows how I represent them by butchering C & L mouldings.

With chairs and other such details added, the rails are painted with acrylic (see Chapter 10).

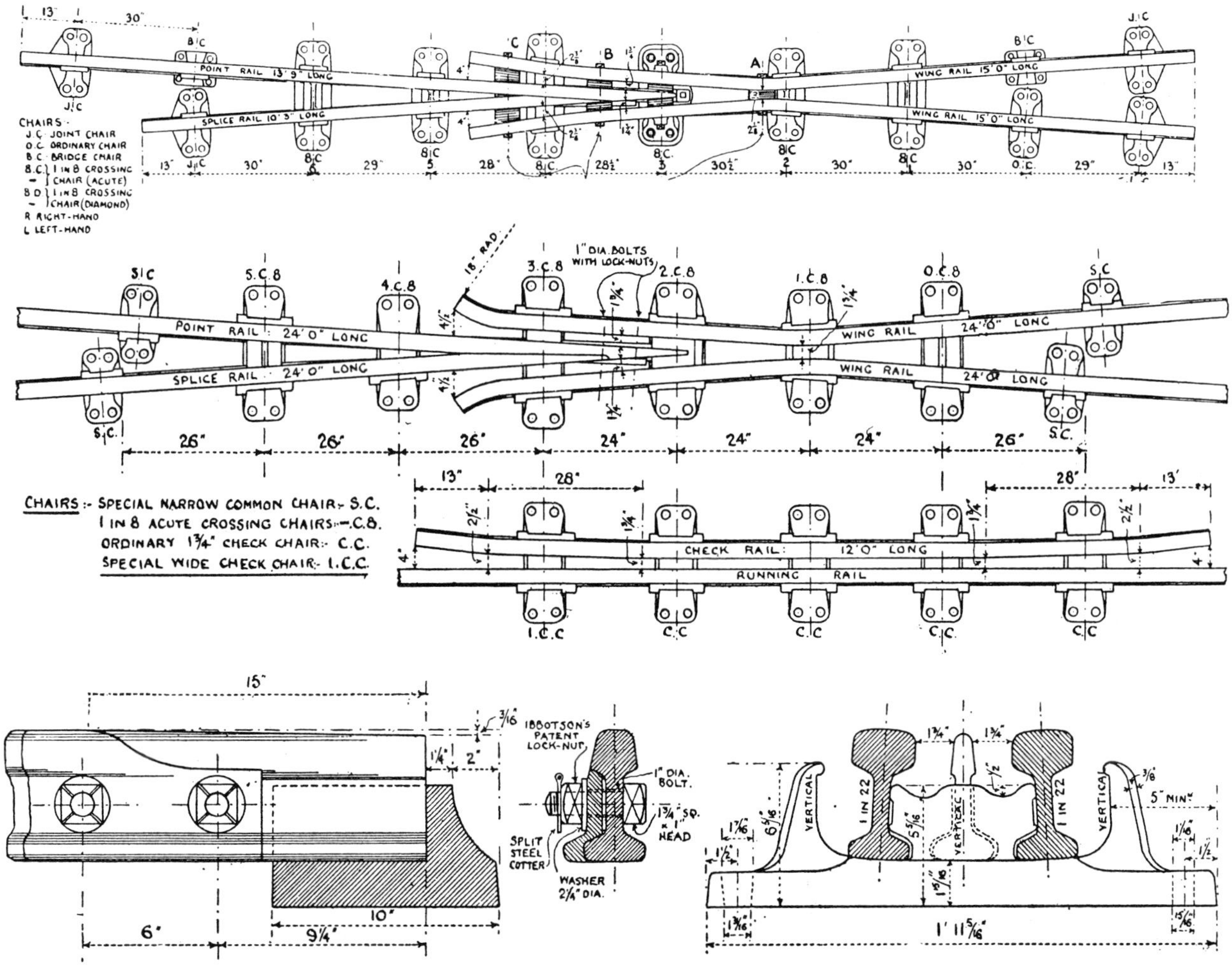

CHAIRS:
J.C. JOINT CHAIR
O.C. ORDINARY CHAIR
B.C. BRIDGE CHAIR
8.C. 1 IN 8 CROSSING CHAIR (ACUTE)
8.D. 1 IN 8 CROSSING CHAIR (DIAMOND)
R RIGHT-HAND
L LEFT-HAND

CHAIRS:- SPECIAL NARROW COMMON CHAIR - S.C.
1 IN 8 ACUTE CROSSING CHAIRS - C.8.
ORDINARY 1¾" CHECK CHAIR:- C.C.
SPECIAL WIDE CHECK CHAIR - I.C.C.

Fig. 7:18 Prototype chairs at common crossing.

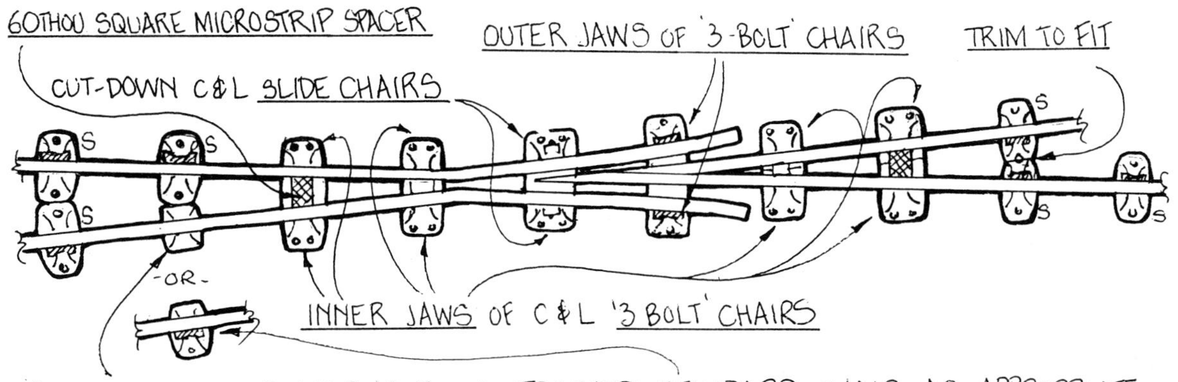

Fig. 7:19 Chairing a common crossing with C & L parts.

VITAL CONNECTIONS

One last aspect of miniature PW that must not be overlooked before we actually get onto the business of assembling the final job is the unprototypical but essential business of ensuring the electrical integrity of the trackwork. Obviously, with wooden sleepers, insulation is no problem, so it's feeds and jumpers that concern us here. Given my brief for fully-concealed wiring, then these do demand a little thought and attention at this stage. In fact, they will already have required a bit of thought at a much earlier stage, in the actual designing of the layout, when the locations and boundaries of feeds and sections will have been decided – information that I transfer to the full-sized 'layout template'.

I've a bit to say on wiring in Chapter 9, but for now I'm simply concerned with providing for any feed droppers or jumpers that might need including in the structure of the track as it is assembled. There are a number of ways of introducing power to track, and carrying it around P & C work as required. I use a bare wire, routed beneath the paper overlay on which my track is built; provided that care is taken to ensure that wires of opposite polarities are kept apart, there's no need to use bulky insulated wiring. The 28 SWG soft copper wire sold by Eileen's Emporium ('Sources' appendix) is ideal, having low resistance, and being easy to form into complex routes. This wiring can be surface-laid if you're not using my paper-based PW system; paint in a dull grey-brown and bury it in the ballast, and no-one will be any the wiser.

I solder feed-wires to the apposite rail foot in a position where I can pass it down through the punched hole in a sleeper not carrying a rivet, where it can be completely concealed by the C & L chair cut in half and used cosmetically. The wire is poked down a hole pricked in the paper trackbase overlay, and a good long tail 'fed through' into the space between overlay and workboard – the wire is soft enough to permit this. Jumper wires are fed down in two halves, attached at each end, to be joined later once the paper is removed from the workboard but before it is laid onto the foam underlay strip.

A lot of the 'internal wiring' in a turnout does not even call for this; the crossing assembly is bonded into one electrical unit by the piece of flat strip beneath the crossing 'V' and wing rails, already noted. The bonding between stockrails and accompanying point blades I accomplish with more fine flat strip, used to represent the prototype bracing at this point. If your turnouts don't have this bracing (a feature of 'standard' bullhead), then use flat strip over a sleeper but beneath the rails, in a position where it can be disguised by C&L chairs modified to represent switch heel chairs. I usually solder these strips to the foot of the stockrails before building them into pointwork.

ASSEMBLY AT LAST!

Having bored you for many a tortuous page with all manner of preparations and preliminaries, at last we come to the stage where all the bits can be brought together into finished PW. Not only is this relatively quick and easy, but it's also very satisfying. Fun, even! Rather than try and cover this very visual process in further pages of tortured prose, I shall now take refuge behind the trusty Contax and try to secure a sufficiency of in-focus photographs for the whole business to become blissfully apparent. 'Trerice', the layout here seen at an embryonic stage, is a Cornish china-clay branch depicted towards the end of the steam era – giving me an excuse for a few concrete sleepers, though not, in all conscience, for any flat-bottom track; most of the extant clay lines are still awaiting that refinement! 'Trerice' was designed to incorporate an interesting selection of P & C work, but for this first sequence we are considering straight and curved plain track and a simple turnout.

This is what it's supposed *to look like.*

CHAPTER EIGHT

DIAMONDS, SLIPS AND COMPOUNDS SPECIAL SITUATIONS

Many railway modellers of my acquaintance exhibit a distaste akin to a phobia when confronted by diamonds, slipped diamonds or compound turnouts. Like a lot of apparently complex phenomena, such convoluted specimens of the platelayer's art can be broken down into a series of simple elements, combined in multiple. As I've pointed out in my prototype anatomy sketch, all P & C work, no matter how involved, consists of just four basic units: switches, common crossings, obtuse crossings, and plain rail joining it all together. The only one of these elements that I've not so far covered is the obtuse crossing, so I'll start with that.

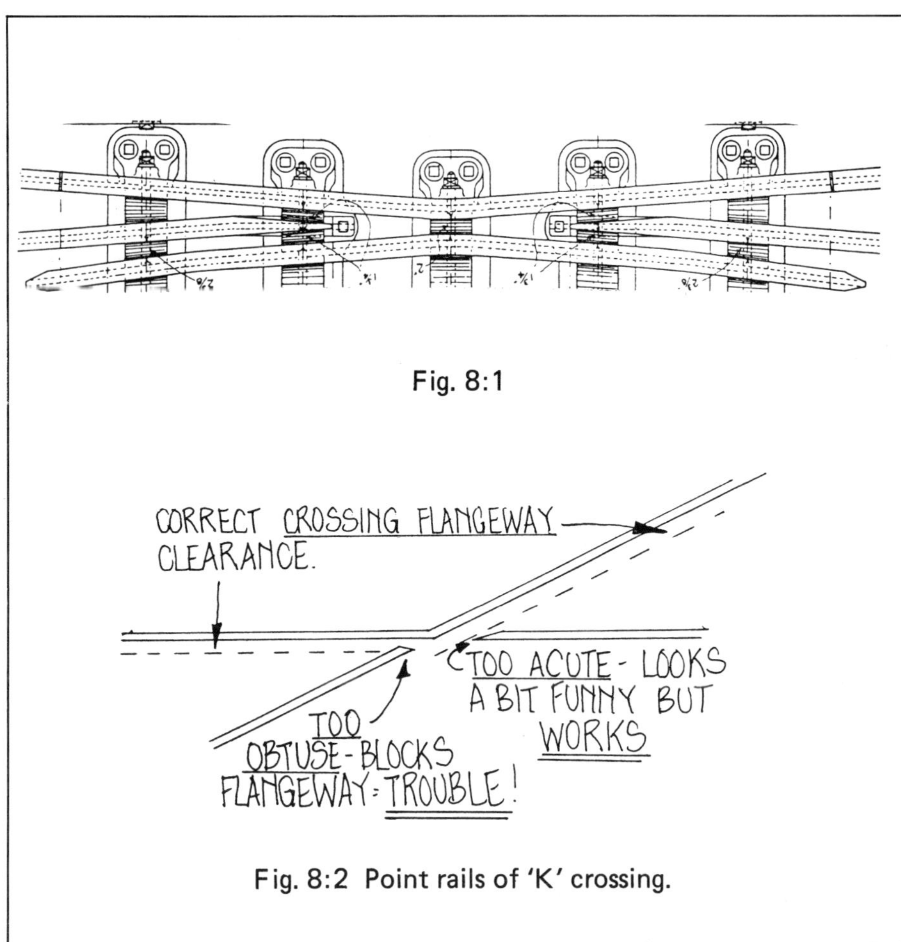

Fig. 8:1

Fig. 8:2 Point rails of 'K' crossing.

OBTUSE CROSSINGS

As can be seen from the first diagram, once more lifted from Allen's book, the obtuse crossing is, in effect, an inverted common crossing, in that the relative positions of the point rail and knuckle are reversed. In fact, this makes life a lot easier, as the knuckle rail and point rails are a lot easier to make than the components of the 'V' of a common crossing. It's all a lot less critical, too; so long as the knuckle bend is nice and crisp (that filed nick in the rail-side), there's not a lot to go wrong with an obtuse crossing, so long as it is of suitable angle. Suitable angle? Well, a moment's thought will serve to suggest that, as the angle of the crossing becomes smaller, the 'knuckle' rail becomes nearer and nearer to a straight, while the gap from knuckle to point rail – fixed by the flangeway width – becomes wider and wider, until a situation is reached where the wheels tend to follow the knuckle and 'turn the corner', rather than traversing the crossing as intended. This 'accidental slip' propensity is not unknown on the prototype, especially with stock having SWB bogies – bogie bolster wagons were particularly prone to going 'the wrong way'. In full-sized practice, 'plain diamond' crossings are limited to a common crossing angle of 1 in 8 or less; from 1 in 9 up, some form of 'switched' diamond would have been employed, where the point rails of the obtuse crossing are made movable, able to close against the sides of the knuckle to provide a continuous path for the wheels, and eliminating that potentially troublesome gap.

It is rare for railway modellers to employ diamonds above 1 in 8; in fact, it's relatively rare for diamonds to be employed at all, for, along with slips and compounds, they are 'fought shy of' by a lot of modellers, leading to rather sterile and unconvincing track plans comprised entirely of plain turnouts. Call me perverse, but I've always rather enjoyed a bit of out-of-the-ordinary track, and there have been few Rice layouts that didn't employ a single slip and at least one three-way point. Contrary to appearances, I would argue that such formations are inherently no more difficult to construct than plain P & C work, as I shall show.

The construction of the last basic element, the obtuse crossing, is actually the easiest job of the lot. I've touched on the need for a crisp bend to the knuckle; the only other component of significance is the point rail, which is a simple filing job, no different to the similar component in the 'V' of the common, or acute, crossing. The same 'tolerance rule' applies, exactly; you can get away with making it too acute, but not with it being insufficiently angled, when the effect is to reduce the (critical) width of the flangeway, as shown in the diagram.

THE PLAIN DIAMOND

This is a straightforward crossing, one pair of rails across another. It consists of a pair of acute, or 'common' crossings, as in a normal turnout, and a pair of equivalent-angle obtuse crossings, sometimes described from their shape as 'K crossings'. As with a turnout, diamonds are classified principally by the angle of the acute crossing, as 'a one-in-six plain diamond crossing, right or left-hand'. That is, a crossing of that angle where the crossing road trails in from the left and leads out to the right will be described as 'right-hand', and the opposite situation as 'left-hand'. The 'plain' in the description refers to the nature of the obtuse crossings, which would be of the simple fixed type. If they were of the 'spring guarded' or 'movable' type, the crossing would be referred to as a 'guarded' or 'switched' diamond crossing.

In constructional terms at 4mm scale, a plain diamond crossing is simpler than a

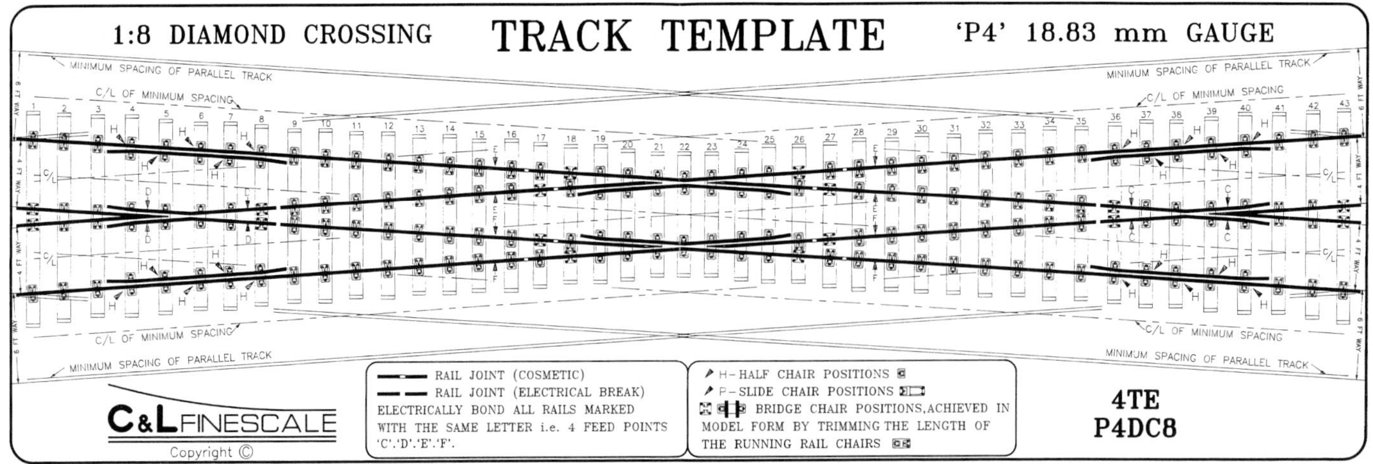

turnout, as the obtuse crossings are easier (and quicker) to make than switches. The timbering is prepared in much the same way, and the same basic rules apply to rivet positioning. As with turnouts, there are 'critical' timber positions – beneath the crossing noses of the common crossings, and beneath both noses and the knuckle centre of the obtuse crossing. What is different about diamonds is that the timbering will not normally be set at right-angles to either road, but rather will be aligned with a line drawn between the noses of the common crossings, as in the diagram.

The exception to this timbering rule for diamond crossings comes where the diamond is an integral part of a larger formation, where the alignment of the timbering may be determined by the main roads of the formation. Thus, in double junctions, the diamond will be on sleepering at right-angles to the straight 'through' road, rather than the curved road of which it is also a part. However, whatever the angle the sleepers are set at, the rules as to sleeper positioning at the critical points will still need to be observed. As with most things in modelling, the best guide to correct procedure is direct observation of the prototype.

Such observation of the prototype might also show up one or two other features of diamond crossings that will need to be accommodated in any model. By no means all diamond crossings occur on straight track, and one or both roads might well be curved. In these circumstances, the various crossings will have differing angles (the GWR, a great user of curved crossings in standard double-junction sets, had crossing angles going up in 'quarters', to allow for these variations). In model terms, the simplest way to build such crossings is to fabricate them – crossing 'Vs' and all – *in situ*. It is far more important to produce trackwork with good visual and actual alignments than it is to observe the niceties of exactitude in crossing angles; the difference between a 1 in $6\frac{1}{2}$ and a 1 in $6\frac{3}{4}$ crossing hardly shouts at you in 4mm scale!

The normal checkrailing of diamond crossings – the usual set-up associated with common crossings, plus the pair of knuckled checkrails of the obtuse crossings – could vary. Curved crossings – often on fairly sharp curves – can call for continuous check rails on the inside rail of the curve. As with pointwork, the various special chairs incorporated in crossings will need representing by a little butchery on the C & L mouldings.

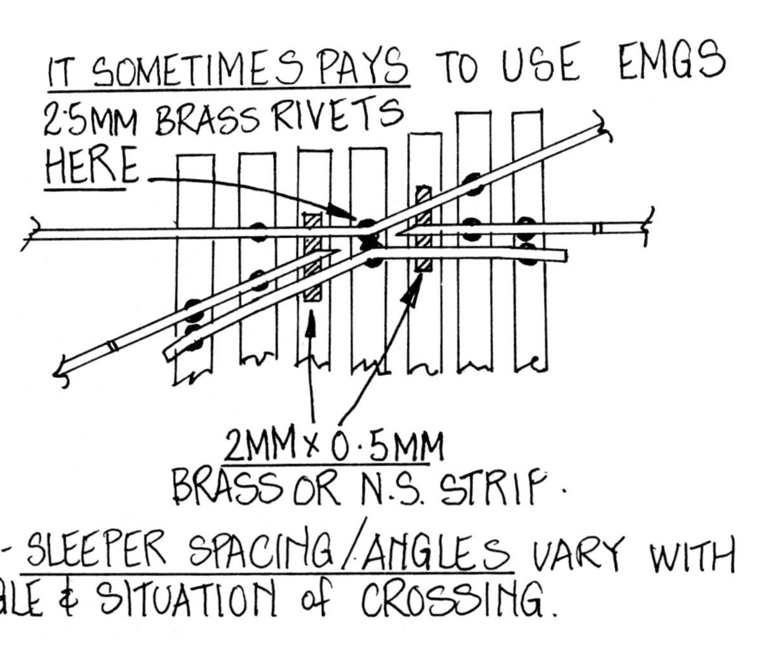

Fig. 8.3 Anchoring noses of 'K' crossings.

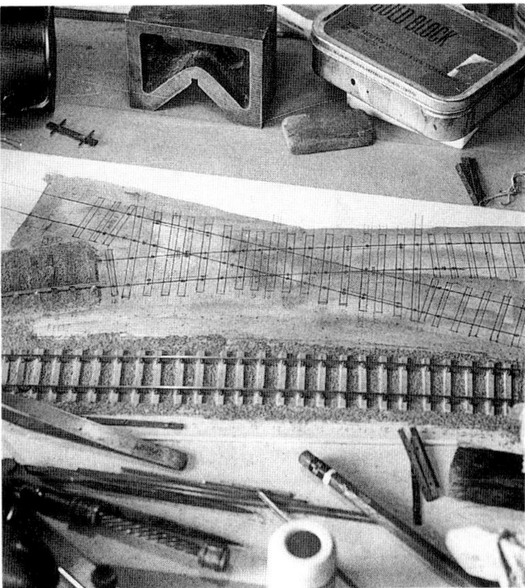

The completed home-drawn template for the diamond receives a wash of grey/brown acrylic paint, and has sleepers and ballast laid as for other track.

With the riveted sleepers laid, rail positions are clearly evident. A length of rail is taken and offered up for marking of the knuckle bend (splodge of felt pen and scriber method). The track gauge is merely serving to hold the rail upright, while the V-block is holding it in position. The bend is then made, and the knuckle rail laid and soldered in place. The rest of the formation is 'built off' this rail.

The second knuckle rail is gauged from the first. The block-type gauge is especially useful here. I tacked the right-hand end of the rail, then swapped the gauge to the 'other road' to check for accuracy in both directions. When all was well, the knuckle rail was finally soldered in place – keep checking! The crossing 'V' could then be set up using 3-point gauges, being filed to fit on site.

The rest of the acute crossing was then laid in as for a turnout, using 3-point and flangeway gauges. This diamond, with its relatively wide crossing angle (nearly 40°) calls for short knuckle/wing rails on the acute crossing; shallower crossing angles give you a bit more to get hold of!

The short crossing nose rails can then be marked off, filed, and fitted. I anchored the noses by soldering short lengths of 1mm x 10-thou NS strip beneath the knuckle rails, as in Fig. 8:3. They are a bit of a fiddle to fit on so short a diamond. Tweezers and a fine soldering iron bit are a help.

Final job in basic sequence is to fit the obtuse crossing wing rails, accomplished with a pair of checkrail gauges, and the acute crossing check rails, no different from those on a turnout. A rolling check with a vehicle will soon tell you how well-aligned the noses of the obtuse crossings are!

The diamond basically complete, with all remaining check-rails in place and all soldered joints made. The cosmetic chairs can now be added, from suitably butchered C & L mouldings, and any easing/fettling of the crossings undertaken. Here, I'm using a fine jeweller's riffling file to impart a bit of 'wear and tear' to the crossing noses. Below is the finished diamond, fully chaired. The turnout by which it joins the 'main line' in the foreground was also built onto a 'custom' template.

'INSIDE' SLIP DIAMONDS

These come in two varieties – single or double. I append a diagram of the 'guts' of a double, which shows the basic construction. A single slip is essentially two pairs of points, superimposed; a double is a pair of compound points, likewise overlapped. (A double slip is sometimes referred to as a 'compound slip' or even 'compound diamond'.) In terms of the bits needed, they amount to much the same thing as the equivalent in pointwork, with the saving of an extra common crossing in the case of the compound version. So – a single slip is two common crossings, two obtuse crossings and two pairs of switches (four blades), while a double has four pairs of switches (eight blades). The actual slip roads are simple enough to arrange, and the only other complication is the extra closure rails contained within the diamond. Tackled logically and in the right order, slips are not really that bad, and their space-saving utility certainly makes them worth the effort.

Contrary to what might be expected, the finer clearances (and hence more compact crossings) of P4 trackwork make these rather 'crowded' formations simpler in that standard than in EM or OO; indeed, in coarser-scale OO, they become fiendishly awkward, simply because the narrower-than-scale gauge coupled with wider-than-scale flangeways tends to leave you with barely enough room to squeeze all the bits in. It may be this hangover from the days of crude compromise that has given the double-slip its unjustified reputation as the 'north face of the Eiger' of model trackbuilding.

I have found that the real key to the construction of successful slip points lies in the order in which the job is tackled. At first glance, it may seem simplest to lay the stock/slip rails first, and 'work in' to the diamond. But a moment's reflection will suggest the opposite, in that the gauging requirement calls for the outer rail of the curve – that is, the closure rail lying within the diamond – to be the determinant of rail position. Also, all the critical, tricky-to-adjust stuff goes on inside the diamond; it's far easier to fiddle about with the easier-to-get-at slip roads if a touch of fiddling be needed. (It usually is!) Rather than tying up a few more pages trying to describe all this, there's another photosequence covering the single slip at 'Trerice'; a double slip would be similar. Inside slips can be built only in a narrow range of crossing angles – 1 in 6 to 1 in 8; angles below 1 in 6 are too short to accommodate the switches within the length of the diamond, and 1 in 8 is, as we've noted, the shallowest angle permitted for a plain diamond. The length of the formation at a very acute angle would anyway be such that there would be little, if any, space saving on

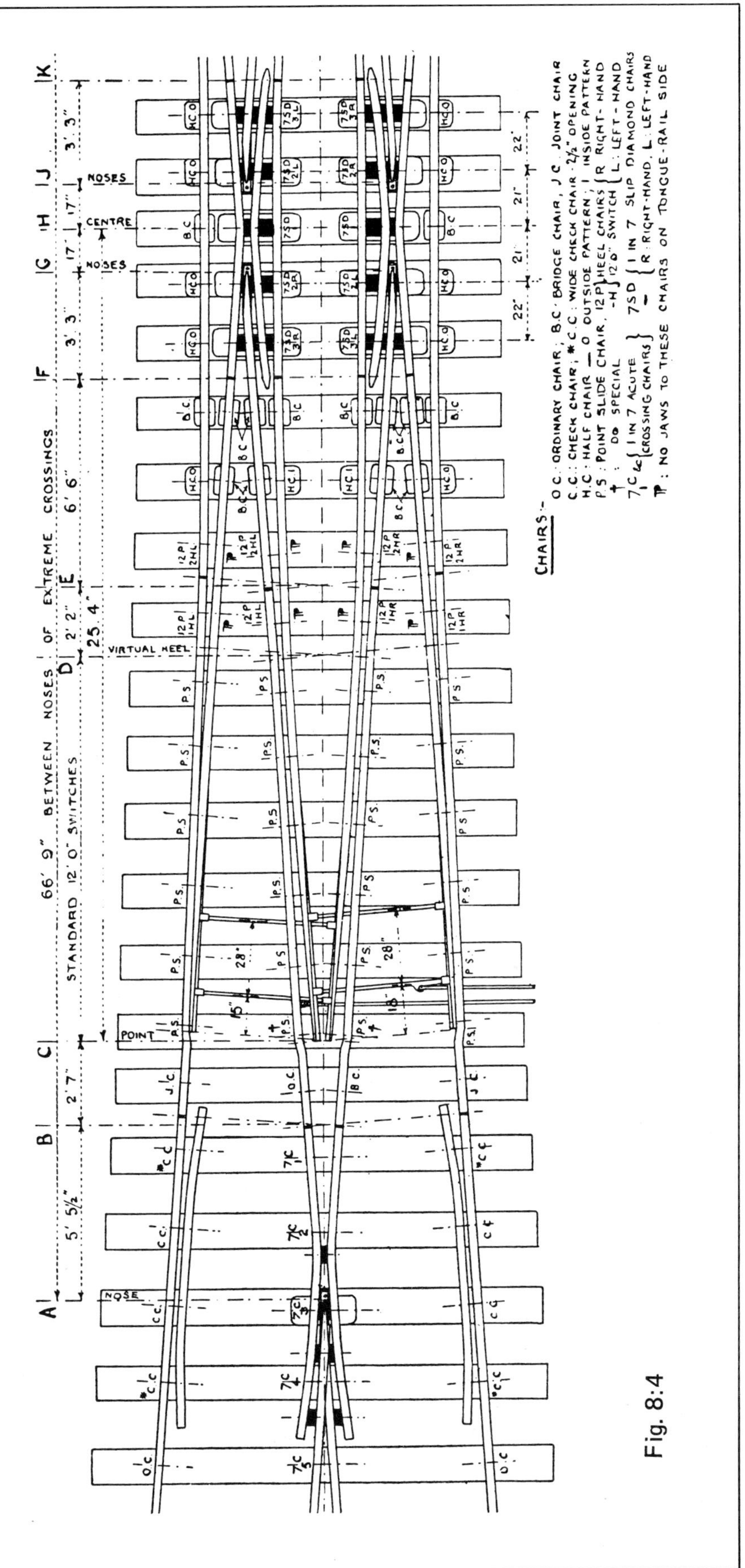

Fig. 8:4

the pair of conventional turnouts that, toe-to-toe, would do the same job.

'OUTSIDE' SLIPS

Thus far, I have been describing 'inside' slip diamonds – those where the switches and closures are all contained within the actual diamond, between the noses of the common crossings. These are the most common type of slip point, but, as noted, they come only in a very limited range of crossing angles. Where a wider crossing angle gives a diamond too short to accommodate the switches and closures, these may be moved to lie wholly or partly outside the diamond, giving formations referred to as 'outside' and 'semi-outside' slips.

An 'outside' slip is really two complete turnouts and a plain diamond crossing built as one formation, close-coupled. Constructionally, at both full-size and in miniature, it amounts to just that. Much more interesting and challenging is the semi-outside slip, a compact and visually attractive piece of PW. C & L now produce a set of templates for such a formation, with a 1 in 4.5 diamond and common crossings on the slip road at 1 in 6.5. It's a superb piece of work, reproduced alongside, and will hopefully inspire a few more people to have a go at this charismatic bit of trackwork. Constructionally, it is all familiar stuff, the difference over a conventional inside slip amounting to an extra pair of common crossings. As with any slip, I'd start in the middle and work outwards to the slip road.

'Trerice' provided me with the excuse to tackle a favourite formation – a semi-outside single slip, for which C & L conveniently produce a template.

The sequence makes the usual start – a wash of 'ballast colour', followed by marking, drilling and staining of the timbers.

Sleepers and ballast, as usual, go down together. With a large and complex piece of P & C work such as this, I cut down the opportunities for confusion by laying timbers in small batches of 6 or 8, as soon as they're riveted; it's awfully easy to mix things up when you've got 60-plus timbers lying about!

Riveted and ballasted timbers, ready for rail. I start with the knuckle rail, as here, building the rest of the formation off it, much as for the diamond.

The first pair of common crossings go down next, together with the adjoining obtuse crossing.

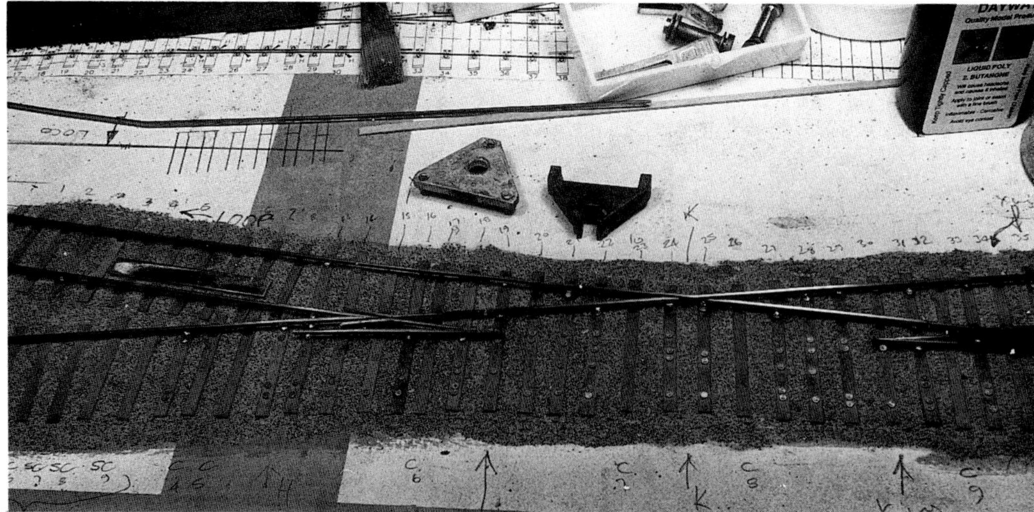

With the 'primary' crossings in place, I lay the 'Vs' of the secondary crossings on the slip road . . .

. . . followed by the knuckle rails and closure. C & L have an electrical error on their template, showing an extra, unnecessary gap in this section of rail. They do the same thing on their 3-way turnout, leading to extra wiring complications. One gap – here close to the RH crossing – suffices.

With something to gauge from, the second knuckle rail is now installed . . .

. . . followed by the knuckle rails of the secondary common crossings, and the rest of the second 'K' crossing. Note the reinforcing/bonding strip being installed using a spare timber to hold it in place for soldering. The 'wing' checkrail at the obtuse crossing ideally calls for two checkrail gauges, being otherwise a 'tack, check, adjust' job.

Checkrails for the common crossings are added exactly as on a turnout. A spot of track-testing can then take place.

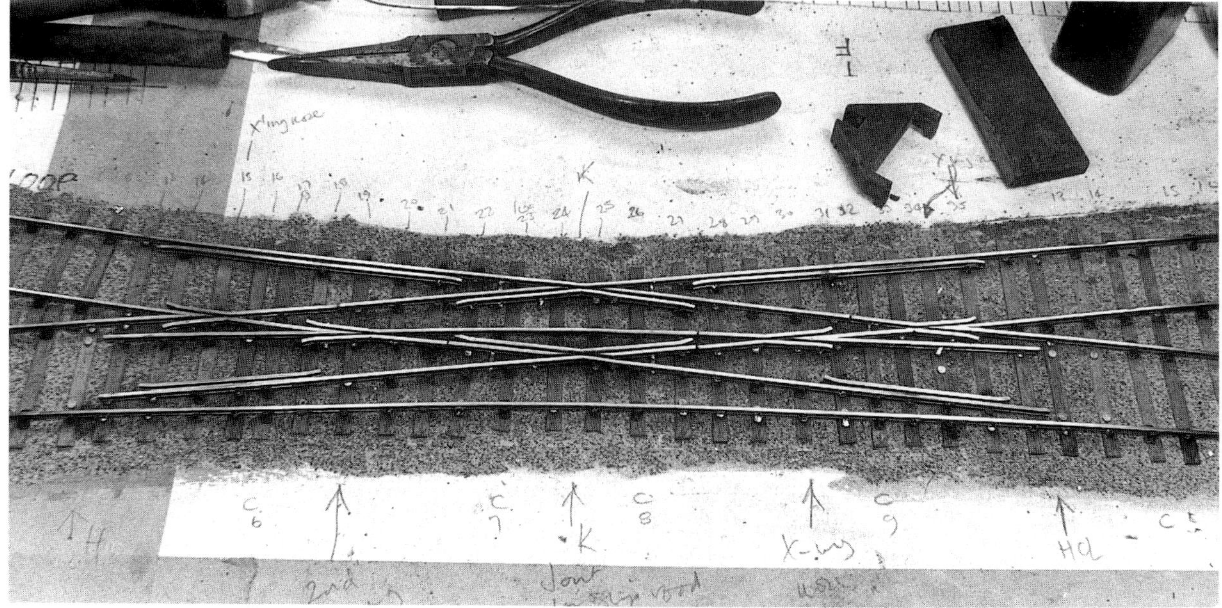

Above: *The slip road can now be added, gauged off of the closure rails, etc., already in place within the diamond.* Left: *Installing point blades on this slip (or any other slip) is no more complex than fitting them to a turnout – and here they are. I'd run out of slide chairs at this juncture, hence the gaps. Note that, on a double slip with 4 blades, it is quite in order in most instances to couple them all to one actuator unit (see next chapter) so that they move together. Only in circumstances calling for 1 pair of blades only to move at a time (usually to provide a 'trap' in an interlocked layout) is it necessar to use separate pairs of stretchers, as in Fig. 8:4, in which case use the offset linkage shown in Fig. 8:5.*

Final stage is, as always, a test, preferably under power. One of my 57XX panniers obliges.

COMPOUND TURNOUTS

A compound turnout is one involving more than one set of switch tongues. It can be a three-way or four-way point, either in tandem (diverging roads on both sides) or 'handed' format. It can be 'overlapped', where both sets of switches coincide, or it can be 'staggered', when they come in sequence. It can also be 'opposed', when the switches face in opposite directions. I append thumbnail sketches of these variants, all of which are possible at 4mm scale.

The most common type of compound turnout is a staggered tandem, where roads diverge on either hand from separate sets of switches within the turnout. Apart from the common timbering, the only other difference from a pair of plain turnouts is the provision of the extra common crossing where the two sets of closure rails intersect. In terms of building a model, there really are no problems; if you can build a plain turnout, you can certainly build a staggered compound. Again, C & L do an excellent template for this formation, in B6L, B8R or the converse. If you need other combinations, such as the B6L, B6R I've used on 'Trerice', you can produce a template by splicing together the appropriate plain turnout templates and doing a spot of simple drawing.

Not many people try four-way points, which were more common on the prototype than many folk think. Apart from the famous example at King's Cross, at the 'country' end of Platform 10, they turn up quite regularly; the GWR had one at Snow Hill, while the GER peppered them around at such vital locations as Stowmarket goods yard!

I can't, as yet, claim to have built a 4-way, but I can't see any real problems that wouldn't be met in 'simpler' formations. Actually, I'd rather be faced with a 4-way than an overlapped 3-way (a formation of which both the Midland and the GER were oddly fond) where the coincidence of the two sets of switches makes for merry old fun when it comes to making it all work. The prototype resorts to unequal-length switch tongues and umpteen sets of tiebars, as shown in the diagram of the GER 'three-throw switch' from Allen's book. In model form, it's just a case of replicating all this, which can make things pretty crowded, especially in the matter of the below-decks actuating department. I think that the answer is to offset one set of dummy-tiebar linkages, as in my sketch.

Leaving aside the overlapped tandem and the joys of three-throw switches, an 'average' compound turnout is no problem to build, and takes about as much effort as a pair of conventional turnouts, with the extra effort of making the additional common crossing being offset by a saving in the amount of timbering required. It is no problem to make it work electrically – as Chapter 9 will show.

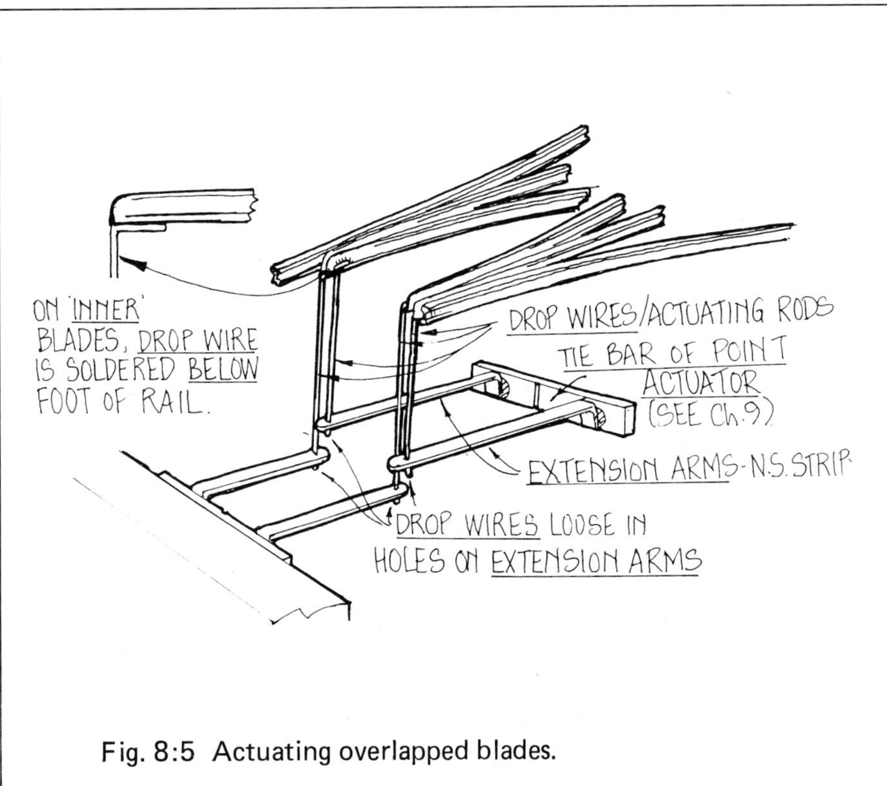

Fig. 8:5 Actuating overlapped blades.

① TAKE TWO ORDINARY TURNOUT TEMPLATES....

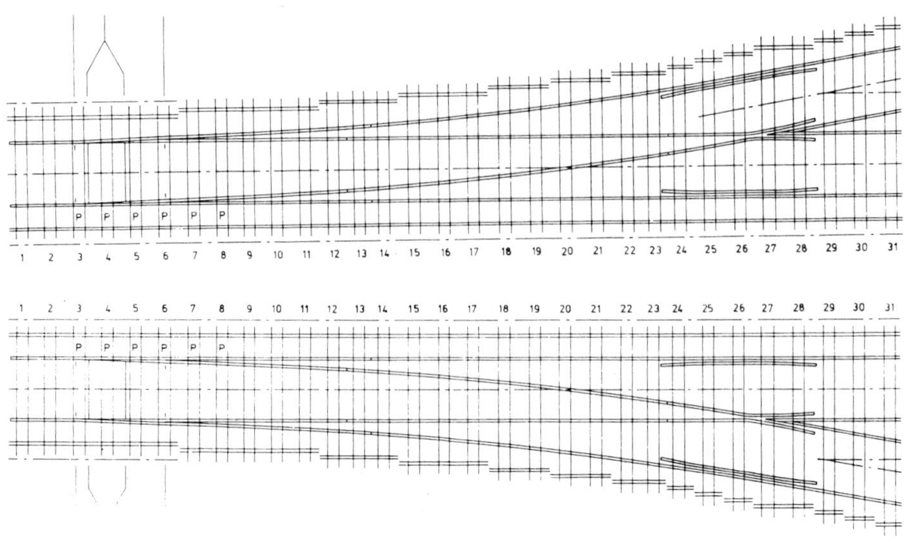

② SLIT IN HALF & JOIN THUS....

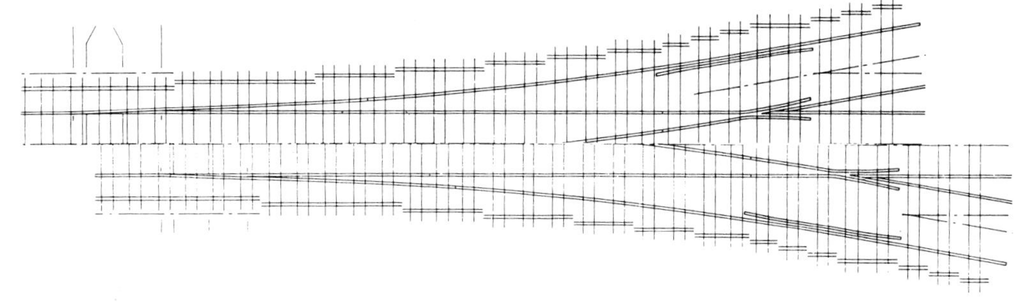

③ DRAW IN MISSING BITS. THE SLIGHTLY MISALIGNED TIMBERS ARE OF NO SIGNIFICANCE - A SMALL ADJUSTMENT DURING CONSTRUCTION ACCOMMODATES.

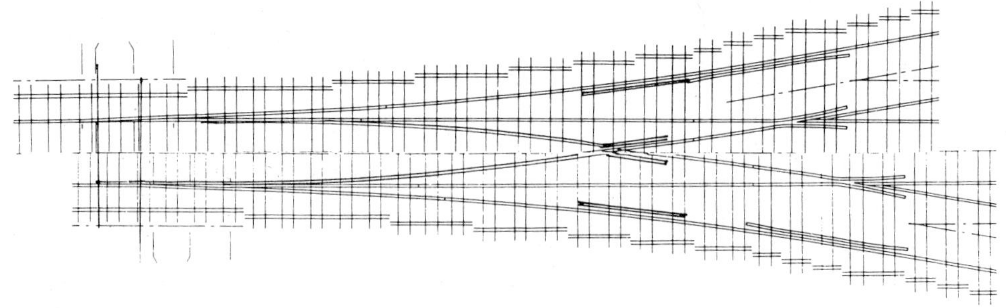

Fig. 8:6 Splicing point templates.

SPECIAL TRACKWORK

Thus far, I have been discussing what are, relatively speaking, 'normal' or commonplace formations. Reality is never that convenient, however, and these more-or-less standardized bits of hardware don't always meet the case. Enter the specialized formation. Examples? Well, quite a common one is the bisected turnout, where a road crosses a turnout in a species of interlaced 'double diamond' across stock rails and closures. It amounts to two diamond crossings of slightly differing angle, and is tedious to build but not particularly problematic. A like case is an 'opposed interlaced' turnout – two plain turnouts overlapped toe to toe. Depending on whether they are of the same or opposite hands, the work amounts to two ordinary turnouts or one single slip. Other such formations might be designed as the need arises, but, once again, they will be constructed from the common building-blocks of switches, acute and obtuse crossings, and plain rail closures; it is only the timbering which will present a unique problem.

Some complex track, however, may employ a radically different form of construction. This is where the level of traffic might call for a greater strength and resistance to wear than can be offered by standard components; the usual solution was to build up the formation from specially-produced extra-hard manganese steel castings, often bolted down to a massive form of timber raft. The most famous examples are probably the crossings on the up side of Newcastle Central, and at Borough Market Junction, between London Bridge, Cannon Street and Charing Cross stations. These castings incorporate all the necessary check-rails, often continuous, plus all manner of reinforcements and locating devices. The 'rail section' is usually truly massive, and a form far removed from normal BH or FB rail. I must confess that I've never attempted to model this sort of PW, nor do I know anyone who has. I think that something fairly drastic, like machining it out of the solid, might be called for; or it could be lost-wax cast from Plastikard patterns. Either way, it's scarcely a run-of-the-mill job, and rather falls outside the scope of the sort of 'soldering iron and kitchen table' engineering most of us have to rely on.

There is one last class of special trackwork that is far more common, and far more readily reproduced, and that is track used where a normal ballasted roadbed is not possible. Three main types spring to mind: bridge track, track incorporating inspection pits, and paved track. The first two are rather similar, employing a form of 'baulk road',

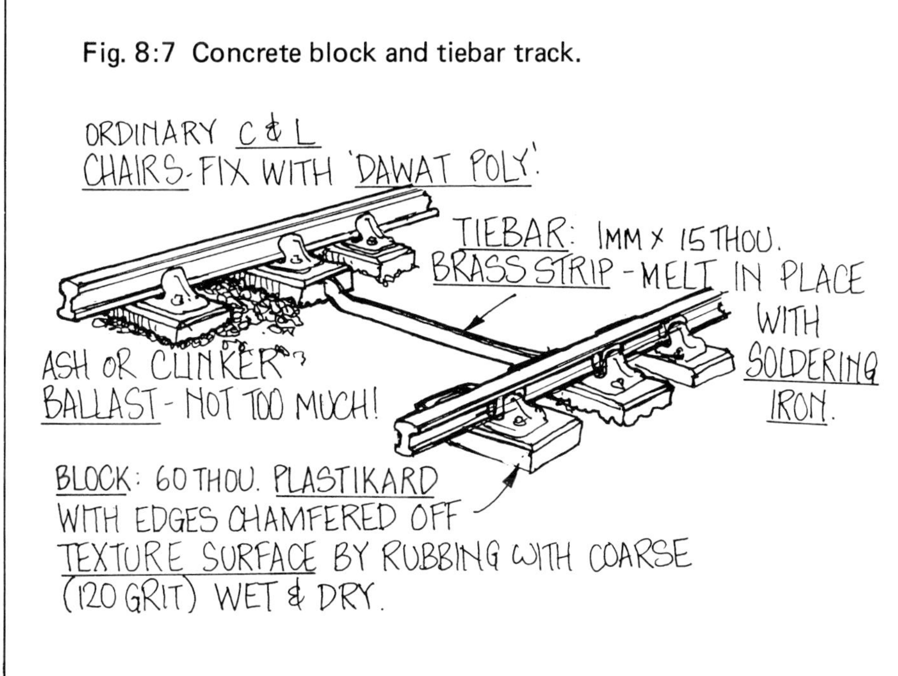

Fig. 8:7 Concrete block and tiebar track.

Concrete block and tiebar track – note extra tiebars either side of rail joint.

with hefty longitudinal timbers beneath the rails, braced and kept to gauge by steel tie-rods, and carrying the rail in special narrow-based chairs. The sketches show how I model this type of 'special track' – Plastikard is the ideal material to work in, as the C & L chairs are readily and firmly bonded with the Daywat Poly.

Paved track is really a doddle, unless it's inset in granite blocks or bricks, which can be tedious to reproduce. The actual track I build from PCB sleepers, with the rail soldered direct to them. Wire and test it before burying! I start off with card infill, then surface with a textured groundmix (sand and tinted Polyfilla is good) or, if I'm faced with setts or bricks, I use Das and duly scribe same – not an exciting chore, but mighty effective if well done. Flangeways are cleared out with a bit of broken hacksaw blade – make sure that wheel-tyres are in full and continuous contact with the rail-head if you want your locos to pick-up when running over inset track. I've scribbled the usual sketch to show all this.

There are one or two other 'oddball' track types that can add a bit of variety to your PW. On 'Trerice' I've laid one siding in GWR 'concrete block and tiebar' sleepers, which were quite a characteristic form of light-duty track in many locations, usually ash-ballasted. I made my blocks from 60-thou Plastikard and melted in the brass strip tiebars. C & L chairs finished it all off. Locations such as cattle docks and locomotive standing places often had a paved trackbase, into which were set wooden sleeper-blocks to carry the chairs. There was usually a central drainage gulley, with a suitable fall on the concrete to direct spillage towards same. Plastikard is, once again, the answer. In fact, it's the answer to most such features, especially in combination with the C & L chairs, which make it so simple to locate and fix the rail. Wagon turntables, weighbridges, sector plates and other similar bits of PW associated hardware, can usually be contrived in short order. I've drawn and photographed a few to round out the nuts-and-bolts part of track construction.

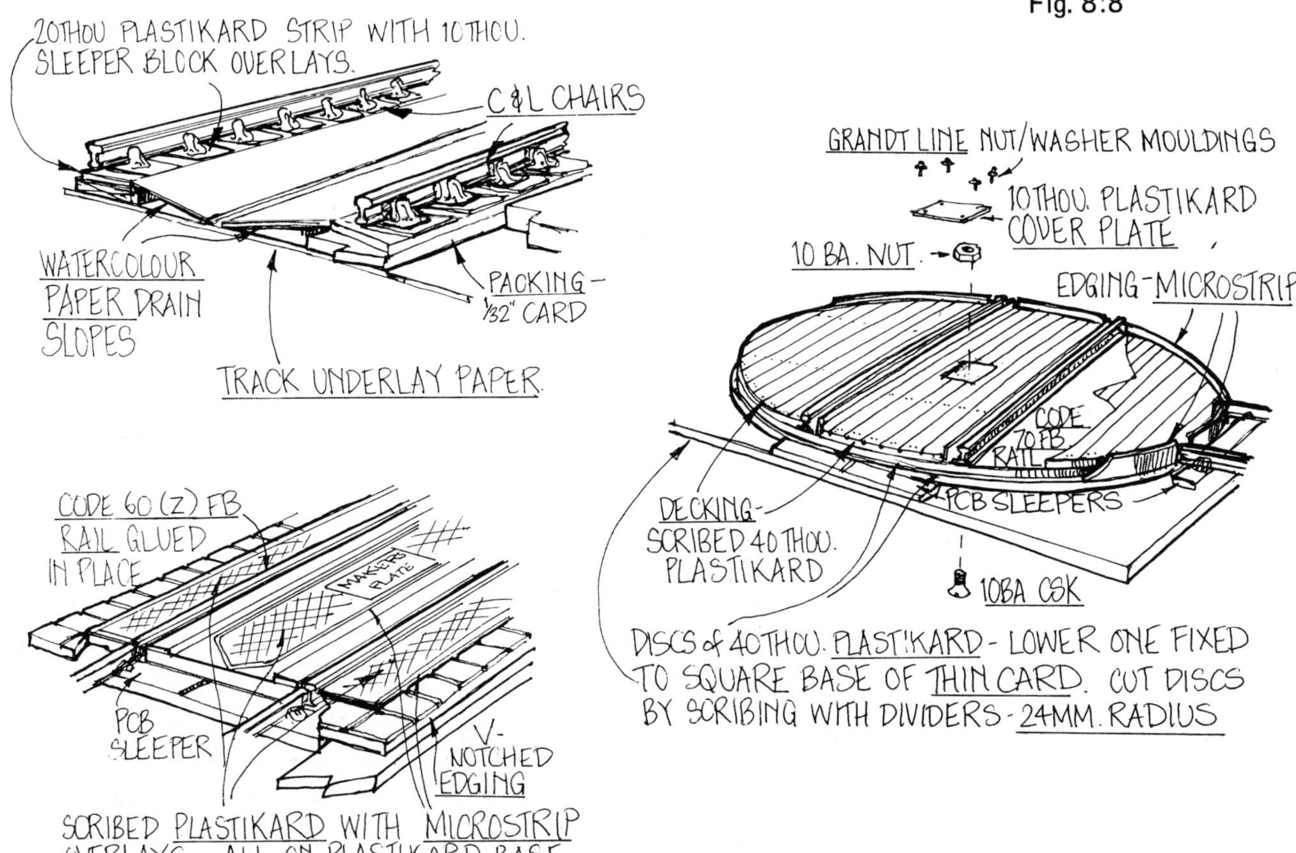

Fig. 8:8

CHAPTER NINE

INSTALLATION AND ACTUATION

Finescale track just doesn't look good, it should work well into the bargain. How well it works depends not only on quality of construction, but also on the care with which it is installed on the layout and the quality of the ancillary systems required to make it function. I've touched on the topic of baseboards elsewhere; vital though they are to the success of a model railway, in the context of this book I'm going to assume that something suitable has been provided, so I'm not delving below trackbase level. Likewise, I can't really consider the question of control other than *en passant,* for all that it has a direct bearing on the functioning of trackwork. What I want to consider here are three factors: the installation of the trackbase, (including underlay and trackwork); the mechanical actuation of pointwork, and the 'internal' wiring associated with the various P & C formations already described in the building stages.

TRACKBASE INSTALLATION

I have said, at several points throughout this rambling essay, that I like to get my trackwork to as advanced a stage as is possible on the workbench before I install it on the layout – and so I do. Starting with the unit of trackwork that has been constructed on the paper underlay in my 'one hit' approach, I aim to have this secured to the underlay and trackbase, internally wired, fitted with point actuators (all tested and working), and painted, detailed and weathered before I finally fit it in place, leaving just the input to the point actuators and the electrical feeds to be hooked up.

First stage in the installation process is to cut the paper underlay, complete with track, free from the workboard. I do this with a good, stout craftknife, cutting along a line corresponding to the boundary of the trackbase section on which that particular formation is destined to go. Making a good, firm pass with a Stanley knife not only cuts out the paper underlay, it also marks the MDFB beneath – which, you may recall, was the piece of that estimable material from which I intended to cut the trackbase.

With the trackwork/underlay cut out, the residual paper and parcels tape is peeled off the MDFB, which is then cut to the required size and shape using a jigsaw. This, in turn, can be used as a template to cut out the foam track underlay from the hapless camping mat. Generally speaking, I'm modelling 'yard limits', where there is no 'ballast shoulder' to the track underpinnings, so I cut the foam to cover the whole of the trackbase section. If I do encounter a length of 'shouldered' track, then I cut the foam into a strip

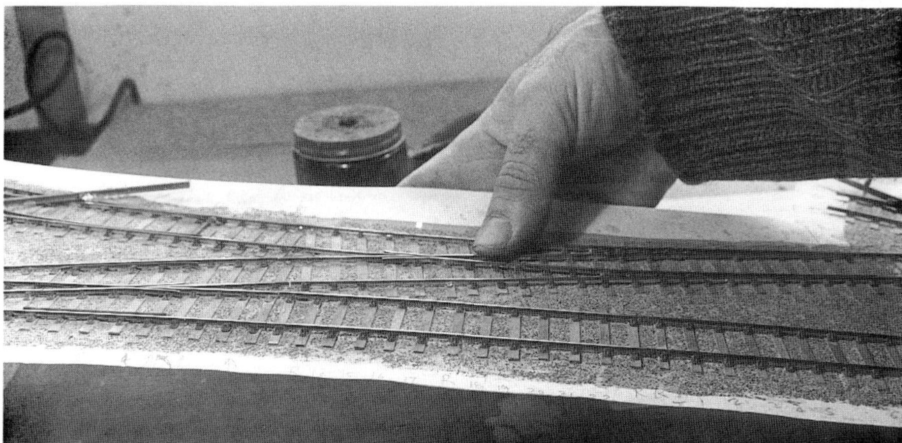

Separating the track and paper underlay from the MDFB workboard ready for laying. I have tack-soldered some odd bits of Peco Code 125 'O' gauge rail to reinforce the track and keep it aligned during laying, although, in fact, the paper does a pretty good job – it's all quite robust.

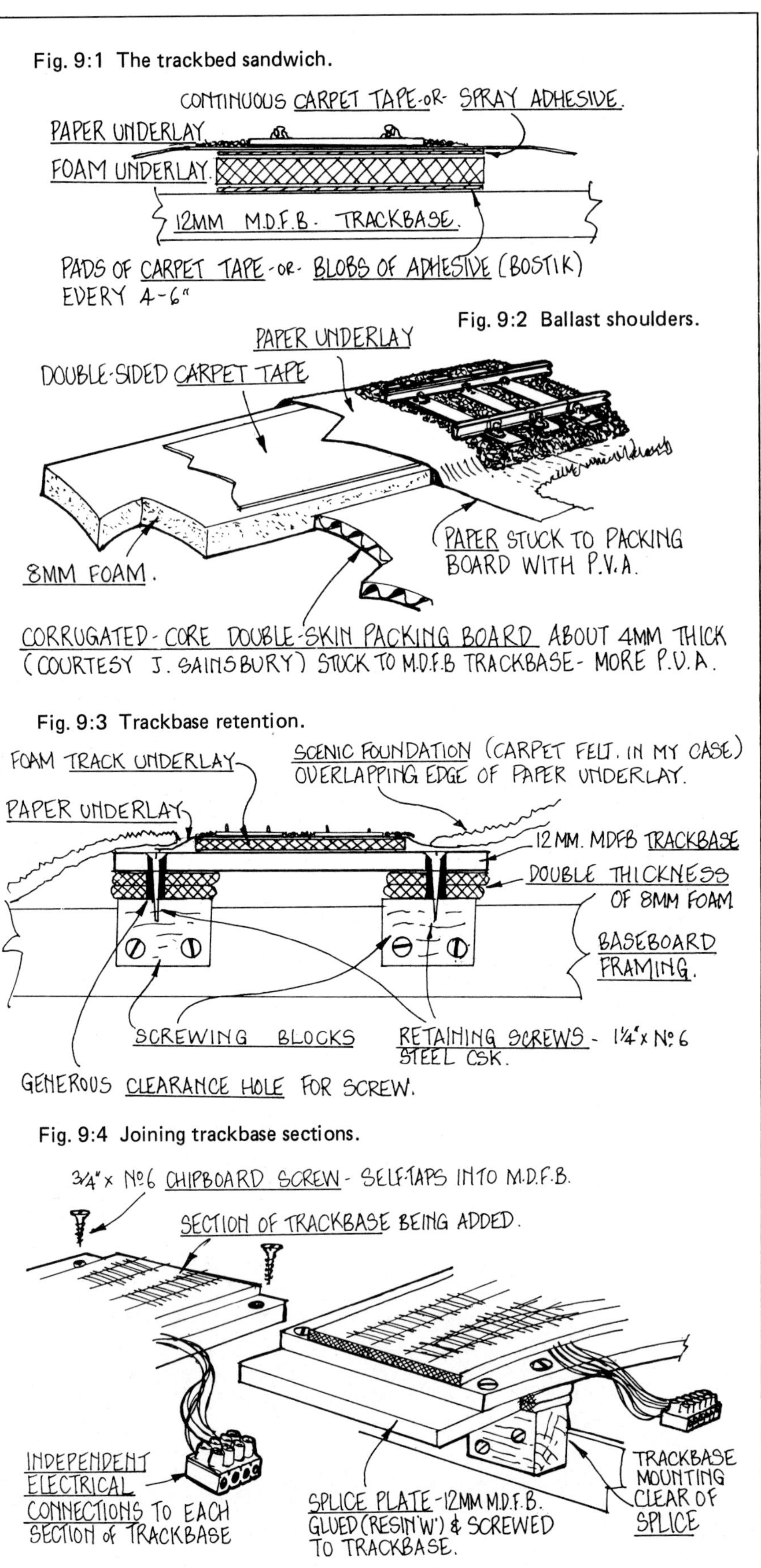

Fig. 9:1 The trackbed sandwich.

Fig. 9:2 Ballast shoulders.

Fig. 9:3 Trackbase retention.

Fig. 9:4 Joining trackbase sections.

of appropriate width for the number of tracks to be carried, and trim the paper underlay to a similarly apposite width. Then I can simply apply Ken Northwood's well-tried system, and form the ballast shoulders by turning the edges of the paper strip down at an appropriate angle. The 8mm foam I use is a bit on the thick side for traditional BH trackwork, so I lay further strips of 3mm double-flute (skinned corrugated) packing board either side of the foam, to which the edges of my paper can be glued (see diagram). Get this board from any supermarket – it's what the majority of cartons are made of. One good-sized box (wine-cases being ideal) provides a pretty good supply. For contemporary deep-bed ballast, the 8mm is about right as it comes.

TRACKBASE PREPARATION

Before the track and underlay paper are installed on the trackbase, a bit of drilling and fitting will be called for. Firstly, the means by which the trackbase is to be attached to the rest of the baseboard structure must be determined. I generally install 'screwing blocks' at appropriate locations on the main baseboard structure – a pair about every 6 inches seems adequate for trackbases up to around 9in wide; over this width, I generally whang in another block somewhere near the centreline, with due allowance for the location of the various tracks. The trackbase is screwed to these blocks, using, in my case, 1¼in No. 6 countersunk steel woodscrews. These screws pass through holes of a generous clearing size drilled in the MDFB trackbase, then through a doubled block of the foam camping mat in which more clearance holes are cut, and finally into the screwing block in the baseboard framing. Again, I've sketched all this. The idea is not only to retain the trackbase, but also to acoustically decouple it from the rest of the baseboard, and to provide a means of adjusting the 'level' of the track.

The different sections of the trackbase also need joining together and aligning, which I accomplish using MDFB 'splice plates' and coarse-thread chipboard screws. The splice plate is glued and screwed to one section of trackbase (Resin 'W' and ordinary ¾in No. 6 screws), forming a locating shelf on which the adjoining section can 'sit'. When all is aligned, the sections are secured together using the chipboard screws (also ¾in No. 6) through clearance holes in the trackbase, 'self tapping' into the splice plate. Once again, there's a spot of illustrative artwork to make it all crystal clear. Although I prepare all this before the track and underlay are laid, I don't actually screw the various sections of trackbase together until they're being installed on the layout.

The last set of holes and clearances that need providing are those for the point and signal actuators, signals usually being in such close proximity to the track as to demand consideration as part of the track-base system. More on point actuators in a page or two – all that I'm concerned with here are the clearance holes needed beneath the switch tongues to transmit the drive from actuator to switch. I drill two generous ($\frac{5}{16}$in) holes in the MDFB sub-base, and cut a similarly expansive clearance in the foam underlay; only in the paper ballast underlay do I cut precise openings, in the form of two narrow slots no more than 5mm long and about 1.5mm wide – pretty unobtrusive. The sketches accompanying the section on point actuators should make these requirements clear – the big holes in trackbase and foam merely allow me some scope for error and adjustment.

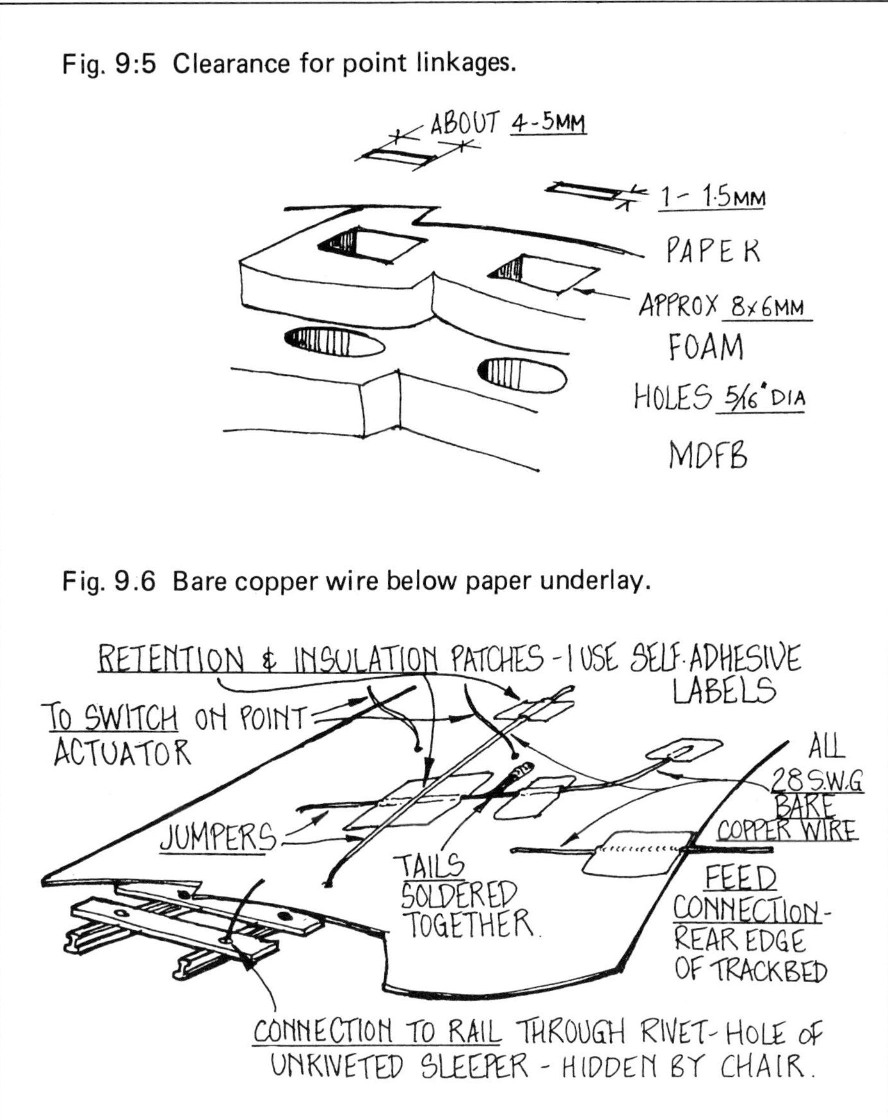

Fig. 9:5 Clearance for point linkages.

Fig. 9.6 Bare copper wire below paper underlay.

ELECTRICAL FEEDS AND JUMPERS

You will recollect that I try and attach these, in the form of soft bare 28SWG copper wire, during construction. I generally forget quite a few, though, and now is the time to add these, poking the wire through pinholes in the paper underlay. Jumpers can be connected-up beneath the paper, and any feeds run out to the edge. I generally build in a spot of redundancy, doubling up any feed or jumper that's going to be hard to get at once everything's installed. The copper wire is flattened down beneath the paper, and taped over to keep it in place. If the bare wires cross each other, insulation is simply provided by tape or paper. I test for continuity and insulation at all stages of this preliminary wiring work, which well repays care and attention to detail.

Much of this wiring will be trapped between paper and foam in the underlay 'sandwich'. I find that, provided solder joints are neatly made and the wire kept as flat as possible to the underside of the paper, it does not affect the level of the 'top' of the track – the foam deforms to accommodate it readily enough. Some feeds – principally those from the crossings and stockrails to feed the below-trackbase microswitches incorporated in the point actuators, will need clearance holes in underlay and trackbase. These are cut and drilled in the same way as those for point drive rods, though without such generous clearance; about $\frac{1}{8}$in is enough.

TRACKLAYING

With the trackbase ready for installation, the track itself can now be laid. In my case, with my biggish chunks of PW on their paper underlay, this is a pretty quick and painless operation. To fix the track to the foam, I use either spray carpet glue or double-sided high-tack carpet-layer's tape, both of which are surprisingly cheap. On balance, I find I tend to use the tape more often, as it's easier to control and hence cleaner. The same adhesives serve to fix underlay to trackbase, but here I don't aim for the overall fix that I use to secure the track to the underlay; I content myself with a strip of tape or blob of adhesive about every 4–6in across the width of the trackbase – it seems to add a spot more flexibility to the system. So long as the underlay is held flat to the base, no benefit derives from additional retention.

Although I sometimes combine several 'paper' units onto one chunk of MDFB trackbase, I never bridge trackbase joints with the paper plus PW, as this would defeat two of the main objects of my system. It would mitigate against my getting everything working before trackbase installation, and it would prevent the independent removal of individual units of trackage for repair or remodelling at a future date. I like each piece of my 'jigsaw to be discrete and self-contained as far as possible. As I usually make my PW in the largest possible units that I can handle on the bench (about 36in × 12in seems the practical maximum), the same constraint applies to the MDFB trackbase sections. So, by and large, it seems logical to make the boundaries coincide so far as the match-up to adjoining trackwork is concerned, although what happens at the sides of the track is dictated by scenic, rather than structural, considerations.

When laying adjoining units of track, the two sections of trackbase are lined up on their splice, and retained either by clamping, or by driving home a couple of the chipboard-screw fixings. The track is aligned and fitted as accurately as possible, ready for final union when the various sections are installed together onto the baseboard. I use the same fishplating techniques to unite rail-ends between the various units of PW as are used within the sections – a Colin Waite etched fishplate, soldered in place. If an expansion joint is needed, then a slide-on

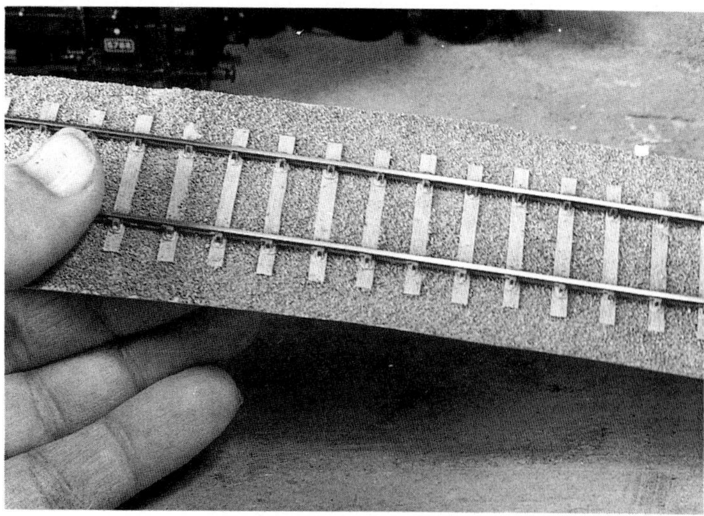

The paper underlay is cut free from the workboard, complete with track and ballast, and laid onto the foam rubber trackbed using spray carpet adhesive. The finished result would normally come over the edge of the foam, but I've cut it short to show the nature of the 'sandwich'. The actual track sub-base in this case is 6mm ply; I prefer 12mm MDFB these days.

fishplate is required. I use Peco's smallest type; it doesn't look very nice, but it does a good locating job. But, as I've said somewhere else, I find that the various gaps left for electrical isolation purposes take care of the expansion requirement in most circumstances.

ELECTRICS – INTERNAL WIRING OF POINTWORK

I mentioned the wherefore of internal wiring (by which I mean the connections and switches necessary for the electrical functioning of units of track within themselves, rather than the external system by which they are fed and controlled) without really describing the why. As this is most simply portrayed in diagram form, I've made a series of drawings covering the formations described in this book. But perhaps a word or two on the general theory and practice of 'internal' track wiring might not go amiss. Electronic whizzkids had better skip the whole of this section and go straight to point actuators.

In the context of finescale trackwork, there's only one possible system of point electrification – the 'all-live' approach that used to be described as 'live frog'. Quelling visions of small green amphibians hopping gaily about the trackwork, I shall proffer the term 'switched common crossing' as an accurate alternative, although taking care to point out (before the writers-to-the-publisher do) that this is a different thing to a switched crossing, where that term refers to a diamond with movable point rails. A moment's consideration of an ordinary turnout will suggest that the common crossings will need to change its polarity when the blades are reversed. This calls for a simple changeover switch capable of connecting the common crossing to whichever stockrail is appropriate; a type of switch known as a single pole, double throw – one circuit, capable of two routes through the switch.

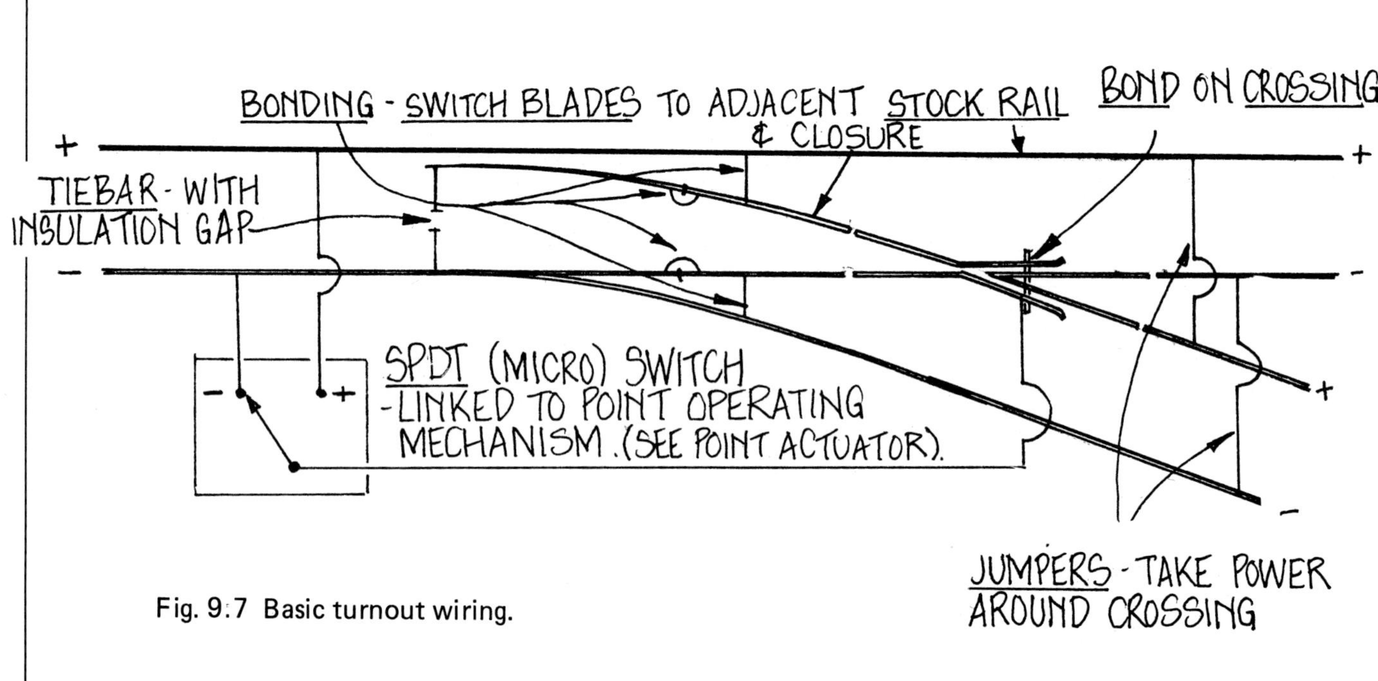

Fig. 9:7 Basic turnout wiring.

This is normally abbreviated to SPDT, and is the type of switch usually incorporated in point motors.

I'll confess straight away that I don't like switches incorporated in point motors – at least, the sort of switch incorporated in the type of point motor that I can afford! I'll have a word or two to say on point motors in the next section of this chapter, but, for now, considering the purely electrical side of the matter, I have to come out in favour of encapsulated microswitches as the simplest and most reliable means of changing common crossing polarity on pointwork. If it comes to it, I plump for this type of switch for virtually *all* switching functions associated with trackwork. I incorporate this switchgear into the actuators of the actual point switches, as will be revealed.

It is the correct orientation of common crossing polarity that is the prime concern of virtually all the 'internal' switching of PW wiring. There is a general rule that relates

Fig. 9:8 Types of changeover switch.

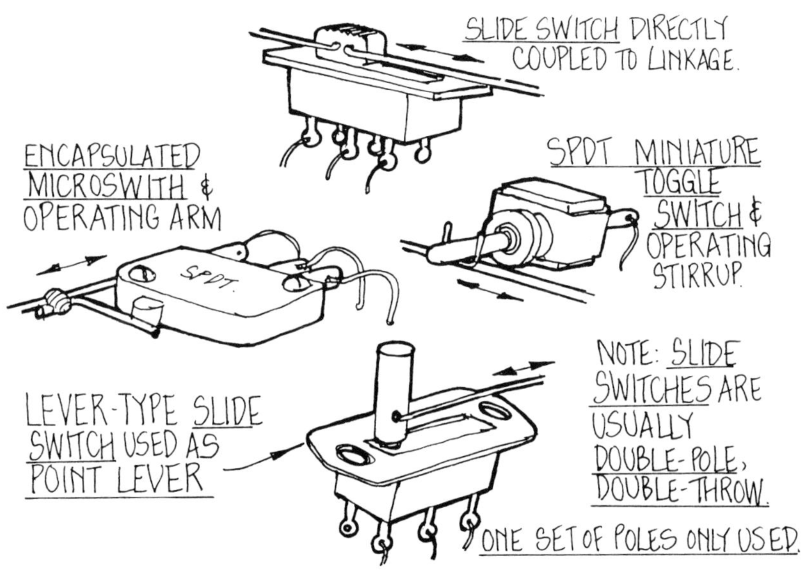

SLIDE SWITCH DIRECTLY COUPLED TO LINKAGE.
ENCAPSULATED MICROSWITH & OPERATING ARM
SPDT
SPDT MINIATURE TOGGLE SWITCH & OPERATING STIRRUP
NOTE: SLIDE SWITCHES ARE USUALLY DOUBLE-POLE, DOUBLE-THROW.
LEVER-TYPE SLIDE SWITCH USED AS POINT LEVER
ONE SET OF POLES ONLY USED.

JUMPER WIRES
(ASSUMING NO SEPARATE SECTION BEYOND TURNOUT)
CHANGEOVER (MICRO) SWITCHES
SWITCH BLADES BONDED THUS
+
−

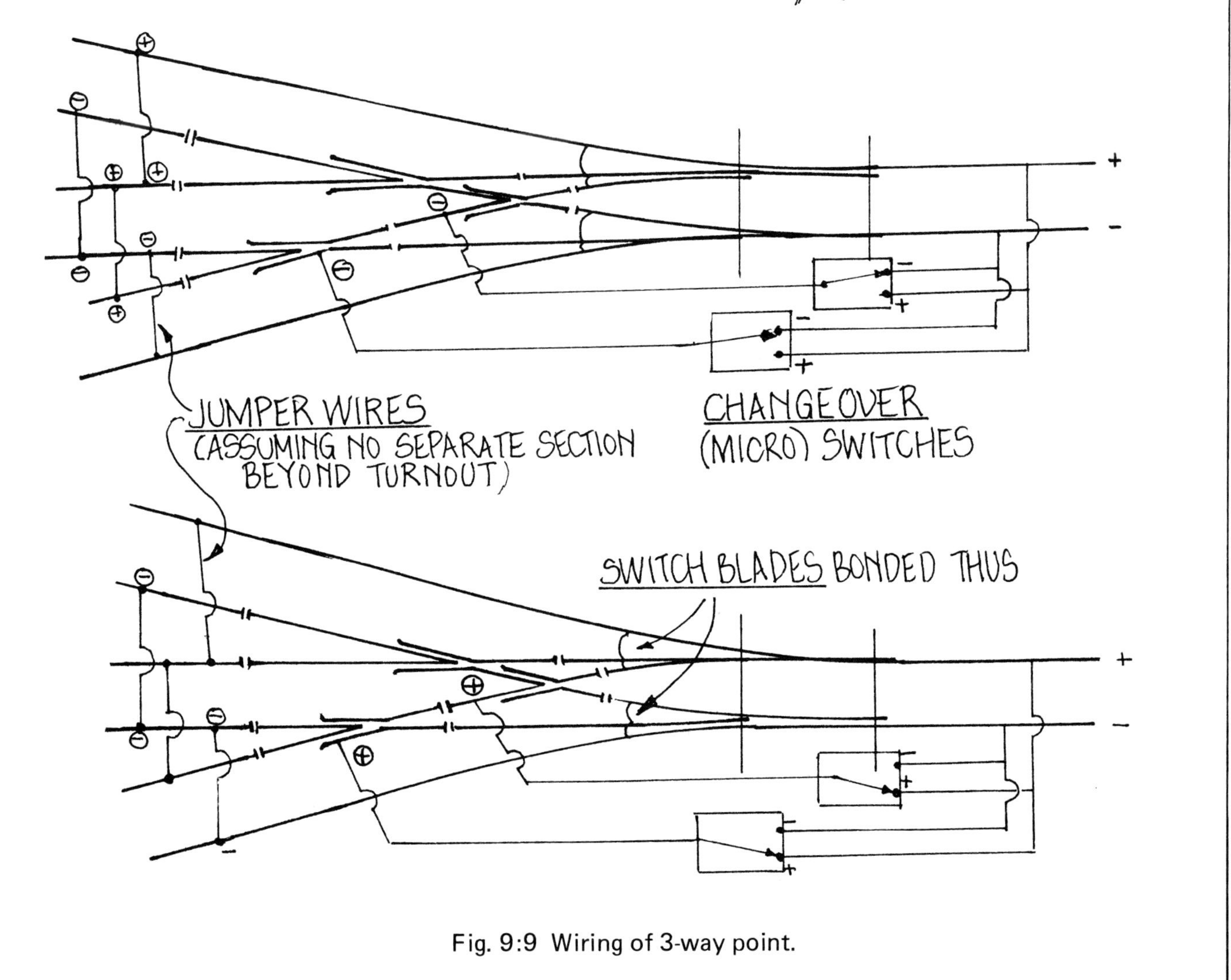

Fig. 9:9 Wiring of 3-way point.

the number of switches to the number of 'throws' of a formation. Hence, a plain turnout, with one pair of blades, and hence one 'throw', needs one microswitch. A tandem or overlapped turnout, with two pairs of blades (even if mixed up in the unholy gaggle of an overlap, there are still two sets of blades for all that it's called a 'three-throw switch' – highly confusing!) has two throws, and hence needs two switches. A single slip likewise has two sets of blades and two 'throws', so also needs two switches. A double slip, for all that it has four sets of blades, still only has two 'throws', as the pairs of blades at each end work in unison and hence only rate one 'throw'. In fact, single and double slips are identical in electrical terms, as might be gathered from the diagram.

Whilst it is true that every switch 'throw' rates a changeover switch, this is not necessarily true of crossings, which may often be linked together and fed by one switch. The most common incidence of this is the good old three-way point, where the third, central common crossing can be simply electrified by grouping it with either (but not of course, both!) of the adjacent crossings. At any time that the road is set for a diverging route, so that the loco will pass over the third crossing, it must obviously be at the same potential as the normal common crossing for that route, and at the opposite potential to the other 'normal' crossing. If, however, the opposing divergence is selected, then the linked common crossing will be at the opposite potential, that is, live to the opposite stockrail – and hence at the correct potential for the route thus selected. With the turnout set for 'straight through' running, it doesn't matter a hang which way the central crossing is switched, as nothing's going to run over it anyway. All this mediaeval Chinese will, hopefully be made clear by *Fig. 9:9*.

It is our old adversary, the plain diamond, that can be a bit of a headache, as it has nil throws and hence doesn't qualify for a switch under Rice's First Law. However, as is patently obvious, the common crossings still need to have their polarities reversed, although this is not the case with the obtuse crossings, which always retain the same polarity. So, some form of external or linked switch is needed, which can be a pain; I always forget about throwing a panel-mounted changeover switch, resulting in red lights and red faces as it all comes to a short-induced halt. It's better, if possible, to look to adjacent pointwork for a 'linked' solution. More often than not, the crossings of pointwork giving access to the diamond can provide the key, and this is a dodge I have often used, as on the East Suffolk Light at Orford Haven, where the set-up sketched at *Fig. 9:11* provided a simple solution.

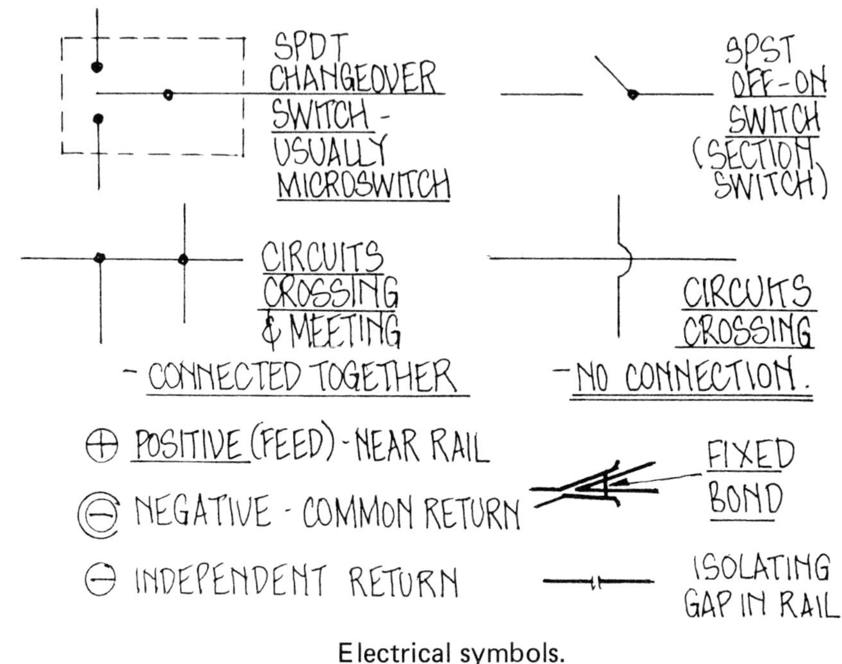

Electrical symbols.

Fig. 9:10 Basic wiring of diamond crossing.

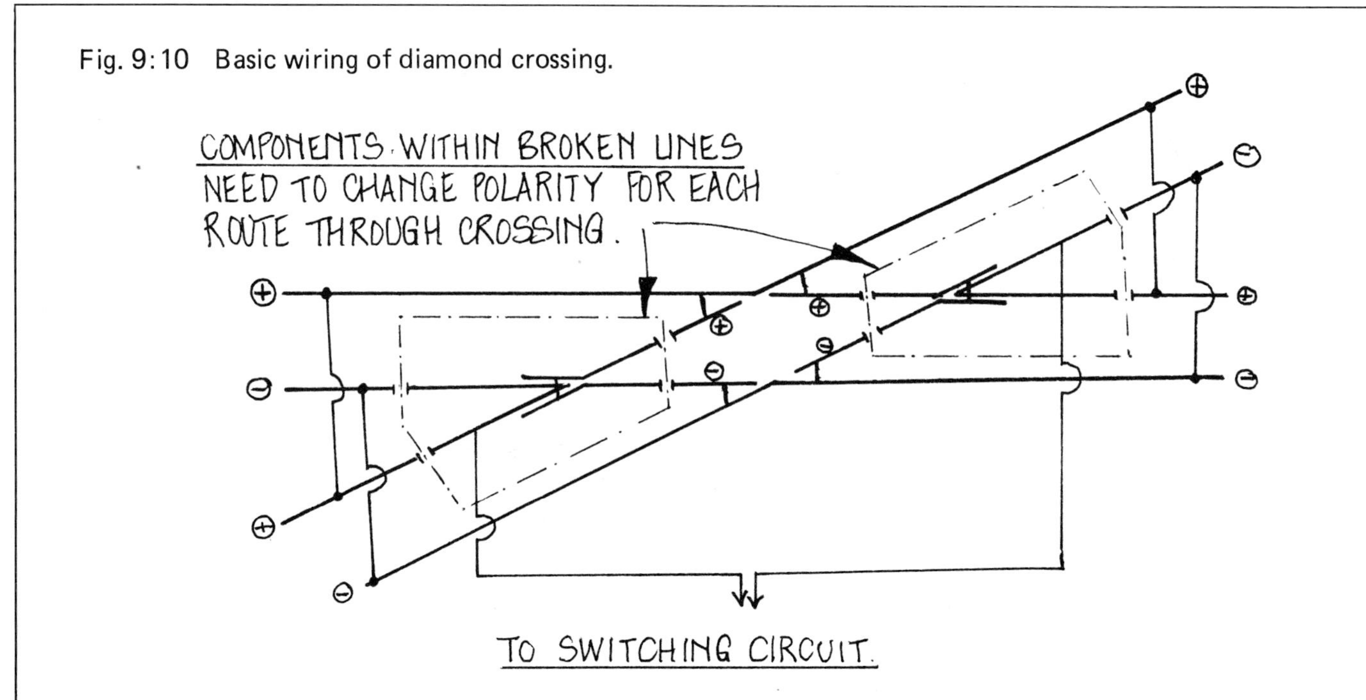

Unfortunately, this noble wheeze only works where all the trackwork concerned is within the same general 'section', the term used in this instance in its commonly understood electrical sense as describing a unit of track energized by a single feed. Where the two routes through the diamond relate to different electrical sections, then 'common linking' cannot be used, as it will tend to bridge around section switches, with interesting but generally undesirable results! The answer in this case is to use 'indirect linking', where the point throw rates two independent switches – or a 'double pole' switch catering for two independent circuits. This is what I did at 'Trerice', where the main line and Benalloch branch are in one section, and the loop is in another. (A quick peek at the track diagram at the start of Chapter 7 should make sense of the geography.) In this case, I utilized additional microswitches incorporated into the actuators of the loop toe points and the actual junction points to control the polarities of the diamond crossing, as in *Fig. 9:12*. The alternative, using a separate (panel mounted? or at least baseboard framing mounted) 'routeing switch', is shown in *Fig. 9:13*. All you need is a good memory to go with it!

The general wiring for a double slip is identical both to a single slip and also to the two turnouts that the system equates to. The changeover switch associated with each pair of switch tongues controls the polarity of the common crossing at the *opposite* end. The rest of the gubbins – switch blades, slip roads, closures and obtuse crossings – is simply split down the middle and wired as two unswitched units. No polarity changes anywhere among this lot, so in spite of the apparent complication, the electrics are very simple. *Fig. 9:14* – a double slip, but no different to a single in these terms – should show how it all works.

The basic principle of applying a changeover switch for every pair of point blades having an independent 'throw', and also of identifying and linking crossings of the same polarity, should take care of most internal 'switching functions'. This leaves only the fixed internal wiring to arrange – bonds and jumpers. Bonding is the linking of different parts of the formation into a single electrical unit – the common crossing is bonded by the strip of metal passing below the 'V' and both wing rails, which is soldered to them all as both a mechanical and electrical link. A similar link unites the parts of an obtuse crossing, and may be extended to incorporate external slip roads and internal closures. Switch blades are likewise bonded to the adjacent stockrails and to the closure rails. I generally bond rail-ends by soldering on the etched brass fishplates, thus killing no less than three birds with one stone; holding the rail-ends in alignment, bonding

Fig. 9:11 Wiring a diamond through adjacent pointwork (common section).

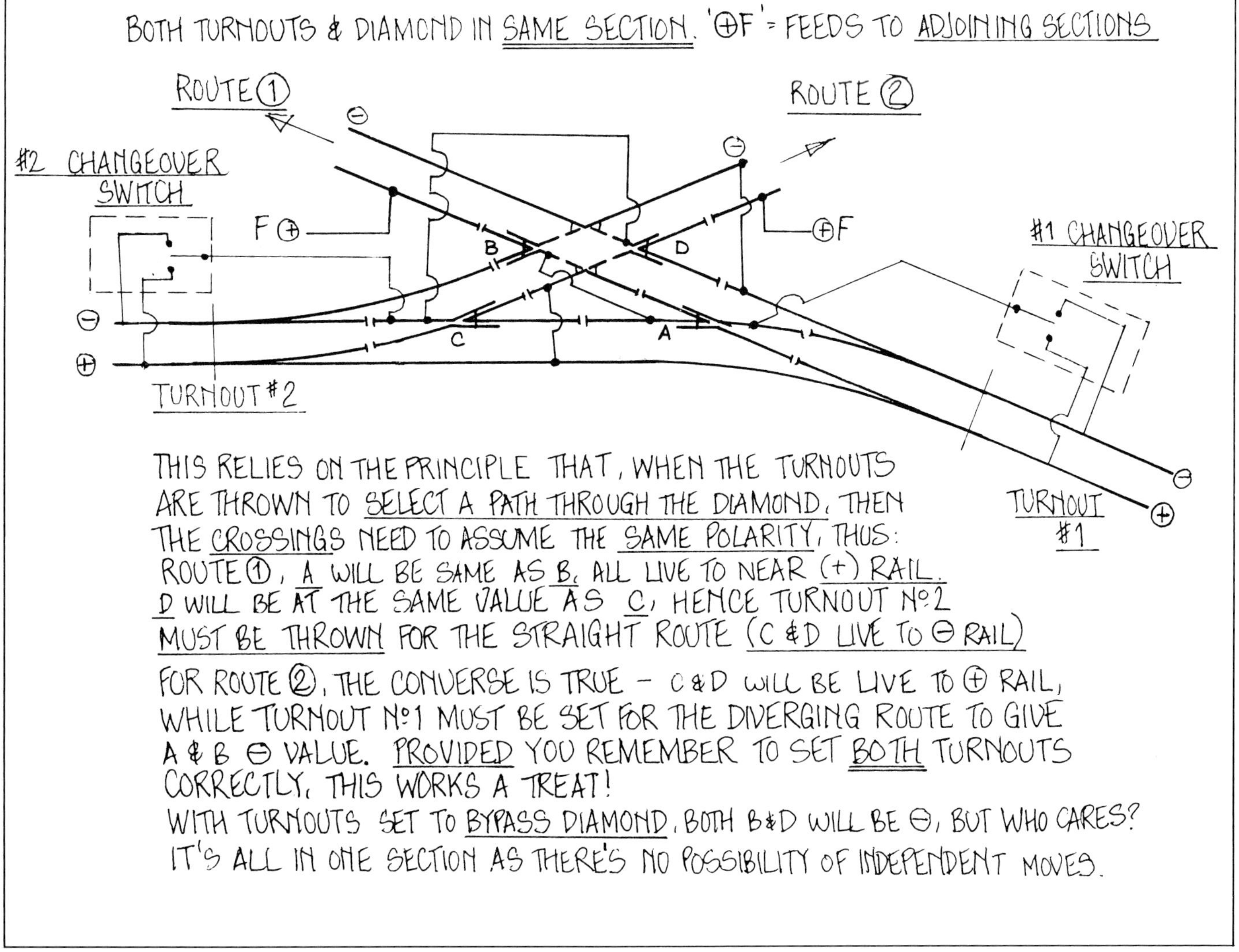

BOTH TURNOUTS & DIAMOND IN SAME SECTION. '⊕F' = FEEDS TO ADJOINING SECTIONS

ROUTE ①

ROUTE ②

#2 CHANGEOVER SWITCH

F ⊕

⊕F

#1 CHANGEOVER SWITCH

B

D

C

A

⊖

⊕

TURNOUT #2

TURNOUT #1

THIS RELIES ON THE PRINCIPLE THAT, WHEN THE TURNOUTS ARE THROWN TO SELECT A PATH THROUGH THE DIAMOND, THEN THE CROSSINGS NEED TO ASSUME THE SAME POLARITY, THUS:
ROUTE ①, A WILL BE SAME AS B, ALL LIVE TO NEAR (+) RAIL.
D WILL BE AT THE SAME VALUE AS C, HENCE TURNOUT Nº2 MUST BE THROWN FOR THE STRAIGHT ROUTE (C & D LIVE TO ⊖ RAIL)
FOR ROUTE ②, THE CONVERSE IS TRUE – C & D WILL BE LIVE TO ⊕ RAIL, WHILE TURNOUT Nº1 MUST BE SET FOR THE DIVERGING ROUTE TO GIVE A & B ⊖ VALUE. PROVIDED YOU REMEMBER TO SET BOTH TURNOUTS CORRECTLY, THIS WORKS A TREAT!
WITH TURNOUTS SET TO BYPASS DIAMOND, BOTH B & D WILL BE ⊖, BUT WHO CARES? IT'S ALL IN ONE SECTION AS THERE'S NO POSSIBILITY OF INDEPENDENT MOVES.

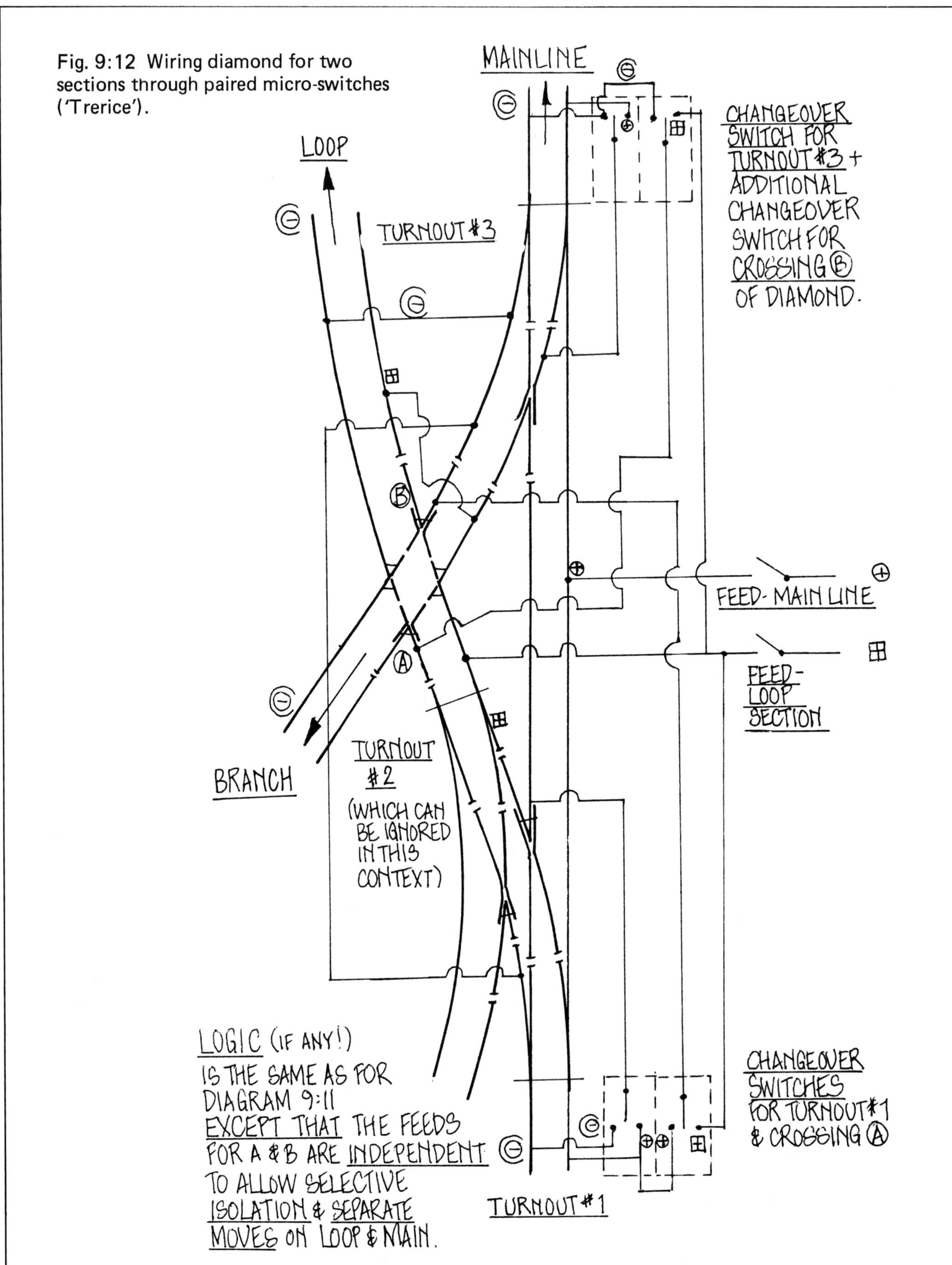

Fig. 9:12 Wiring diamond for two sections through paired micro-switches ('Trerice').

Fig. 9:13 Wiring diamond for independent circuits through routeing switch.

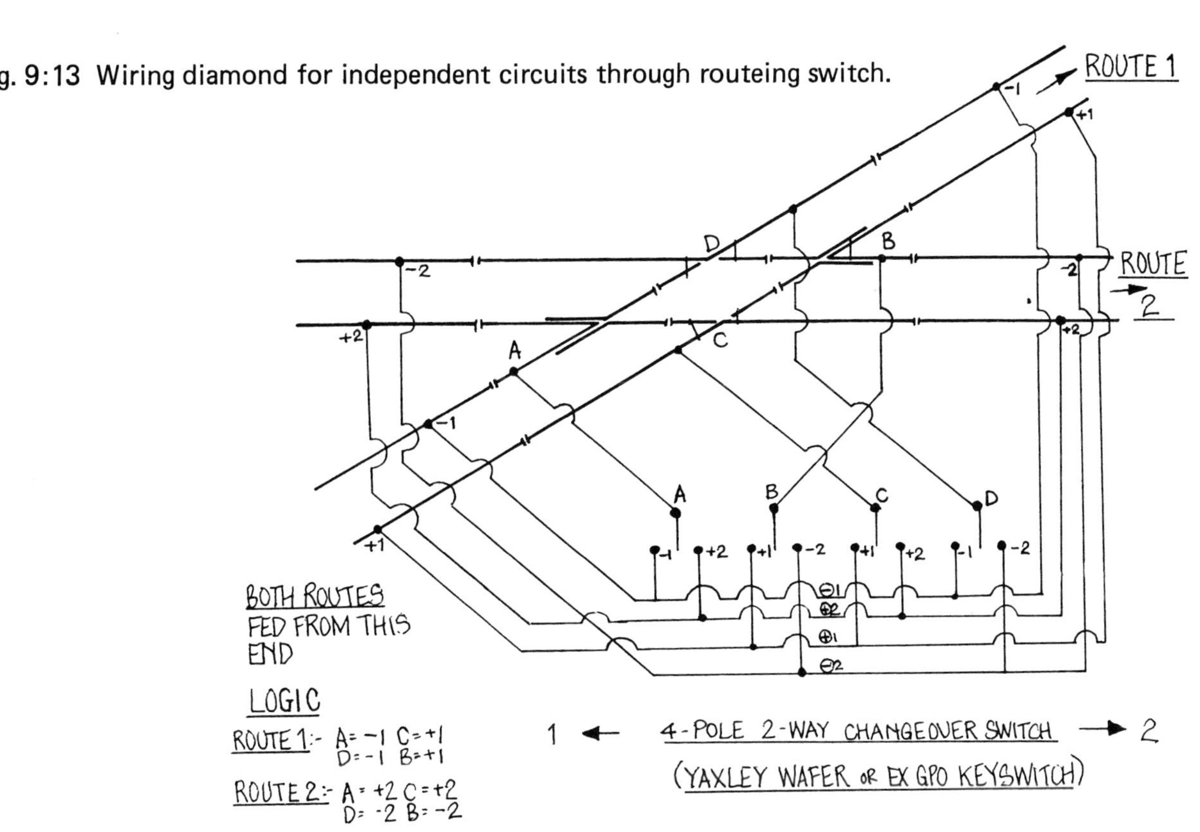

Fig. 9:14 Wiring of double or single slip.

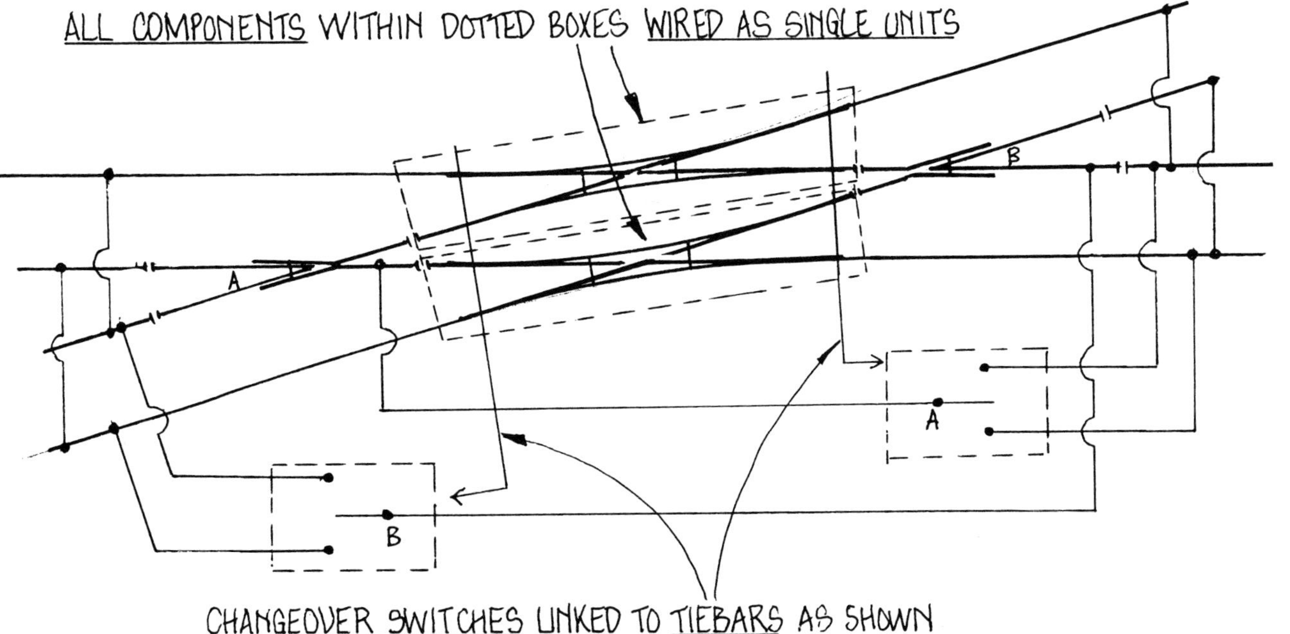

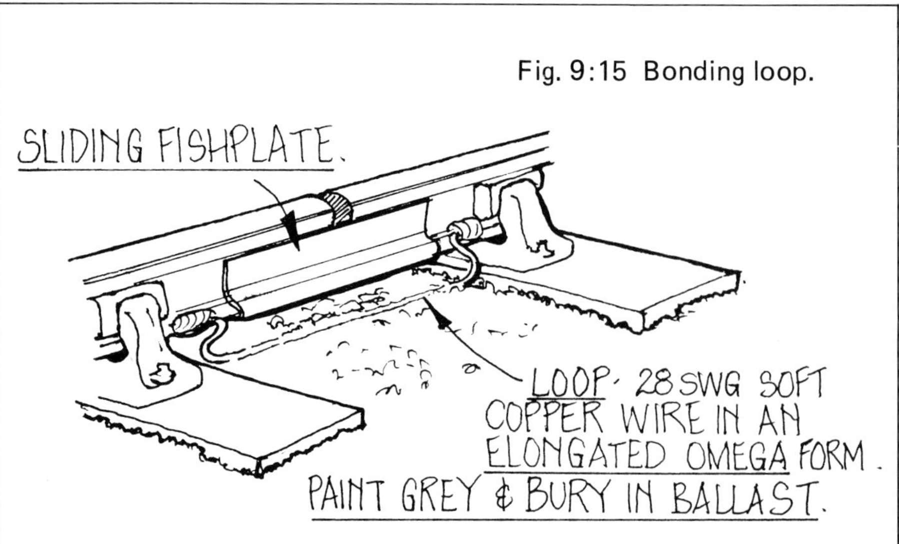

Fig. 9:15 Bonding loop.

them electrically, and decorating the joint cosmetically. If an expansion joint has been left, though, I don't rely on the sliding contact with the fishplate, preferring to add a loop of fine copper bonding wire, as in *Fig. 9:15*.

Jumpers are fixed wires that link different parts of the formation that, whilst not adjacent, need to be at the same polarity. They frequently 'by-pass' units, such as the common crossing, that are switched. As I've already described, I arrange jumper wires to run below the *paper* underlay but on *top* of the foam, where they are both invisible and protected from damage. To be on the safe side, I always duplicate these connections, so that a failed joint or fracture won't be a problem. Mind you, using the 28 SWG copper wire, it isn't the end of the world if a connection 'lets go'; it's easy enough to route a replacement on the surface of the paper, burying it in a little extra ballast. Indeed, if you're modelling the contemporary scene, such connections – part of the track circuiting – are wholly prototypical.

The last class of 'fixed wire' is a track feed, by which power is routed to the various parts of the trackwork from the external part of the wiring system – usually from some form of control panel. I attach feeds to the track using a 'tail' of the 28 SWG bare copper wire, which I run out to the edge of the paper underlay for connection to the wire bringing the power from its source. I have a dislike of below-baseboard wiring, especially on exhibition layouts. I generally arrange as much as possible of my layout wiring in a 'trough' along the rear of the baseboard, often in 'busbar' form. The various feeds are then routed above the baseboard but below the scenery, and the joint with the 'tail' to the track made above ground, disguised by some suitable scenic feature. In my experience, it's joints that give way, not wires – so long as you can get at those, maintenance is no problem. I have, anyway, found the chief cause of fractured joints to be dangling leads below baseboards becoming snagged; my 'buried' wiring is protected against such problems.

A last point on wiring generally – beware over-complication. There is no point in providing wiring to facilitate operational moves that you'll never make (but it's surprising how many people do). A lot of section wiring can be avoided by making use of the 'double positive' principle, where the electrical unit of the crossing is extended back for the whole length of a siding or other dead-end. When the turnout is set 'against' that road, both rails will be at the same potential, so nothing will move; just as effective as isolation, and very simple to achieve.

POINT ACTUATORS

The means by which turnouts are to operate in the broad sense is a matter of control philosophy. Solenoids, slow-action motors, wire-in-tube, rodding, fishing line and rubber bands – the possibilities are almost endless. However, at some stage, the drive, whatever its source, needs transmitting to the point tiebar. It will not have escaped your attention that, thus far, my points don't possess a tiebar! The reason is partly cosmetic, partly practical. Cosmetically, real point tiebars (more properly known as stretcher bars) are pretty small and insignificant, and when reduced to 4mm scale, certainly wouldn't be man enough to do the job. Anyway, we need them to be non-conducting, as our point blades are at opposite polarities – something the prototype doesn't have to worry about. So, I add a nice, fine dummy stretcher bar 'up top' for public consumption, and site the real thing below the trackbase, where it forms part of my 'point actuator'.

After experimenting with all manner of 'turnout operating units' and several types of dummy-tiebar system, I finally evolved the gadget illustrated, which I have dubbed a 'point actuator'. This device performs a number of functions; it incorporates a robust, insulated point tiebar, fitted with limit stops and an over-travel spring (omega loop), which takes care of all the mechanical shocks and loadings associated with turnout operation. This is particularly valuable if solenoid motors are being used, as these can deliver a pretty hefty shock loading, almost guaranteed to fracture the soldered joint to the point blades before too long. To drive this tiebar, there is a lever which, with its range of drillings, provides a considerable range of adjustment so that the input throw can be matched-up to the requirement for operating that particular turnout.

Also incorporated is the changeover switch for the common crossing, in the form of a spring-loaded encapsulated micro-switch of the SPDT configuration already described. I've used two types for this – the little clear-cased French job that the South London Group of the Scalefour Society supplies, or the Radiospares 331–398; both work in the same way, and I operate them by means of an arm soldered to the drive lever. If additional switching circuits are needed – as described for the powering of diamond crossings – then the microswitches can be 'stacked', and the operating arm made wide enough to engage both switches. Last part of the actuator is an input link, of 18 SWG piano wire running in fine brass tube; a short length of the tube soldered to the end of this link takes a standard twin-screw wiring connector (liberated from 'chocolate block' connector strip). A similar arrangement on the end of the drive system enables the actuator to be simply connected up or removed. I also use small chocolate-block connectors to link the wiring from crossing and stockrails to the actuator.

The construction and installation of the actuator should be apparent from the sketches. Nothing is very critical, and each one only costs a few pence to make. The actual connection to the point blades is by means of a couple of dropper wires which pass down through the small clearance slots in the paper underlay, and then through the generous clearance holes provided in the foam and trackbase, to engage in the two small pieces of fine brass capillary tube soldered to the dummy tiebar. The droppers are free in this tube, which means that they can turn with the movement of the mechanism, preventing any distorting torque being applied to the point tongues. This also allows the actuator to be removed if necessary without disturbing the connections to the blades, which are simply slid out of the tubes. The timber bearer on which the actuator is constructed is made long enough to span the track formation above, being

Fig. 9:16 Point actuator.

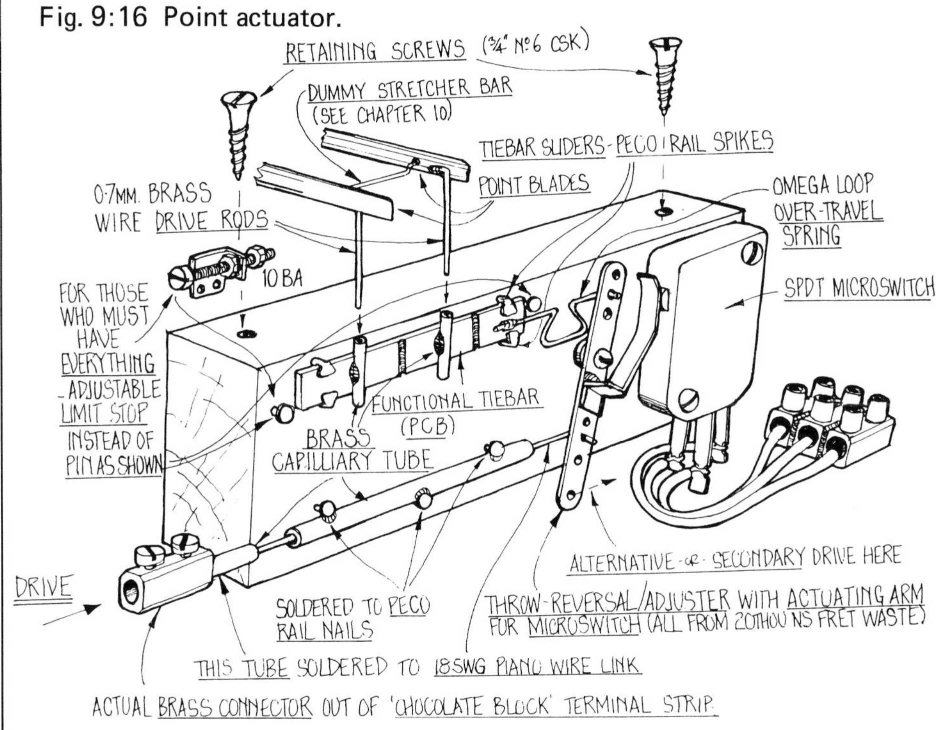

The Rice patent point actuator in all its homespun glory. The microswitch is the Petercem 'Microcontact' CM 3804, obtainable from the South London Area Group of the Scalefour Society (usually on sale at Scalefour events and shows attended by any South London Group layout.

retained by a screw through the trackbase outside the formation width each side.

The actuators are built up and tested on the bench before being installed below the trackbase. Obviously, clearance will be needed beneath the trackbase when this is installed on the layout, not usually a problem – my actuators work out about $1\frac{1}{2}$in deep. You also need to be able to get at the input connection. As this is at one end or other of the actuator, and hence close to (or beyond) the edge of the trackbase, it can be reached from above. However, I also like to be able to gain access from beneath, just in case I need to remove the actuator for service or repair at some future time. Made with reasonable care, though, these actuators are robust, long-lived and trouble-free. I haven't bust one yet. I generally drive my actuators by mechanical linkage – either wire-in-tube or rodding, but they are truly universal in application.

I don't know of any commercially made point actuators of this sort, but there are some turnout operating units (TOU) on the market, Exactoscale having a particularly neat cam-operated design. Point motors I use in moderation, and I'm no great lover of the things, especially solenoids. They are an added complication, with more to go wrong than a mechanical system. The more recent types of motor-drive slow-action units are better, with the Fulgurex and the American 'Tortoise' (see suppliers index) being the best of them, for my money. The only solenoid I will entertain is the Maygib, which is much softer in its action than the 'kerwhallop' H&M. But, taken all-in, I much prefer some form of mechanical point drive, either from a pukka lever frame (with or without full tappet locking) or from a simple slider. I use a rodded system based on John Flack's $\frac{1}{16}$in NS rod and hefty, home-made cranks, all guided by Peco steel track spikes. This is carried across baseboard joints by one or other of the simple little gadgets sketched, and I run the rods along the base of the rear-of-baseboard 'channel' containing the wiring. On 'Trerice', I've arranged the turnouts for dual operation; at exhibitions, they are worked off a bank of 'sliders' in the St Dennis Junction fiddleyard, while at home, an extension rod off the 'other end' of the actuator comes through the front framing of the baseboard and terminates in a little turned brass push-pull knob.

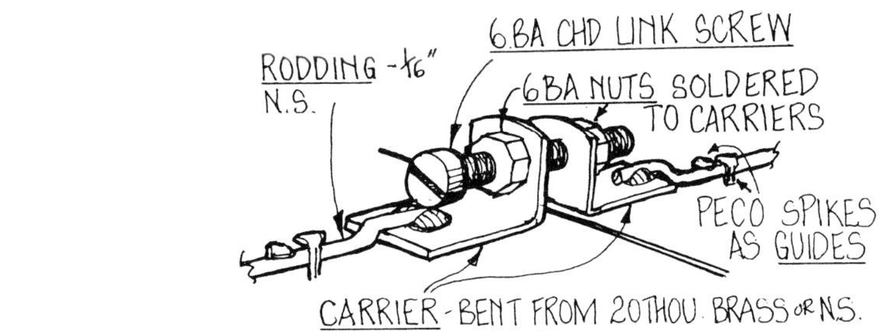

Fig. 9:17 Carrying mechanical point drive across a baseboard joint.

SUMMARY

I could go on discussing the ancillary side of track installation for another couple of chapters – many perfectly workable schemes haven't even rated a mention in these pages. But, at the end of the day, I'm happier describing a system which has evolved over more than fifteen years and nearly a dozen layouts, and which I know to be effective and reliable – not to mention cheap! But one thing that I would stress is the importance of considering the wiring and point actuation schemes at the *design* stage, rather than indulging in a bout of belated headscratching once all the track's down. Robustness and simplicity are the keynotes to success, in my experience. And, if I had to single out one thing that makes a crucial contribution to reliability, I would opt for limit stops in the point actuating mechanism, so that no hefty shock or mechanical loadings are imposed on the ever-weak point blade/tiebar joint.

There's a lot more to permanent way than rail, sleepers and ballast. Real track is rich in texture and detail, resolved in a subtle and complex colouring. L. E. COPELAND

CHAPTER TEN

DETAILING, PAINTING & WEATHERING

It is only comparatively recently that the standard of detailing and finishing of model PW seems to have caught up with the levels now accepted as 'normal' for locomotives, stock and structures. There have been superbly detailed models in these latter spheres for a good half-century, but only in the last few years have we had chairs for our BH track that actually look like the real thing. To my way of thinking, the development of, firstly, the Scalefour/MJT cast whitemetal chairs, followed by the truly excellent C & L mouldings, have been one of the most significant developments in fine-scale railway modelling. Now, it's a bit of a job to get the rest of the PW fixtures and fittings up to the same standard.

The fixing of the actual chairs I undertake, as described, during the track construction; likewise, most of the fishplates are installed as the PW is laid. So, what other details are there to add? The answer depends, as do so many modelling answers, on observation of the prototype. But, to set you looking, try this list for starters: rail anchors, level markers (those small white posts driven into the cess to set the 'top' alignment), AWS ramps, treadles and detectors, detonator placers (ever seen one of those modelled? I bet Frank Dyer's got 'em!), track circuit jumpers, clamp-on tiebars (used where the gauge shows signs of spreading), track alignment pegs, track drains, point stretcher rods and tiebars, facing point locks, stop-blocks, ballast bins (for 'scalpings' – small ballast used to maintain the packing of the sleepers and hence the 'top'). Modellers of the contemporary scene have even more to tangle with – CWR expansion joints, point heaters, lineside cable ducts and relay cabinets, point motors, hot-box detectors and all other manner of techno-gubbins. Most people these days seem to reckon on including such fundamentals as point rodding (although the posts carrying the accompanying signal wires seem to appear less often), while some other lineside features, such as mileposts and gradient markers, instruction boards (Stop! Pin Down Brakes! Whistle!), speed restrictions and trespass notices have long been favourite train-set accessories.

All-in-all, there's plenty of scope for detailing of PW, and there is no doubt that the inclusion of some of these prototype features adds both interest and versimilitude to the track – although it's possible to overdo things! Colin Waite does some exquisite etched phosphor-bronze cranks and proper brass rodding stools which are fiddly but worth the trouble. They go with the ½mm square wire – all available from Scalefour Stores, if you're of that persuasion.

It is with pointwork that the addition of some details can become tricky, as the bothersome but necessary electrics complicate matters. The worst problem is tiebars and stretcher rods, of which there may be three or four on a long pair of switches. I use two methods to add these stretcher rods, and a third method for dummy tiebars. (The difference is that the tiebar, or stretcher bar, is usually of flat plate bolted to the switch tongues with angle brackets, while the stretcher rods have threaded rods and are nutted direct into the web of the switch rails; the bar takes the drive from the operating linkage, while the stretcher rods just reinforce the switch rails and keep them from spreading under load). The complications in representing these vital features arise, of course, from the opposite electrical polarities of the switch blades, calling for some insulation in the equation somewhere.

The sketch shows how I overcome these problems. For stretcher rods, I have generally adapted the original P4 solution, where the rod is soldered to one switch rail, and passes through an oversize hole in the opposing one, the difference being taken up with a suitable insulating medium. The Protofour solution was Araldite; Rice prefers a tiny slice of plastic insulation sleeving off of GPO (telephone cable, the single-core type, or, alternatively, a wrapping of epoxy-soaked tissue paper around the end of the rod where it locates in the oversize hole (see sketch). Alternatively, the two halves of the rod (which is fashioned from 0.45mm brass wire) are separated by a short central sleeve, 'Evo-Stuck' in place; check for electrical insulation *before* installation! And don't dally with the soldering iron or you'll melt

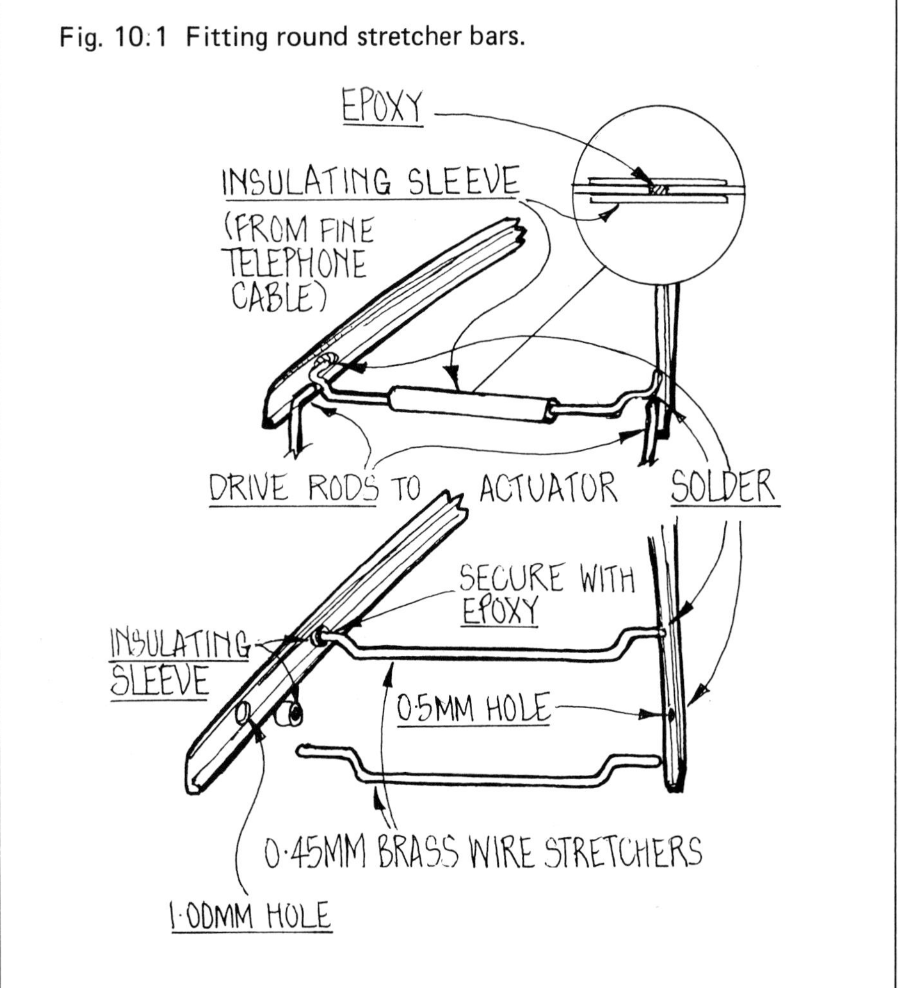

Fig. 10:1 Fitting round stretcher bars.

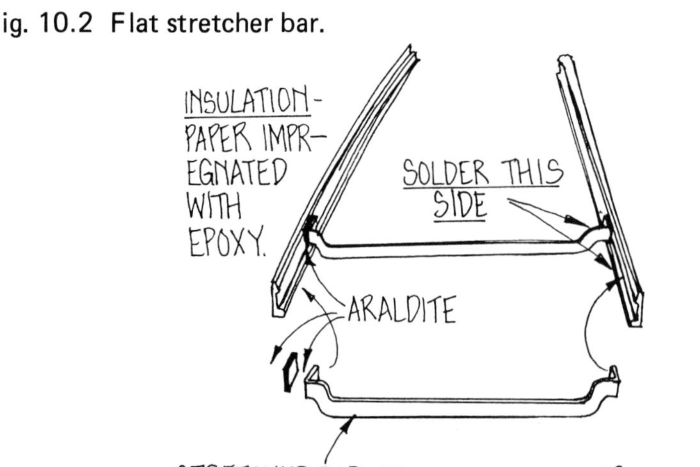

Fig. 10.2 Flat stretcher bar.

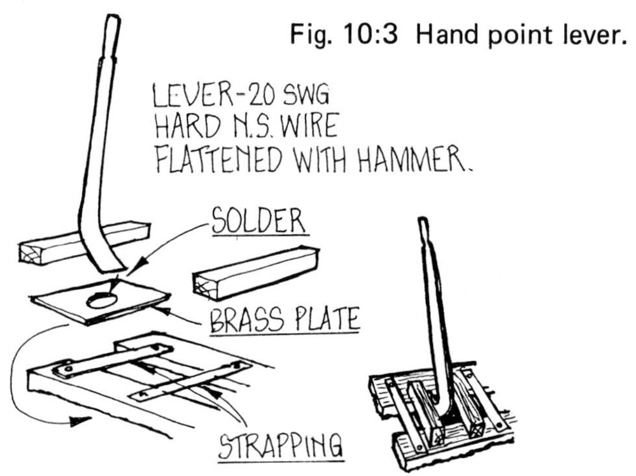

Fig. 10:3 Hand point lever.

Fig. 10.4 Rail-built stop block.

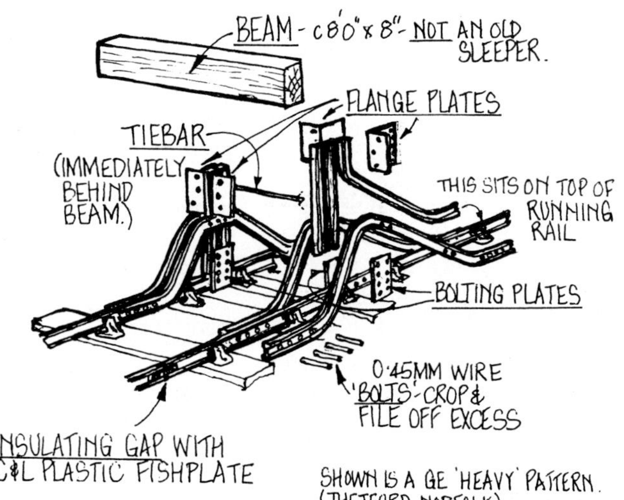

the sleeve. Some prototype stretcher rods have such a sleeve – it's an internally threaded screw adjuster, used to accurately set the length of the stretcher.

Such stretcher bars are not, of course, strong enough to actually locate the switch tongues – this is done by the very substantial below-trackbase tiebar included in the point actuator. All the visible rods and bars are purely cosmetic, none more so than the flat plate tiebar illustrated in my next sketch, fashioned out of fine brass strip (fret waste again!), soldered to one tongue and Araldited to the other, with a paper insulation strip to keep the various volts apart. This is one track detail that can't really be added until the point actuator is installed to take the actual mechanical load of the tongues. If you need to remove the actuator, don't forget to clamp (Dinky curler) and wedge (couple of offcuts of ply sleeper strip) the switch tongues to preserve the delicate dummy stretcher bar – it won't take the strain.

Facing point locks, thankfully, don't have to work, not even on Ray Hammond's layouts, so all that's needed is the cover for this mechanism – although in case you wonder what they're all about, there's a picture of one in the altogether, from which you'll note that an extra tiebar is involved, not to mention divers cranks, rods, strapping plates and linkages; better keep the cover on ... The type of FPL and cover, along with other details such as AWS ramps and point rodding (round or square bar, type of stool?), will vary from one company (or BR Region) to another; consult the prototype for authenticity.

Another telling detail that is omitted on a surprising number of occasions is the ubiquitous hand point lever, a device cleverly designed to give as many railwaymen as possible a long retirement on disability pay with ricked backs and double hernias. There are some nice – but fragile – castings available, so I contrive my own from strip or flattened wire as in the sketch. These are still vulnerable, but can be bent back into shape rather than breaking off. There are, of course, variants on the basic design, the more so as you go back into the pre-grouping area (or wander into more distant sidings still laid with older PW components), so be sure that you are modelling something appropriate.

And then, of course, there are buffer stops, among the most distinctive and 'modellogenic' of PW furniture. Strictly speaking, they lie outside the scope of this narrative, but they are so characteristic that they need careful modelling and accurate research. Provided that it is not called upon to perform its intended function too hard or too often, the rail-built bufferstop is a very long-lived piece of equipment, and plenty of pre-grouping specimens survive unto this day. The modelling world woke up to the enormous variety in bufferstop design when Mike Sharman set about producing a selection in his whitemetal 'Mike's Models' range. These are still available, but aren't really up to the modern finescale mark, having patterns made using the old Code 95 'scale' bullhead rail. Provided you don't need too many of them, rail-built bufferstops are pleasant and rewarding modelling projects, and my sketch shows how I go about it. These are best made in steel rail, which is far easier to bend in the vertical plane than is the much harder drawn nickel-silver.

I could go on describing PW fittings and fixtures for about another *Guardian* leadersworth, but I think that I've said enough to suggest that the application of the observing eye and a bit of scrap rail and Plastikard can transform bald PW into the visually rich and varied path traversed by traditional steam trains or the limestoned techno-desert inhabited by HSTs and the like. The essential point is that the track is just as much a model as it is a functional component of a miniature railway system; and I can't help feeling that most of us – me included – have concentrated on the functional side of our track at the expense of its appearance.

PAINTING AND WEATHERING TRACK

I think that, even in the rather 'bright and shiny' world of 'mainstream' modelling, the train running on the chrome-plated girder carried on bright, shiny brown plastic sleepers (all of identical hue), over a totally uniform (because it is unadorned grey foam rubber) ballast bed, is on the way out. Most people reckon, at the very least, to paint the sides of the rail some suitable shade of grimy rust, while the more percipient modellers find that a blast of matt paint and some variegated ballast can make even standard Code 100 Flexi-track a lot less visually offensive.

Painting the rails and using a 'natural' looking ballast has been standard finescale practice for a long time, but these are really only the basics; real track is a wonderfully subtle and varied mosaic of colours and textures that takes some effort to emulate – something, I must say, that our American cousins have long paid more attention to than the average UK modeller, for all that their basic track's not a patch on ours. So, it's possible to take the track-finishing process a lot further than decent ballast and a spot of rail-paint. The natural variation in sleeper colour that results from the staining process is a good starting point, taking away one of the most common causes of 'over uniform' track. Real sleepers may start off a strong brown-black when freshly creosoted, but once *in situ,* track dust (from the ballast, constantly being broken down by the action of the track as trains pass over it) soon tones the colour down, while the action of rain and sunlight weathers the timber to a grey-brown and finally to a pale fawn/silver. These are the sort of colours that I aim for when staining my ply sleepers – to my eye, nothing looks worse than strong, dark tones that 'leap out' at you.

In the naturalistic world of finescale model railways, the aim is to get everything to harmonize, to blend in seemlessly into a convincing whole. Anything that unduly stands out can easily upset our carefully contrived illusion, where careful attention to that old bogey, colour perspective, is the key to success. So, even with subtly coloured sleepers and naturally variegated ballast, I still go in for some further toning down of the finished PW to help it to 'sit in' with the rest of the landscape modelling. I use two techniques to accomplish this – airbrushing with acrylic paint, and dry-powder dusting.

As well as getting the track to read correctly in its visual context (i.e. look right where it is, if you're not impressed by art-speak), the powder and paint colourings can be used to accentuate the differences between the various areas or types of PW. As I think I remarked about a hundred or two pages ago, one of the oldest modelling chestnuts is the back coal siding ballasted and maintained to main line 'prize length' standard. Having gone to the trouble – I hope – of modelling such track with, say, 30ft panels, pre-group sleepers none too well-aligned, and ash or cinder ballast complete with a due complement of weeds and rubbish, it can be further – if subtly – differentiated from running lines by careful use of colour. The sleepers, for instance, can be 'faded' a bit more by dry-brushing with a pale silvery grey shade of acrylic, while the patchy nature of the ballast can be suggested by some dry powder weathering, using cheap artist's pastels ground up on a coarse file and applied with a soft camel-hair brush. The rail-sides can be a darker, dirtier shade of 'rust' – they have, after all, been there a good long time.

Rusty rails are one of the great problems for the aspirant builder of truly realistic track, as the scenic/visual and electrical requirements are in direct conflict. In truth, only very heavily-used lines would have railheads as shiny as those on the average model railway, while much track should exhibit no degree of 'polish' at all. The back coal-siding should, in truth, have the running surface of the rails fully as rusty and grimed as the rail-sides and chairs. I do this where I can (where only stock, not locos, need access), and I try and keep non-running rails – checkrails and point wing-rails – suitably rusty. All it calls for is occasional touching-up, and a modicum of care when track-cleaning – an operation I find that I only carry out occasionally since adopting steel rail.

I carry out all my track painting – rail sides included – in Humbrol acrylics. Painting rail sides calls for a tolerably good brush – I use a synthetic-bristle Daler 'Dalon' sable substitute, about a No. 3 in the D77 series. I mix my own 'rail' shade, a sort of darkish red ochre, and I generally paint the rail as part of the basic trackmaking process. This includes the chairs as well, and is a fiddly and time-consuming business, but one that needs doing thoroughly and neatly. I did try picking out the wooden keys in a different, grey-brown shade on one length of bullhead, but decided the effect was more fussy than convincing. Just as well, given the probable insanity if undertaken on any amount of PW!

Fishplate bolts on running lines are regularly oiled, which imparts a blackish hue to these components, something that is worth picking out. Likewise, point slide chairs are greased – put a lick of a dark grey on the slide surfaces, and once all the track painting is complete, I spot a tiny 'dob' of Vaseline onto these faces; can't have my blades sticking, can I? And it's a nice finishing touch.

With all this detail painting completed, I then set about toning down the final result. As with most things in our modelled scene, viewing model track at the usual sort of distance of two or three feet is equivalent to looking at real track 50–75 yards away, so a bit of 'atmospheric colour dilution' is in order. I use an 'atmospheric tint' for this – a faintly warm, very pale bluish-grey acrylic, just drifted on as a very fine spray from the airbrush. It's particularly important to take the 'sting' out of the rail paint which, if not tamed in this way, is apt to 'stare' a bit.

The last effect that I try and incorporate is the general unifying weathering – or possibly, contamination – dictated by the nature of the track ballast and also of the traffic passing over it. So, for instance, a main running line might receive a dusting of ground-up pastel of a shade equivalent to, or a tone or two lighter than, the predominant colour of the ballast. This is applied on a big, soft camel-hair brush (a wide make-up 'blusher' brush from Boots), and the surplus blown and tapped off. Other lines might be more affected by the fall-out from the traffic; such was certainly the case on the china-clay branches that inspired 'Trerice', where the ballast – and just about everything else, if it comes to it – was overlaid with a film of china-clay dust, giving a very characteristic whitened appearance to the PW which I have attempted to represent with a hodge-podge of talcum powder, French chalk, pastel and airbrushed acrylic. Lines carrying, say, iron ore, limestone or coal, might be similarly affected, calling for application of appropriately coloured powder weathering and maybe a bit of airbrush tinting as well. I don't know if overgrowth and general weed-infestation counts as 'weathering', but it's certainly a preoccupation if your layout includes anything other than main running lines. Have a look at the picture of Martyn Welch's wonderful 'Hursley' (*Model Railway Journal* No. 40), and see what a bit of couch-grass can do for your dead-ends. It really needs introducing at the constructional stage, being substituted for the ballast when the sleepers are laid – I've tried chopped-up sisal string, plumbers hemp, rayon flock, sieved sawdust, dried teabag contents and pukka ground foam, depending upon the virulence of the vegetation being represented. Other alternatives include lint and carpet felt – it's a field where experiment pays dividends. Colouring can be applied at one of several points – before installation, once *in situ*, but before the rails are added, and at the weathering and finishing stage. I usually end up by having a go at all three stages. Convincing weedy sidings are not easy to achieve, I find!

PAINTING PLASTIC-SLEEPERED TRACK

My remarks so far have been aimed at my own style of all-ply-sleeper trackbuilding, but a lot of folk restrict this to pointwork and use C&L Flexi-track elsewhere. It's quite a job to paint this so that it 'matches in' with ply sleeper, and in this instance, I adopt a rather different approach. I have personally found a mix of stained ply and painted plastic sleepers unconvincing, so I prefer to put them on equal footing by painting the ply as well. To start with, I paint the completed Flexi-track and either the finished point formations (if they're being built on templates, then 'lifted and laid') or the prepared timbering, with an aerosol tin of car spray primer in the usual neutral grey colour.

With the sleepering all of a similar shade, and exhibiting the same general surface texture and absorbency, it's not now too difficult to colour the sleepers with the acrylic paint in my preferred grey-brown shade, either by airbrushing or by dry-brushing with a stiff hogshair brush. The rails and chairs are picked out in the appropriate shade as already described, and the rest of the toning down and weathering process similarly applied once the track has been laid and ballasted. 'Woolverstone' had its track (Ratio bases and individually built P&C work from ply-and-occasional rivet + C & L chairs) painted thus, and it doesn't look too bad, though I still think it lacks the subtlety of the all-ply track on 'Trerice' and other more recent efforts.

Painting. With pre-stained sleepers, the main painting job is the rail and chairs. I use matt acrylic to my own 'rail rust' recipe (black, red, yellow and khakhi) applied in a fairly fluid state using a reasonable sable to keep it neat around the chair-bases. The whole track is then 'toned down' with the airbrush, in this case using a warm pale grey colour just 'misted' on. Track is usually quite a light colour – most model track is far too dark.

I must confess that I haven't, thus far, experimented with a mix of C&L Flexi-track and 'built *in situ*' P&C work as described in this book. I suppose that I'm getting old and finicky (as well as tending to build relatively modest layouts, at least so far as the amount of track involved), but I find the appearance of even the C&L Flexi-track a bit lacking beside the subtly-coloured and more characterful, fully-keyed track that I can build by my own methods, so I'm not inclined to try, though I can't see why there should be any difficulty.

TIME TO RIDE INTO THE SUNSET

Well, there you have it. I'm not making any claims as to the scope and completeness of this tome, for all its not-inconsiderable length. It is not a definitive work, merely a particular and partisan approach to the business of making finescale track in 4mm scale. It has, to be frank, taken a lot of writing, and been subject to the odd spot of revision (spot the joins!). I'm still experimenting with different methods of doing the job, with underlay materials, painting techniques, ballast and different ways of wiring. What is in these pages, I know works; a good deal of the dodges I dreamed up and tried, didn't. There's still a lot more to do before the question of truly excellent model PW is really sewn up definitively, but if what I've suggested is a step on the way, then I'll retire, happy, to my cell. Happy platelaying!

GLOSSARY

GENERAL TERMS

Formation – The completed earthworks along a line of railway.

Track formation – An assemblage of P & C work forming a complex of track.

Sub-roadbed – The underlying structure on which track is laid, including earthworks, hardcores, drainage media and structures.

Roadbed – The material immediately beneath the track, usually a free-draining coarse rubble foundation topped with ballast.

A road – a single line of railway.

Permanent Way – The finished trackwork on a railway, so called to distinguish it from the 'temporary way' laid down to facilitate construction.

The works – The engineering features needed by a railway – bridges, earthworks, etc. 'Way & works' = engineering plus trackwork.

Ruling – Applied to a gradient, curve or clearance. The most critical situation on a given stretch of railway, the determinant of that which can operate over it.

P & C work – Point and crossing work – the fabrication of turnouts and other more complex formations.

Easement – The practice of connecting straight and curved sections of track by a progressively tightening or transitional curve.

Cant – An inclination applied either to individual rails (to match 'coning' of wheels) or to a road, to produce super-elevation.

Super-elevation – The practice of raising the outer rail on curved track to help counter the effects of centrifugal force.

'Top' – The vertical alignment of the permanent way.

'Creep' – The propensity of a line of track to try and advance in the general direction of the traffic passing over it.

'Bearing' – The load imposed by PW or individual PW components on that which lies beneath them, i.e. bearing of chair on sleeper. Often expressed in tons per square inch.

Running rail – A rail or part of a rail over which the wheels of traffic pass – called thus to distinguish it from passive rails, such as check-rails, wing-rails and guards.

Running line – A road carrying through traffic, part of a route, as opposed to a siding, loop, bay or dock, etc.

Turnout - Track formation where two roads diverge. Can be described as semi-curved (one straight, one curved road), curved (both roads curved on same hand) and 'Y' (both roads curved, opposite hands). Consists of one set of switches and one crossing.

Compound turnout – Formation where two or more roads diverge. Turnout using more than one set of switches and three or more crossings. Takes various forms: Most common as '3-way', either tandem (diverging roads opposite hands) or overlapped (roads same hand).

Diamond crossing – Two roads crossing at an angle; no connection between roads.

Slip diamond – As above, with connections between roads. Two routes only connected give a single slip; all four routes give a double or compound slip. The slip roads can be within the diamond (inside), partly within (semi-outside) or outside.

Lead – The internal length of a turnout – the distance from nose of switch to nose of crossing.

Nominal radius – The averaged radius of a transitioned curve.

'Railway curves' – Draughtsman's templates for drawing out easements and curves in one operation; the standard relationship of transition to fixed radius.

Crossing angle – The method of defining the degree of divergence of two lines of rail or roads in P & C work; expressed as a gradient, i.e. 1 in 8 (or No. 8).

BASIC PW COMPONENTS

Ballast – The material used to locate the track, being packed below and between the sleepers, and in some cases covering the entire PW up to the railheads

Sleepering – The timber, stone, metal or concrete baulks or blocks used to support rail and hold the track in gauge. Principally – cross sleepering, the normal PW practice, at 90° to rails, and longitudinal, lying parallel to and beneath the rails. Often referred to as 'timbers', especially in respect of P & C work, or 'baulks' if longitudinal.

Transom – The cross-timber used to set the gauge in longitudinally-sleepered track.

Chair – An iron casting used in conjunction with bullhead or double-headed rail, to support and locate the rail, and to improve the bearing on the sleeper. The rail is normally kept in place by use of a resilient wedge fixing, or key.

Baseplate – An iron casting functioning in a similar way to a chair, but used with flat-bottom or Vignoles rail. The rail is held by spikes, clips or bolts.

Spike – A claw-headed square section nail used to hold down flat-bottom rail.

Screw spike (rail screw, chair screw) – A tapered screw having a square-section head with a large flange beneath it. Used both to hold down FB rail and to locate and retain chairs onto sleepers.

Lockspike – A form of spike incorporating a sprung shank designed to expand and lock into timber sleepers.

Elastic spike – A sprung head spike for use with flat-bottom rail, designed to impart vertical resilience without loss of lateral location.

Trenail – An oak peg used to hold a chair down to a sleeper.

Fang bolt – A nut-and-bolt assembly incorporating a large square cast and cleated washer used to hold down chairs in place of screw spikes and trenails.

Slide chair or slide plate – A special type of chair used beneath point blades. It is bolted to the stock-rail, and incorporates a lubricated surface on which the blades slide.

Special chairs – Chairs used in situations other than plain track; includes crossing nose chairs, switch heel chairs, and check-rail chairs – these 'multiple rail' chairs are sometimes confusingly referred to as 'bridge chairs'.

Bridge chair – As above, or, more commonly, a chair having a narrower but longer base than a standard chair, designed for use on rail bearer baulks – the longitudinal sleepers often used on bridge deckings. These chairs are used in other situations where the standard chair base did not suit, e.g. for inspection pits and in some P & C work.

Pandrol clip – a modern sprung steel clip fastening for flat-bottom rail.

Key – A hardwood wedge or sprung steel block used to provide a resilient locating packing between bullhead rail and a chair.

Rail anchor – A cast or forged bracket designed to fasten to the foot of a rail and bear against the side of a chair or baseplate to counter the effects of rail creep.

Double-headed rail – An early form, being of symmetrical section, with head and foot designed to be interchanged, potentially doubling rail life. It didn't work, so one head was increased to give bullhead.

Bullhead rail – A form of 'double head' rail where one head is increased in section to give greater strength and a greater wearing surface.

Flat-bottom rail – A rail having a wide, flat flange at the foot, designed to give a low bearing on the sleeper, allowing it to be, in some instances, fastened direct to the timber without chairs or baseplates.

Vignoles rail – A form of FB rail for light applications, advocated by the French railway engineer of that name.

Bridge rail – The low 'inverted T' section rail designed by Brunel for the GW broad gauge 'baulk road' longitudinally-sleepered track.

Rail section – The form and weight of rail, classified thus: '85 lb to the yard bullhead'. In model terminology, the section is classified by the form and the height in thou, thus flat-bottom, Code 70 (70-thou high).

Rail webb – The narrow portion of the rail profile separating head and foot.

Check-rail – A non-running rail designed to limit or 'check' the movement of a wheelset in relation to the running rails.

Wing rail – The continuation of the knuckle rail of a common crossing to form check-rails either side of the crossing nose. Can also be applied to the check-rail opposite the knuckle on an obtuse or 'K' crossing.

Knuckle rail – The bent sections of rail in P & C work that have the set of the bend away from the flange of the wheelsets. Found in both common and obtuse crossings.

Point rail – A rail having a horizontal taper planed on the end of it – a constituent part of a common crossing.

Splice rail – Similar to above, but planed to lie against the side of a point rail to give a crossing 'V'.

Crossing nose – The point of a crossing 'V'. It has quite a subtle shape, and does not come to a sharp point.

Crossing splice – The practice of locating the end of a splice rail in a recess machined in the side of the point rail in a crossing 'V'.

Crossing block – A set of iron spacers cast to keep the components of a common or obtuse crossing in the correct relationship.

Common (or acute) crossing – An assembly consisting of point and splice rails, knuckle and wing rails, crossing nose and wing bridge chairs, crossing block and cross bolts, designed to pass a flanged wheel over a rail at a facing angle of less than 90°.

Obtuse or 'K' crossing – Similar to above, but used in situations where the facing angle is greater than 90°. There are no splice rails in a 'K' crossing, and the knuckle and wing rails are opposite rather than adjoining.

Crossing set – All the components, excluding sleepers, needed to construct a crossing

Switch – The assembly of point blades, stock rails, stretcher bars, slide chairs and heel bridge chairs used to divert vehicles from one road to another.

Switch blades (point blades or point tongues) – Sections of rail planed to a fine taper in the horizontal plane to fit against the stock rails, and specially profiled to guide the wheelsets with minimal jolting.

Stretcher bars – Flat strip or round section bars holding the point blades in the correct alignment and at the appropriate setting.

Drive stretcher – The stretcher connected to the point-changing mechanism – what modellers refer to as a 'point tiebar'.

Locking bar or stretcher – Stretcher notched or drilled to accept the bolt of a point lock.

Point lock – A device to ensure that, once thrown and locked, a switch cannot move, especially under passing traffic. Usually used where the switch is negotiated by trains in a facing direction (facing point lock), either locked by linkage from the signal box frame, or by approaching trains operating a treadle (locking treadle or locking bar). Also used to secure sidings and other tracks which can only be 'opened' using a special key, usual on single-track branches where the key is part of the train staff (Annett's key system).

Tiebar – A bar, threaded and bolted into rail web or rail bearer, designed to prevent gauge spreading.

Stock rail – The running rails of a turnout at the outside of the formation, incorporating any sets, joggles or rebates for the housing of point blades.

Joggle – An offset forged into a rail to provide a recess into which a point-blade may fit. Designed to protect crossing nose. FB rail cannot be joggled, so a similar recess (rebate) is milled out of the rail.

Set – An angled bend made in rail, as when the diverging road of a turnout leaves the straight alignment.

Fished joint – The practice of joining adjacent lengths of rail by means of a fishplate, secured by fish bolts.

Suspended joint – Where the join between adjacent rail lengths does not occur over a sleeper, but in the space between sleepers.

Fishplate – drilled and forged steel plate designed to support rail joints vertically while allowing freedom of movement longitudinally. The retaining bolts are not tightened, and locate through oval or oversize holes in the rail web. Can be of 2 or 4 bolt pattern.

Chaired joint – Older type of joint, where the ends of adjacent rails are supported in, and keyed to, a special 'joint chair', with the joint thus over a sleeper.

Track panel – A length of track, complete. A term generally relating to prefabricated PW.

SOURCES

Acme Model Co., P.O. Box 69, Hampton, Middlesex, TW12 3NA.
'Tortoise' slow-action point motor (the best one I've found).

Ambis Engineering, 27 Stanhope Gardens, Ilford, Essex, IG1 3LQ.
Lever frames with interlocking. Point motors.

C & L Components, Martin House, 80 Wollaston Way, Burnt Mills Industrial Estate, Basildon, Essex, SS13 1DJ.
Moulded plastic trackbase, chairs and sleepers, etc. Nickel silver and steel Code 75 BH rail. Flex track (BH) in 16.5, EM and P4. Point templates.

Eileen's Emporium, 55 Reedsdale Gardens, Gildersome, Leeds, LS27 7JD.
Metals – strip various. Wires, including 28 SWG soft copper for wiring.

EM Gauge Society, Membership Secretary, Ted Butler, 2 Chesham Crescent, London, SE20 7RL.
Ply and rivet components. Rail. Track gauges. Templates, EM and P4. Fishplates, etc. Mail order service to members. Public sales at 'Expo' functions.

Exactoscale Ltd., 29 Couchmore Avenue, Esher, Surrey, KT10 9AS.
Track gauges, P4. Turnout operating units. Some PW components – SC & LE range. Foam underlay. Technical manual. Stocks Eileen's Emporium wire.

John K. Flack, 107 Hillcrest Road, Bromley, Kent, BR1 4SA.
Metals, including wire and strip in wide range of sizes. I use his 1/16in nickel silver rod for point operating linkages.

Kean-Maygib Precision Engineering Ltd., Wendover Road, Rackheath Industrial Estate, Norwich, Norfolk, NR13 6LH.
A decent solenoid point motor – certainly my choice.

Model Signal Engineering, PO Box 13, Leamington Spa, Warwickshire, CV31 1GN.
Mechanical lever frame system.

Peco Ltd., Beer, Seaton, Devon, EX12 3NA.
'Individulay' FS track components for FB track – OO, EM and P4. Code 60, 70 and 83 FB NS rail. Moulded plastic sleepers and rail fixings.

Puffers Ltd., 134A Kenton Road, Harrow, Middlesex, HA3 0HG.
Good general model shop, stocks PW components including C & L.

Scalefour Society, Membership Secretary, B. K. Pearce, 1 Eastcote Road, Pinner, Middlesex, HA5 1DS.
Stores – full range of gauges, C & L parts, ply and rivet, steel and NS BH rail, templates, etc. P4 only. Mail order to members, direct sales at Scalefour events and some shows.

Shestos, Unit 2 Shapcote Trading Centre, 374 High Street, Willesden, London NW10 2DH.
Tools – everything you'll ever need to build PW except track gauges.

Victors, 116 Pentonville Road, London N1 9JL.
American rail sections, including Rail Craft. Fulgurex point motors, also Kemtron.